LAND OF MANY SHORES

Land of Many Shores

PERSPECTIVES FROM A DIVERSE NEWFOUNDLAND AND LABRADOR

Edited by

Ainsley Hawthorn

Breakwater Books
P.O. Box 2188, St. John's, NL, Canada, A1C 6E6
www.breakwaterbooks.com

A CIP catalogue record for this book is available from Library and
Archives Canada.

ISBN 978-1-55081-896-3 (softcover)

We acknowledge the support of the Canada Council for the Arts and the
City of St. John's.

We acknowledge the financial support of the Government of Canada through
the Department of Heritage and the Government of Newfoundland and
Labrador through the Department of Tourism, Culture, Arts and Recreation
for our publishing activities.

Printed and bound in Canada.

Breakwater Books is committed to choosing papers and materials for our
books that help to protect our environment.

To this end, this book is printed on a recycled paper and other sources that
are certified by the Forest Stewardship Council®.

To all those who have come before
and those who will come after

Contents

Preface and Resources

The stories shared in this book are deeply personal and delve into subjects like suicide, grief, mental illness, substance use, colonialism, racism, ableism, homophobia, transphobia, and gender dysphoria. You may find some of these topics difficult to read about, especially if you've experienced them in your own life. If at any time you feel psychologically unwell, are concerned for your safety, or need help accessing community supports, below is a list of some of the resources that are available to you free of charge in the province of Newfoundland and Labrador.

Mental Health Crisis Line (24-Hour)
Call: 1-888-737-4668
Professionally trained crisis interveners are available to assist anyone in distress, as well as their loved ones or caregivers. Mental health crises can include, but aren't limited to, having suicidal thoughts, experiencing abuse or trauma, or struggling to cope with work, school, or relationships.

Crisis Text Line (24-Hour)
Text: 741741 (Adults), 686868 (Children and Youth)
Text from anywhere in Canada to chat confidentially with a live, trained crisis responder who can help you through a painful emotional or mental

health episode. You don't need a data plan or Internet connection to use this service.

CHANNAL Peer Support Warm Line

Call: 1-855-753-2560

The Warm Line is a non-judgmental talk line and referral service for anyone with a mental health concern that does not require urgent care. The line is operated by trained peer supporters with lived experience of mental illness and is open from 10 a.m. to 12 midnight Newfoundland time, seven days a week.

The Recovery Centre

Call: 1-877-752-4980

The Recovery Centre in St. John's provides round-the-clock nursing and medical care to adults aged sixteen and over from any part of the province who need help while withdrawing from alcohol, drugs, or gambling. If this is the right service for you, the centre can usually offer a bed within 24 hours.

Mental Health and Addictions Systems Navigator

Call: 1-877-999-7589

If you're having trouble accessing mental health or addictions services, the systems navigator can connect you with care.

Hope for Wellness for Indigenous Peoples (24-Hour)

Call: 1-855-242-3310; Chat: www.hopeforwellness.ca

Hope for Wellness offers culturally competent counselling and crisis intervention in Inuktitut, Cree, Ojibway, English, and French. Counsellors can also help you find supports in your local area.

Indian Residential School Survivor Hotlines

Call: 1-866-925-4419 (24-Hour Crisis Line), 1-866-414-8111 (Info Line)

Residential school survivors and their families can access counselling, cultural, and emotional support through these hotlines. The 24-hour crisis line is staffed by Indigenous counsellors who are trained to assist anyone experiencing distress as a result of their residential school experience.

Kids Help Phone (24-Hour)

Call: 1-800-668-6868; Text: 686868

Children, teens, and young adults anywhere in Canada can call Kids Help Phone to speak anonymously with a professional counsellor in English, French, or Arabic. Counsellors are ready to chat about topics like bullying and abuse, friends and family, and emotional well-being.

2SLGBTQ+ Youth Line

Call: 1-800-268-9688; Text: (647) 694-4275; Chat: www.youthline.ca

The Youth Line is a queer, trans, and Two Spirit–led organization that offers peer support to 2SLGBTQ+ individuals aged 29 and under. The line is open from 5:30 p.m. to 11:00 p.m. Newfoundland time, every day except Saturday.

Trans LifeLine (24-Hour)

Call: 1-877-330-6366

The LifeLine provides trans and questioning callers, as well as their friends and family, with trans peer support. Operators will not assume your gender identity based on your voice and will not call rescue services such as 911 or law enforcement without your consent.

NL Association of the Deaf

Call or Text: (709) 726-6672; Text: (709) 728-5763 (Counselling);
Email: nlad@nlad.org

The NL Association of the Deaf offers health and wellness counselling, employment services, and community support in American Sign Language and English to members of the Deaf community in the province.

Domestic Violence Help Line (24-Hour)

Call or Text: 1-888-709-7090

Contact the Help Line to chat with a trained professional who can counsel you, work with you on a safety plan, or connect you with shelter at your nearest transition house.

Sexual Assault Support and Information Line (24-Hour)
Call: 1-800-726-2743
Empathetic volunteers are on hand to provide guidance to anyone in the province who's been impacted by sexual violence. In the St. John's area, the support line can connect you with a volunteer to accompany you to St. Clare's Hospital or the RNC following an assault.

Safe Harbour Outreach Project (SHOP)
Call or Text: (709) 771-1077 or (709) 771-7171
SHOP offers individual support, health care referrals, community gatherings, and advocacy for sex workers in Newfoundland and Labrador. They serve anyone who identifies as a current or former sex worker, in any part of the industry.

NL Human Rights Commission
Call: 1-800-563-5808; Email: humanrights@gov.nl.ca
If you've experienced harassment or discrimination, you can contact the Human Rights Commission to learn about your rights or to file a complaint.

This isn't a comprehensive list, and it is intended as a starting point only. The contacts above can offer immediate assistance and put you in touch with the many other community organizations and government institutions providing services in Newfoundland and Labrador and the rest of the country.

A Note about Language Usage

Readers may notice that, occasionally, vocabulary and references to persons or groups do not follow standard editorial practice. This choice was made in order to maintain the voices of the authors in this collection as they express their experiences on their own terms and in their own words.

Mapping a Diverse Newfoundland and Labrador

by

AINSLEY HAWTHORN

"New wave of immigrants brings diversity to rural NL"
"Local businesses adapt to the needs of a multicultural workforce"
"Conference shines a spotlight on inclusion as NL demographics change"

Headlines like these frustrate me to no end, popping up with ever greater frequency over the past decade, implying that diversity is new to this place. Headlines like these are what motivated me to create this book.

There's a myth that diversity *comes to* Newfoundland and Labrador but isn't *of* Newfoundland and Labrador. That it's an import, albeit a desirable one, like flour, tea, or fresh fruit in winter. For a people renowned for pride in our heritage, we have a staggeringly limited view of our history and society. As some tell it, we're a group of English and Irish descendants, Anglicans and Catholics, who have had this region more or less to ourselves for centuries, and it's only now, with the arrival of international immigrants, that we are becoming culturally, racially, and otherwise diverse. But this narrative is a fiction, a fantasy. When we accept it as true, we not only misjudge who we are today, we diminish who we were in the past.

When did we become so narrow-minded about who we are and where we come from? In a March 9, 2015, article for *TheIndependent.ca*, geographer and author Maura Hanrahan suggested that we owe our collective cultural amnesia, at least in part, to a very effective marketing strategy. The cod moratorium and subsequent recession that hit Newfoundland and Labrador in the 1990s led the provincial government, under then premier Brian Tobin, to lean hard into tourism as an antidote to our economic woes.

"In a series of embarrassing developments," Hanrahan writes, "the province sent the world the clear message that we were all redheads, dancing jigs in meadows while a nearby cousin played the fiddle."

The government's standpoint on our Irishness has changed little in the intervening years, at least as far as their PR is concerned. The provincial tourism website still proclaims Newfoundland and Labrador "the most Irish place outside of Ireland," though fact-checking by the *Newfoundland Quarterly* showed that distinction should rightfully go to Australia, where 35 per cent of the population claims Irish ancestry compared to a mere 21 per cent in Newfoundland and Labrador.

Tourism campaigns over the past thirty years may have recast our province in shades of kelly green, but marketers weren't the first to dilute Newfoundland and Labrador's complex heritage. We have a longstanding tradition of reducing our culture to a simple hybrid of English and Irish influences. To find the source of this tendency, we have to look back quite a bit further than the 1990s, to 1840 and the establishment of the Newfoundland Natives' Society. If that name puts you in mind of Indigenous cultures, don't be fooled. The society was actually founded by Newfoundlanders of British and Irish descent.

The French Revolution and the Napoleonic Wars that followed it had disrupted Europe's fisheries, and significant numbers of Europeans whose ancestors had fished seasonally along the coast of Newfoundland decided to immigrate permanently to the island, where the fishery was stable. As a result, Newfoundland's settler population almost quadrupled in less than twenty years, from 11,382 people in 1797 to 40,568 in 1815. Most of these immigrants hailed from southwest England and southeast Ireland, but their children, growing up far from the British Isles, felt a stronger attachment to Newfoundland than to the homelands of their parents. They also resented the colonial government, which was composed mostly of elite British-born men who occasionally expressed disdain for the local population, implying that they were uneducated yokels.

On September 12, 1840, almost three hundred men met in a fish store in St. John's to inaugurate the Newfoundland Natives' Society. The majority of them were members of the urban middle class—businessmen, doctors, and lawyers—rather than the rural livyers who made up most of the settler population. The society's goal was to promote the political, educational, and professional interests of people like its founders: men of Anglo-Celtic descent who had been born on the island. Despite the religious rivalries that had been imported from the United Kingdom with their immigrant forebears, the group's members were a mix of Catholics and Protestants, united in the belief that all would be better off if they presented a united front against the foreign-born merchants and politicians they believed were exploiting them.

That evening, Newfoundland identity as we know it began to coalesce. The men referred to themselves as "Newfoundlanders," in contrast to the island's foreign-born "inhabitants." Together, they unanimously approved a design for a society flag depicting aspects of Newfoundland settler culture: a fisherman and a woodsman, a sealing vessel and a plough. These images were encircled by a rose, thistle, and shamrock wreath, representing England, Scotland, and Ireland. According to an article published in the *Patriot*—a nationalist St. John's newspaper—three days later, society members considered these countries "the stock from whence the Newfoundlander derives his origin."

According to the newspaper, its editor R. J. Parsons had declared in a passionate speech: "Until [this] moment [the natives of Newfoundland] were strangers in their own country—they had no influence in any department of the Government—aliens had usurped their birth rights....This night we proclaim ourselves a people—we proclaim our nationality, and we shall fail to do our duty, if henceforward we do not make that nationality to be respected."

The parameters of Newfoundland identity as laid out in that first meeting of the Natives' Society have stayed with us to this day, although the

Scottish component has been largely forgotten. The society's vision of what it meant to be a Newfoundlander, though, was extremely short-sighted, extending only as far as the boundaries of middle-class St. John's society. The men who met that fall evening neglected, and perhaps were hardly aware of, other populations of European descent on the island, like the French settlers of the west coast. By dismissing the possibility that people born elsewhere in the world could ever qualify as Newfoundlanders, they set the stage for the exclusion of later immigrants from our understanding of Newfoundland identity, so that the cultural contributions of the hundreds of Chinese, Lebanese, and Jewish people who settled here beginning in the late nineteenth century are widely ignored.

There's no small irony, either, in the society's total omission of the region's various Indigenous Peoples from their concept of a "native-born Newfoundlander," since R. J. Parson's screed about aliens overwhelming native populations and subjecting them to foreign rule reads like an account of the European colonization of Indigenous territories. Had the society wanted to accurately represent the native-born population of Newfoundland and Labrador at the time, their definition would have had to include the Innu and Inuit of the Big Land as well as the Mi'kmaq of the island. While the last known member of the Beothuk people, Shanawdithit, had died a decade earlier, Mi'kmaw Oral Tradition holds that Beothuk refugees, sick and starving as European colonists encroached on their land, integrated with the Mi'kmaw community.

Our idea of who we are as a populace is anemic in other ways, too—ways that reflect the composition of the Natives' Society and the backgrounds of the individuals who were most prominent in the colony's public life during the nineteenth century. Who was missing from the meeting that night? Working-class and rural Newfoundlanders, for one, though the organization was intended to represent them as well. Likewise, our current concept of Newfoundland identity romanticizes outport culture while, at the same time, failing to recognize the wide range of backgrounds, lifestyles, and needs of the people who actually live outside the confines of the capital city. Rural Newfoundlanders might be idealized, but at the cost of being reduced to a stereotype. As for Labradorians, they're an afterthought at best—never mentioned at the Natives' Society meeting and regularly overlooked today.

Women were glaringly absent from the room, too, though the society flag itself had been designed by a local woman. She goes unnamed in the meeting records, referred to only as a "fair daughter of 'Terra Nova.'" Since then, we've managed to incorporate women into our collective imagination about this place—what would Newfoundland and Labrador be without its nans, after all?—and, to a lesser extent, into our political institutions, though work remains to be done on both fronts. We still rarely hear about the critical roles women played in shaping our history, and less than a quarter of Newfoundland and Labrador's MHAs and mayors are women.

There are other perspectives that we've barely begun to integrate into our self-conception. Voices that existed here but went unheard in the nineteenth century, voices that we downplay even now. Members of the 2SLGBTQ+ community, practitioners of religions other than Christianity, people who are neurodivergent, who are disabled, who live with a mental illness or addiction—we exclude them from the public image of Newfoundland and Labrador; we relegate them to the status of outsiders in their own home. We stigmatize our sex workers and reject the residents of our prisons, treating them as if they're not here, though they're our neighbours, our relatives, ourselves.

So, who are we really? Out of every hundred Newfoundlanders and Labradorians:

- Nine of us are Indigenous, the third-largest proportion of any province in the country, and eleven have Indigenous ancestry.
- Two are Black or non-Indigenous people of colour.
- Two are of Asian heritage, with ancestors from East Asia, South Asia, West Central Asia, or the Middle East.
- One is of African or Caribbean heritage.
- Five are descended from French settlers, five are bilingual in English and French, and one speaks French as a first language.
- Two have a first language other than English or French. The most common are Innu-aimun, Arabic, Tagalog (Filipino), and Mandarin Chinese.
- Two are immigrants. One arrived before 2001 and the other after.

- One practises a religion other than Christianity, and six profess no religion whatsoever.
- Fourteen have a disability. Of these, three have an intellectual disability.
- Ten have a mood disorder, such as depression, anxiety, or bipolar disorder.
- Eighteen regularly drink more than experts consider safe.
- Two have been harmed by their use of cocaine, speed, ecstasy, hallucinogens, or heroin.

Why is it important to recognize this diversity? Some people argue that acknowledging the differences amongst us is divisive—that labels are limiting. But we are already labelling ourselves: we are already assuming a white, straight, Anglo-Irish, Christian identity that fits many of us poorly. Making those false generalizations about ourselves is what's limiting. It's a barrier that stands between us and self-knowledge. Until we can broaden our perspective to allow for variety within our population, we will have only the most superficial grasp of who we are. For as long as we pigeonhole our culture, we will inhibit who we have the potential to become.

In a July 2009 talk for TEDGlobal, award-winning author Chimamanda Ngozi Adichie spoke of the danger of a single story. "The single story creates stereotypes," she said, "and the problem with stereotypes is not that they are untrue but that they are incomplete." Our English and Irish cultural heritage and our Catholic and Protestant religious traditions are meaningful aspects of our identity, but so are our Mi'kmaw and Lebanese heritage, our Muslim and Hindu traditions. Some of us play the accordion, step dance, and eat Jiggs' Dinner. Others play the qilaut, dance salsa, or eat shawarma. Some of us roll down Broadway in our wheelchairs instead of strolling on foot. Some of us go to work in the sex trade instead of in an office in Atlantic Place. All of these experiences make us who we are as a people. To dismiss them is to erase the richness of our culture, to discount our collective wisdom, and to alienate members of our own communities. To dismiss these experiences is to impoverish ourselves.

The stories and essays in this book are written from viewpoints we seldom have the chance to hear. They may surprise you or baffle you. They may give you insight into lives that are very different from your own or give you the reassurance that there are people like you in this place, too. If nothing else, I hope you will come away with an appreciation of how multi-faceted we are, we who live at the edge of the continent, at the boundary between land and sea. As you read, remember that the authors in this collection aren't writing on behalf of any groups they might belong to— personal identity is far too complicated and many-layered to expect anyone to represent a whole subset of the population. Instead, consider these postcards from a province you might not know as well as you think you do.

This is a portrait of us. The question now is: Who do we want to become next?

Where I'm From

by

JULIE BULL

I'm from crashing waves and wood smoke burning
From cold winter days and life-long learning
I'm from mustard pickles and bottled beets
From trapping and fishing and hunting for meat
From country roads to city streets
I'm from "everything happens for a reason" and "you will
    because you can"
I'm from a dipper, not a saucepan
I'm from administering junk mail and playing school
Imagination my most prized tool
I'm from trying it first and pioneering
From helping others and volunteering
I'm from power in numbers and strength of community
From no immunity to discontinuity
From every opportunity to search for unity
My vision is in my dreams for that which is unseen

I'm from unnamed dirt roads to the 401
Why am I the one? Leaving the midnight sun
Doing what I can with that which is undone
From everyone in my business to anonymity
The proximity of creativity
From strong Bull women, from generation to generation
From the formation of my own creation
I'm from confrontation and contemplation
A demonstration of determination
I'm from the fluctuation of incarnation
From not knowing one day to the next to doing my best
From the normalization of aggravation
From the visualization of beautification
From a conversation to convocation
I'm from concrete jungles and hugging trees
I'm from snowbanks taller than me and a cool summer's breeze
I'm from "throw salt over your shoulder" and "if you've got nothing
    nice to say, don't say anything at all"
From a free-for-all to protocol

I'm from bungalows and ocean views
From piercings and tattoos
I'm from being judged by them and not by me
From humility and agility
From susceptibility to possibility
I'm from pedagogies and philosophies
From paradoxes and curiosities
I'm from consent and confidentiality
From thinking about it critically
From the practicality of morality
I'm from conflicts of interest
I know that I'm different
I'm from justice and autonomy
Mutual exclusivity is not for me
It's all a false dichotomy

It's the space between when we feed the machine
The *ethical space* that we find in that place
My identity not bound artificially
To be free is authenticity
From poverty to prosperity
I'm from the gifts that were put in me

I'm from basic literacy to decolonizing the academy
From "the road less travelled" to a life unravelled
To demystify and exemplify
From getting lost at a marginal cost
To finding myself, the myth dispelled
From captivity to freedom
From the Grand Canyon to the Colosseum
My sensitivity is my reflexivity
No room for negativity or inactivity
The inspection of introspection
I'm from Vienna sausages to "that's just the way it is"
From standing still to flying the world
I'm from the ancient land, my netherworld
With northern lights trapped in the rock
This is not what I planned, I didn't understand
Labradorite in my line of sight
I'm my own prototype
From writer's block to the path that I walk
I cannot lose but I can choose
I'm from "an eye for an eye makes the whole world blind"
Leave no one behind
The forget-me-not from the one you forgot

I'm from the land and the sea
The animosity of atrocities
From a preoccupation of being mismatched, the outcast
From the devastation of domination
From the aftermath of backlash to fighting back

I'm from traditions and technologies
Blank stares and apologies
My existence is resistance
I tried to keep my distance but my persistence is optimistic
The probability of my success, "statistically significant"
The predicament not definitive
My willingness is no coincidence, it's serendipitous
That the impetus from my imagination is the acceleration
    of exploration
It was in the instant that I went against it
"You're still here" echoes in my mind
As my heart breaks for those who are gone
I'm here for them. For you. For me.
My resiliency runs deep in my veins
I will not take in vain that I remain not to refrain but to retrain

I'm from Tom Petty and Kenny Rogers
From "we get what we give" and "we share what we've got"
I went in head first, for better or worst
We are who we are, distance from afar
Objects in the rear-view mirror appear closer than they are
Force-fed a single story
Pain and poverty in all their glory
Though a chapter, it's not the book
I found my hook from the way you look when I speak my truths
I'm from the aurora borealis
From the chaos and the balance
I'm from the mountains and the land
To understand a dreamland where the ocean meets the sand
I personify darkness to light, stars in the night
I know I'm alright and I'm not afraid to fight
The power of my ancestors in me
Power and love in equal proportions
Life's distortions

I'm from the vision of my grandmother
And the prayers of her ancestors
Her independence weaved into my existence
I'm from "practice makes perfect" and the Doppler effect
To learn to connect
From overprotection to misdirection
From retrospection to resurrection
The opportunistic infection at the intersections of natural selection
I'm from ethics review and collaboration
A fascination with innovation
From punctuation to publication
From suffocation to restoration
From policy to practice
The global atlas
I'm provocative
A paradox
Pandora's box
From the equinox
Who we are is in the stars
I'm from ideologies and institutions
From apologies to resolutions
From "whatever doesn't kill you makes you stronger" and "laughter makes you live longer"
It makes me a fighter and the load feels lighter
It's my grit that bit that you can't describe
A heartbeat deep inside
The window seat in the flight of life

Compassion through interaction
Satisfaction with my own expansion
Extraction, just a fraction of my own distraction
It's relational not sensational
I take personal responsibility
It's my own self-advocacy
I have the right to be myself, to love myself. To honour me.

It's all about hope, a slippery slope to learn to cope
My resiliency, my legacy
Reclaiming my identity

Tokenism. Animism. The instinctual bit you bury inside.
You make it hide in this game of seek. What's this you speak?
The serenity of my identity is not up for debate
My name's sake. You activate this welfare state while I accommodate
    a heart full of hate.
From epistemological collision
To making tough decisions
From being scared to tears to facing fears
From holding on to letting go
From questioning why to starting to know
A discursive analysis of society's paralysis
What's here for us? Where do we go?
This much I know
We let go of ego and follow our heart
That's the only start
Instead of criticize I realize my own potential and that's essential

The danger of a single story
That I could've become
Destined to become
Started to become
When that narrative overpowered
No happy hour
Spirit devoured
But I've overcome with no rule of thumb from the beat of the drum
From statistical analysis to individual variance
From philosophical debate to examining my own self
From skirting sickness to weaving wellness and asking for help
From imaginary friends to a visionary end
From "just do your best" and "forget all the rest"
From ethical theory to the way we actually act

Not a question of fact but a matter of fact
To look back from humble beginnings to nine round innings
A nomadic life not tamed by the skyscrapers that tower over the city
My own standing committee on how to do me
From simplicity to complexity and to weave them together
A proud carrier of my eagle feather

From the inaugural student member on the REB
To dipping my toes in the Baltic Sea
From shy and timid to challenging my limits
To testing my strength and doing it anyway
Healing is the pathway from my spirit wound
As the trauma runs through my blood
But there's a flood
Of resiliency that carries me
Through the animosity and uncertainty
From my ancestors who prayed
That I'd be here one day
With who I am and what they knew
To try anew a different way
The road less travelled and here I stand
On the blessed land that takes my hand
To be true to myself and do the right thing
To examine my life and the adventures it brings
The consequences of putting up fences
Leave people defenceless
To hoard what we find and to push people out

From contemplating a moral imperative
To engaging with my own narrative
From second guesses to life's lessons
The integration of me and life to illustrate the complexity
It's not perplex to me for me to be
The social justice freedom fighter
Not just for me but for anyone who needs me to be

I use the voice that's been given to me
To challenge the dominant view
Contributing to the danger of a single story
Exploratory
To find the power of love
Instead of the love of power
It's my superpower to be empowered
To learn to let go
To absolve
To dissolve the single story
To evolve in all my glory
The theory and practice of social change
To rearrange the action of exchange
From the first to graduate high school to breaking the cycle
From moving away yet not leaving it behind to finding mine
From 'you can do it if you put your mind to it' and 'to do it you just
    have to go through it'
Empathy, breathlessly, conscious
To walk a mile. To think a while.
I shoot for the moon but sometimes I'm too busy gazing at stars
    from afar
My strength through resiliency from the communities that trust
    in me
The legacy I want to see that came before me
My ancestors were investors in me
My identity
So much to question and so much to learn
The fire inside burns, with no limitation
My foundation is *All My Relations*

House

by

GEMMA HICKEY

"Why does your voice sound so patchy?" asked my aunt, her soft voice heavy with concern. "Do you have a cold?"

"Not at all," I replied. "I just started testosterone, so my voice is cracking like a teenage boy."

"What's that, Paula? Gemma wants to be a boy?" my 96-year-old grandmother bawled out.

I had stopped in to visit my grandmother before hiking the trail on Signal Hill. Her house, where she raised her large Irish Catholic family, was based in the historic Battery overlooking the St. John's Harbour. Cradled in the arms of the surrounding hills, the community mirrored a rural outport in the heart of the capital city. Pocket-sized houses and fishing stages draped in colourful hues were strung along the hill's base. From a distance they resembled the decorative trinkets on a charm bracelet, like the hopes so many islanders hung on the fishery. The slopes enclosing the harbour were full of trails, first beaten by foot soldiers during both World Wars as they scurried between forts like ants on a hill.

When my grandmother married my grandfather, they rented a small house, located on Power's Court, along the other side of Signal Hill from the church. But, when the church made plans to build a school, the property was set to be demolished. They had nowhere else to go once they received an eviction notice. With six children to care for, my grandmother marched over to the rectory and bartered with the priest. She offered to have another baby if he could find her family a place to live. He informed her that there was a rundown house available for rent in the Battery for a little over thirty dollars a month, which was a lot of money back then. There was no electricity or running water, and there were cracks in the roof as well as the foundation. Out of desperation, my grandparents moved their family in the following day, and, within weeks of moving, Holy Mother Church had another member, as my grandmother was pregnant again. They raised nine children and managed to build a life together, transforming a decrepit house into a beautiful home. Their resilience served as both shelter and foundation. Times were tough, but they made a great team.

My grandfather, who came from poverty, was street-smart and a jack-of-all-trades. He only had a grade eight education but, when he got a job at a local bakery, worked his way up the line to become the Master Baker. My grandmother was intelligent and well-read. Her father, an artist hired to paint religious art in church buildings, was offered housing and education for his family while he was employed with the church, so my grandmother and her two siblings went to the same schools as children who came from privilege. When he died and the church evicted his family, her mother found an apartment in downtown St. John's, and, to make ends meet, took in boarders, knitted and mended garments, and set up a tea room serving hot meals and desserts. My grandmother and her siblings all had jobs to do, and that's how her family survived The Great Depression. Her mother even refused the dole.

Not long after my grandmother had a hearing aid placed in her ear, it was common among my family members to joke about her so-called "selective hearing." Nothing ever slipped by her. One day during a visit as she was dozing on the couch, I decided to take advantage of the situation by changing the channel while her favourite soap opera, *Another World*, was on the television.

"Mind yourself, now, child," she warned.

When we were kids, my cousins and I wondered if she possessed magical powers because she always seemed to know our every move, even if she wasn't looking in our direction.

"Is she a witch?" asked my cousin Michael while he paced the floor, arms flailing in the air as if he were about to surrender himself to the other side in battle. We were both feeling defeated, having been exiled to the spare bedroom without supper by our parents at the annual Good Friday gathering, which, on that particular day, consisted of a traditional feed of deep-fried codfish caught by my uncle, and homemade fries. But what made it even more unbearable was the fact that we weren't allowed to have dessert. And considering that his father and my mother, the most devout of the siblings, gave up sweets for Lent, Michael and I had already gone forty days without it.

"Nah, my teacher told me that only Protestants can be witches," I answered as I curled up on the bed, knowing full well we wouldn't be tasting freedom any time soon either. "Nan's more Catholic than the Pope!"

Earlier that evening Michael had had an idea. There were no toys readily available, so he asked all the smokers in our family—there were quite a few at the time—if he could have the foil from their cigarette packages. He then snuck into the back pantry undetected and stole some aluminum foil. When he resurfaced, he proudly presented me with a silver ball for us to play catch with. I hustled to the other side of the kitchen, anxiously waiting for him to toss it into the air. But, when he did, instead of aiming it in my direction he whipped it at the dark wooden cupboards. It hit the counter then bounced into a black plastic pipe attached to the washing machine. Michael and I rushed over to look down the pipe. Though he was exactly one year older, as we shared a birthday, he and I were roughly the same height. I pulled a chair out from the table, and Michael climbed on top. When he didn't see the shiny ball, he assumed it had rolled down the drain and into the main sewer line. We rejoined the rest of our family in the living room.

We were all having a time singing old Irish songs while our uncle Tony played guitar until one of our younger cousins got sick and vomited on our grandmother's hand-knitted quilt draped over the back of the couch. Our aunt Margie acted quickly and threw it in the washer so it wouldn't stain.

When the cycle completed, the water backed up, and the washer, which was a small spin machine, began to gallop steadily, causing white suds to fly into the air. Like a bucking bull at a rodeo, the washer leapt and spun wildly, refusing to be tamed. My grandmother quickly took over the reins and instructed my uncle Tony, who happened to be a plumber, to go fetch the snake from his truck.

"Those youngsters clogged that drain with some kind of makeshift ball," she insisted. "Mark my words."

She was right. As usual.

"She's on testosterone, Mom," my aunt responded in an awkward tone.

My heart sank when my aunt referred to me as "she." I wasn't prepared for the emotional response it evoked in me, nor was I ready to engage in a larger discussion on pronouns. I felt the anxiety swell like a wave from deep within, anticipating a negative response from my grandmother. I braced myself between the arms of the flower-patterned Queen Anne–inspired chair nestled in the corner of her living room.

She was sitting in her rocking chair, and though her eyes peered at me over the top of her bifocals, the knitting needles in her hands choreographed the dancing wool in her lap without missing a beat.

"I told your mother you were a boy," she proudly stated, "and that put me in her bad books then."

"But you're a bad boy," she added. "Gets away with it, too, on account of that devilish grin and handsome face you got on you."

Apparently, a few years prior my mother went to my grandmother in tears after she took me to a movie at the Avalon Mall. An elderly man in a wheelchair, accompanied by his daughter, was having a difficult time getting the push button to work on the automatic door at the main entrance so I rushed over and held the door open for them. The woman told my mother that I was a "real gentleman."

"That's my daughter!" my mother shouted in response.

It wasn't the first time someone mistook me for a boy, and my mother, whose beauty reflects every notion of conventional femininity, had had her fill. I was a tomboy when I was little, and after my high school gradua-tion I got a buzz cut and came out as a butch lesbian. The clothing I chose to wear was masculine, which I liked, but for some reason the skin I was in never seemed to fit right. I didn't know what that meant at the time.

I was conditioned to believe that being gay was a sin because I was raised in a devout Catholic family. As a teenager, I sought the help of a conver-sion therapist in an effort to try to change. When that didn't work, I made a decision to end my life. One flask and two bottles of pills later, I found myself alive, but barely, in the emergency room at the Health Sciences Centre. Once I became physically well, I was moved to the psychiatric ward on another wing of the hospital. The short time I spent there was life-alter-ing because the psychiatrist assigned to me was so refreshingly progressive. He told me that there was nothing wrong with me and sent me home.

"What will you do with your breasts?" my grandmother asked.

"I'm going to get them removed, Nan," I responded.

"Proper thing," she said with a wink. "Sure, you won't miss them. Got your pick of breasts with them girls you're with.

"Will you grow a bird I wonder?" she asked.

"No, but my clitoris will get bigger," I answered.

"Well, that's all right for you then," she said with a chuckle. "If I had that maybe I'd like having sex with your grandfather."

We all laughed.

"Nan, what if I don't want to be a boy or a girl?" I asked.

"Just be Gemma," she answered. "That's all Nan wants."

———

There are so many layers to trauma. Years of therapy helped to peel some of them away, but when I began to pay attention to my body, many more became apparent. I had recently completed a month-long, 908-kilometre walk across Newfoundland to raise funds and awareness for Pathways, an organization I founded for survivors who, like me, were abused by a mem-ber of the clergy. Before the walk I put myself through a rigorous training schedule in order to be successful at my goal of walking across the island. I lost seventy-five pounds, but all that weight loss heightened my dysphoria.

My breasts became more noticeable. I tried binding them, but—no matter how hard I tried to smother them—they were still there. They felt like lumps on my chest. Scar tissue from the wounds of my sexual assaults. Reminders of why I was raped. Because I was a woman. Was I betraying my own kind for wanting them gone, especially when so many of my female friends had lost theirs to breast cancer? Suddenly the cultural weight of breasts was becoming too heavy to lift.

During the long hours of solitude along the shoulder of the Trans-Canada Highway, I reflected on my past. Revisiting my childhood brought me back to myself. It was a homecoming of continuous arrival with each step. I came to the realization that claiming an identity within a binary constricted me to a singular gender script rooted in coloniality. Growing up, all of my notions on gender and sexuality were continually reinforced by the heteropatriarchy within the Catholic Church. I began to reclaim not only my body, but my mind as well. After the walk, I made a decision to pursue hormone therapy, which felt freeing, but it was my grandmother's words that gave me wings. She lifted me out of the house I was living in—i.e., my body. Just be Gemma. Of course. Why didn't I think of that? I don't need to be trapped within this binary of male or female. I can just be me. For thirty-eight years of my life I was socialized as a woman. I was abused as a woman. And though I never really felt like a woman, which is the main reason why I never wanted to dress like one, I didn't want to erase parts of myself that could inform the person I was becoming. I decided to keep my name and give up my breasts. I made an appointment with a private clinic in Mississauga, Ontario, for top surgery.

My grandmother had a bad fall a month before my mother and I were booked to fly to Ontario. She couldn't wait to get out of hospital and go back to her home, which she loved so dearly. My family took turns looking in on her, including my cousin Ann-Marie, who is a nurse. When it came time for her medication, my cousin warned my grandmother that the pill she was about to take was unusually large and therefore may be difficult to swallow. My grandmother, who never minced words, offered some wise ones in response.

"Ann-Marie, the biggest pill I ever had to swallow was acceptance, and, once I did, everything in my life got better."

A week or so later my grandmother had another fall. She began to hemorrhage in the middle of the night and had to be rushed to hospital. I caught a cold so wasn't able to visit her, but I spoke to her every day by phone. I had just picked up my car from the garage when my mother called me, her voice quivering, telling me to hurry in to the hospital. By the time I got there, my grandmother had died. I wept over her body, still warm.

"Nan would've wanted you to get your surgery," said my cousin Kelly. "You have to go."

When the tears ceased, I asked my uncle John to lead us in a prayer. I knew that's what my grandmother would've wanted. We held hands and prayed the Hail Mary to honour her, as her first name was Mary.

My family moved the wake and funeral ahead so that my mother and I could take part. We were scheduled to leave a few days after she had passed.

At the funeral home during the wake my mother and aunts motioned for me to come up to the coffin. My aunt Paula took my grandmother's prayer card—which she used to pray with every day—from her cold hands, kissed it, then passed it to her sister to kiss and then to my mother. After my mother kissed the card, she crossed it over my breasts while the three of them prayed the Our Father. Of all the prayers to pray over my breasts before I had them removed...the Our Father...seriously...like, WTF? But, whatever. In that moment, given where we were, I made a game-time decision not to challenge the patriarchy.

My grandmother told me later that the reason she knew what everyone was up to was because she had mirrors strategically placed in the house.

"You don't feed nine youngsters and keep an eye to them without having a few tricks up your sleeve," she confessed.

As for her selective hearing...well, once she figured out how to adjust the volume on the hearing aid, she decided that she could tune in and out of conversations.

"I don't be bothered with foolishness," she said, "but I dies for a bit of news."

I've applied that hearing technique to the negative thoughts in my own head. I don't have time for foolishness either, especially my own. When I look in the mirror now, I can see myself from all different kinds of angles, and I've finally come to a place of acceptance within my own self. Nan was right—everything does get better. The body we live in may not be what we want it to be at first, but, just like my grandparents who made their house a home, I was finally beginning to learn how to live in mine. It was going to take some more work, but I was almost home.

Newfoundland's Offer
How the Baltic People Came to Corner Brook in the 1950s

by

ILGA LEJA

WHY NEWFOUNDLAND?

We were never meant to settle in Newfoundland in 1950, my parents, my brother, and I. My father, Ernest Leja, was never meant to marshal together a delegation of German and Baltic engineers, technicians, and labourers to come to Corner Brook, to take part in Joseph Smallwood's New Industries Program, and to bring more industry to a part of Newfoundland that already had a well-established pulp and paper mill. No, we were meant to eventually return to Latvia, to my parents' homeland, to a free and independent Latvia as it had been before the Second World War.

But history had different plans for us. As my parents told it, Latvia had been abandoned by the West, had been handed over to Stalin to be absorbed into the Soviet Union. It would not be free again for another forty-one years, something my father would not live to see. As it turned out, though, he and my mother were the lucky ones. They were not among those refugees and displaced persons who were forced to return to Latvia under Soviet occupation. They were given an exit strategy. They were offered Newfoundland.

That strategy required a confluence of factors both historical and personal. My parents, together with thousands of their compatriots, had escaped to Germany in 1944 when Soviet troops invaded their country for the second and final time. They knew what would have been in store for them if they had stayed. They had already suffered through the earlier Soviet invasion in 1940, which had lasted a year. That year—until July 1941, when Nazi troops occupied Riga, Latvia's capital city—is known to Latvians as "Baigais Gads" (the "Terrible Year" or "Year of Terror").

The Soviet KGB had set up operations in Riga where they detained Latvian citizens, imprisoning and torturing them. They carried out executions and set the local population against each other, causing them to spy on one another. It was during that year that thousands of Latvians were packed into cattle cars and deported to Siberia. There they were either placed in labour camps or left to survive as best they could in the unforgiving environment. My father's first family was among them. He would have been taken with them, too, if it had not been for the timing. That fateful night when his wife and son were ordered to pack quickly while Russian soldiers looked on, my father was on a train on his way home from St. Petersburg.

On the heels of the second Soviet invasion in 1944, my parents, at that time unmarried, made their way by ship to Germany. My father was in the fortunate position of having been in the employ of German companies as a professional engineer during the days of Latvian independence, primarily in the gypsum/cement industry. Those connections were to prove vital and would turn out to be the unlikely link that would ultimately bring us to Canada.

The war over, my father was given permission to develop new economic enterprises as part of the postwar rebuilding of Germany. These included a gypsum and wallboard plant in Bodenverder which he, working together with a team of other Baltic engineers and technicians, designed and then built. Meanwhile my parents had settled in nearby Stadtoldendorf, where other Baltic Germans and some Latvians also lived. This community was to become the core group that would make the transition to Newfoundland when the time came.

It came on the heels of Newfoundland's confederation with Canada. Joseph Smallwood, the new province's first premier, had a grand vision for Newfoundland: to bring it out of its lingering economic depression by developing it into an industrial powerhouse. No longer wanting to rely so heavily on the fisheries that had historically sustained Newfoundland's population, Smallwood proposed introducing new sectors. He believed that his New Industries Program would not only help boost the economy but would bring more education and expertise to the local labour force as well.

In order to do this, he needed advice and connections. When he turned to the Canadian government for assistance, they recommended Alfred Valdmanis. Valdmanis, at that time acting as a consultant to a number of Canadian government departments, had been Minister of Finance in pre-war Latvia when Latvia enjoyed its short-lived period of independence. He had many contacts in Germany and had worked with prominent Latvians and Baltic Germans during his tenure. One of those Latvians was my father.

Smallwood made Valdmanis his Minister of Economic Development. They developed a close relationship and Smallwood readily took any advice that Valdmanis offered. To build industry in the province, Newfoundland was going to need engineers and technical experts. Many of these existed among the refugee population in postwar Europe. And since Valdmanis's connections lay in Germany among fellow Latvians, he drew on that community for his hiring recommendations to Smallwood. The two made several trips to Germany to meet with potential experts and to collaborate with the German companies who currently employed them.

My father could have stayed on in Germany, could have had a comfortable life with steady and interesting employment. Why did he even consider moving to what must have seemed like the end of the world to him? In a nutshell: fear of Soviet communism. From his experience in the Second World War, when Latvia suffered through a series of occupations from both Germany and Russia, it was the Soviet occupation that frightened Latvians the most. "Baigais Gads" was still a fresh memory. The beginning of the Korean War in 1950 confirmed their suspicion that communism was spreading fast. In addition, some Latvians had been forced to return to Latvia against their will. Suddenly Germany did not seem like such a safe place after all.

I knew my father was hesitant about the decision and did not really want to make the move. By this time he was approaching his mid-fifties and had secure work and a comfortable home. He was living with my mother, Lilija, and two children born in Germany: my brother Gunar and me. It was my fearless mother, twenty-one years younger than my father, who convinced him that moving to Newfoundland was the right decision. An opportunity to begin again and to build a life with this new family.

Decision made, Premier Smallwood was able to fast-track the immigration process for the teams of European experts he needed. My father, together with a number of other German and Latvian colleagues, made the trip to Newfoundland by airplane a few times before resettling. They came to investigate what resources were available, what infrastructure existed, what would need to be built, what would need to be imported, and where the most favourable locations for setting up were. It was determined that Corner Brook was the ideal place to build a cement plant and eventually a gypsum plant, too. Corner Brook, being a port, could ship cement and gypsum products directly to ports in Canada and on the US Eastern Seaboard.

WHO WERE WE?

Although it may have seemed to the local population that we were of a single nationality, the group of approximately seventy immigrants who arrived in Corner Brook in the early 1950s was actually a mix of Latvians, Baltic Germans, and Germans (known among us as "Reichsdeutsche," meaning from Germany proper). Thrown together by history and circumstance, we were differentiated by language, place of birth, culture, and heritage. Within the group, those differences were recognized and each nationality observed its own traditions, holidays, and social customs.

It is true that the Baltic Germans also came from Latvia. They were ethnic Germans who had long settled in Latvia and had lived there for centuries, largely as a result of earlier German occupations of the region. Most of them no longer had ties with Germany itself but continued to speak the language and maintained many of the same cultural traditions.

At the time of the Second World War, their departure from Latvia was not a matter of personal decision, as it was for the Latvians. Their fate was determined by the 1939 Molotov–Ribbentrop Pact (also known as the Hitler–Stalin Pact or the Nazi–Soviet Pact), which divided Eastern Europe between the two superpowers. Because Latvia, together with the other Baltic States of Estonia and Lithuania, was to fall under the Soviet sphere, Germans living there had to move to German-held territory.

In November 1939, Baltic Germans were evacuated from their homes in Latvia and resettled in the Reichsgau of Poland (Reichsgau Wartheland). They were given German citizenship, and the men were expected to serve in the war or otherwise work in factories and businesses that were necessary to Germany's war effort. Among those were the gypsum quarries and cement factories where the Baltic Germans who eventually came to Corner Brook worked.

Near the end of the Second World War, while Latvians were engaged in the largest out-migration in the country's history, the Baltic Germans in Poland were forced to move as well. With word that the Russians were quickly advancing into the German-held Wartheland, ethnic German families packed whatever they could and boarded trains to take them into Germany itself.

One group managed to make their way to the Westphalia region, to a small mid-German town, Stadtoldendorf, and the nearby towns of Bielefeld and Bodenverder. They had agreed while still in Latvia that, if they could, they would try to meet up again at a predetermined place in Germany. Through various circuitous routes, they managed this. When the war ended, they came together to rebuild the former plants in Stadtoldendorf and Bodenverder. Starting from almost nothing, with only pencil and paper to work out the plant design and limited construction materials, they were able to draw on their accumulated expertise and begin producing the cement and gypsum that were essential to the reconstruction of Germany.

The first contingent to arrive in Corner Brook included my father and his team of engineers and technicians who could initiate the plan for a cement plant with a gypsum plant to follow. Since they were needed right away, most of them came by airplane, landing in either Gander or Stephenville. Their families came later, some of them waiting as much as a year before making the journey.

The Latvians and Germans who came to build the cement plant were not the first Balts to arrive in Corner Brook. Several Latvian families (the Langins, Bulins, and Berzins) were already in place before Confederation. Ernest Langins, Karlis Bulins, and Aleksandrs Berzins were engineers recruited by Bowater to work in the company's pulp and paper mill. Their presence formed a core Baltic community and they were able to offer assistance to those who came later.

INTEGRATING INTO LIFE IN NEWFOUNDLAND

Adjusting to life in Newfoundland, so far away from anything that was familiar to them, was a challenge for many of the new immigrants. Some adapted more readily than others. There were those like Richard Kajaks, who built a cabin in Flat Bay and took up fishing and hunting as though he had always lived there. There were those like Jennie Steinbergs, who learned to speak English better than many of the other immigrant women who chose instead to stay close to home and within their own circle. Jennie, with her energetic spirit, became active in various community groups. Junija Langins worked as a dentist and travelled regularly down both shores of the Bay of Islands, where she provided dental care to the residents. There were those like Heimtrud and Stanislaus Rodsewicz, who embraced Newfoundland's nature and never hesitated to expound on its outstanding beauty to anyone who would listen. Others, like my father, became integrated into the community through work, through training local labourers and working side by side with them.

Before any of that could happen, though, the first order of business was to find accommodation in a town that was not prepared for such an influx of new residents. We were among the lucky ones and were housed for a short time at the Glynmill Inn until one of the townhouses on Reid Street became available. Many, though, spent their first months living in the Fern Street Barracks, a set of rudimentary buildings, dormitory-style, that had originally been built to accommodate the construction workers who had come to build the tuberculosis sanatorium nearby.

Eventually families built or bought homes on East Valley Road, Reid Street, and Brookfield Avenue. W. J. Lundrigan Ltd. erected four homes on Caribou Road for their immigrant workers. A number of Baltic Germans and Latvians purchased land near the North Star Cement plant, where they built houses in styles that were reminiscent of their homeland. Ingrid Lane, named for Ingrid Tode who, together with her husband Hans, became instrumental in reviving a vital theatre scene in the town, was dubbed "Little Berlin" by the locals.

This confusion about being German plagued those of us who did not consider ourselves German. It was almost impossible to clarify our difference to the locals. We all spoke German; we were friends with the Germans; we had arrived from Germany; our parents had worked in Germany. Those facts qualified us as German. Few knew about Latvia, where it was or anything about its history. By the 1950s it was a country that no longer existed, having been swallowed up by the Soviet Union.

INSIDER/OUTSIDER TENSION

In his book *Strangers & Others: Newfoundland Essays* (Pedlar Press 2015), Canadian literary critic and professor Stan Dragland describes what he calls the "insider/outsider tension" that is felt by both the local Newfoundlander and the new immigrant: "In any case, the newcomer who settles in Newfoundland will in various ways be inside and outside both, and that until the cows come home."

Mr. Dragland, a mainlander, was himself a CFA—a "Come-From-Away." We were CFFAS—"Come-From-Far-Aways." In true Newfoundland fashion, we were welcomed with open arms. The Lundrigan clan took us in, befriended us, and showed us how to make our way in this new world. Neighbours were curious about us. They gathered around us, visited us, shared food and local advice. Neighbourhood children included us in their games and birthday parties. School principals made sure that we were taken care of, especially those older children who still did not speak English but had to be placed in the higher grades. Local workers were grateful for the employment opportunities we brought. My father enjoyed a kind of reverent respect and was referred to by everyone as "Doctor Leja" or "the Doctor," even though he did not have a doctorate.

I will never know what the Corner Brookers really thought of us. We must have been a topic of some conversation and speculation, especially in the beginning, with those strange, unpronounceable names: Sermuksnis, Rodsewicz, Prorins, Obrascova, Jaunzems, Leja (pronounced LAY-ah). And why did we complain about the food, or rather, the lack of the kind of food we were used to? What were those unusual holidays we celebrated? Why was November 18 (Latvian Independence Day) such a big deal? Why did we make such a fuss about flowers? What were we really saying when we spoke our own language?

What I can be sure of is that the speculation and comparison went both ways. At home and in the homes of other Latvians, I heard about all the ways in which we were different from the local Newfoundlanders. And yet here I was, growing up among them, playing with them, going to school with them, learning everything they learned, speaking the same language. I was becoming one of them without ever being one of them. I would never be able to play the "Who's your father?" game, never be able to name a relation between us.

What neither the Newfoundlanders nor the Latvians seemed to have realized was how similar their historical experiences were. Like Newfoundland, once a proud, independent country whose sovereignty had been taken away by an imperial power, so Latvia had lost its independence to the Soviet Union. Like Newfoundland, which had lived through the ills of colonialism, so Latvia had suffered under repeated invasions and domination by its more powerful neighbours. Like Newfoundland, which had its own unique culture fostered in its outports and recorded in its folksongs and folklore, so, too, Latvia had hung on to its identity by relying on the "dainas" (Latvian folksongs) and Latvian mythology.

OUR LEGACY

To write about the Baltic community in Corner Brook raises the question of legacy. Did we have an impact? Does it matter? Most of us no longer live in Newfoundland. The first generation, our parents, are now gone, and those of us who were children in the 1950s have moved on to live in other places. Except for a very few instances, it would be easy to think that we did not leave a mark, or at least none of any consequence. We came, we lived there for a while, and then we disappeared.

I do believe that the European influx into Corner Brook brought with it change and growth that went beyond the obvious—beyond the building of industry and jobs for the locals. The Latvians and Germans brought with them their own experiences and expectations and were not willing to abandon them just because they landed in a place that had no prior knowledge of them.

They did not leave their passions behind in Europe. They brought them along. The Todes brought their love of theatre and invigorated a new community of performance that included both newcomers and locals. They sought out local talent and brought it to the fore. Music, too, had a central role among the Balts who made arrangements to bring the Atlantic Symphony and other musical groups to town. Today Corner Brook resounds with music, art, and culture to a degree that is unusual for a community of its size. One can point to the existence of Grenfell College to explain this dynamic creative energy, but it was already there before the college arrived.

It can also be said that skiing would not have attained the prominence that it currently enjoys in Corner Brook had it not been for people like Ernest Langins and Jennie Steinbergs, two of the kingpins behind the development of the Corner Brook Ski Club and, eventually, Marble Mountain ski resort. Because of their commitment and efforts, we children grew up on skis, enjoyed every winter weekend outdoors, and developed a circle of new friends who shared the sport with us.

As for me, my legacy comes in a more personal form, in the shape of my daughter Maija— Latvian and Newfoundlander both—who was born in Corner Brook and who visits her Newfoundland family frequently. She has a home there and, like me, regards Newfoundland as God's land, a place more resplendent than any other place on earth. Her connection to Newfoundland, its people, and its culture is unbreakable. As is mine, even if I am a CFFA.

The Pains We Lie About

Mental Illness in Rural NL

by

T. J. SMITH

The coastline is dangerous and rugged. The weather is dynamic and unpredictable. The ocean is volatile and unforgiving.

Men in rural Newfoundland are shaped by these surroundings. Almost all of the rural communities in Newfoundland are located within a few kilometres of the Atlantic Ocean. Traditionally, the men of these communities grew up on the ocean. They were rough and tough, strong and unwavering.

I grew up in the 1990s and early 2000s in St. Anthony, Newfoundland, a community of just over 2,000 people. Mental illness was never, ever spoken of. It was taboo, except for vague descriptions such as "He's crazy," "She's insane," "Buddy's bipolar," and "He got 'er gone b'y." These "sayings" were accepted. We didn't know any different as youth or teenagers.

Our health classes didn't cover depression. Our parents wouldn't dare speak of anxiety. Our grandparents certainly didn't discuss bipolar disorder with us. We simply were not educated by any of the role models in our lives.

It wasn't their fault. In that era, it was accepted and expected in our rural communities that there would be no talk of mental health or mental illness.

Ignoring mental illness, though, doesn't make it go away. It's a widely known stat that one in five Canadians will experience some type of mental illness in their life. There are over 500,000 people in Newfoundland and Labrador. My math skills tell me that equates to about 100,000 Newfoundlanders and Labradorians who will encounter a mental illness in their lifespan.

A lady who attended one of our local Mental Health Peer Support Group meetings shared that, "back in the day," schooners would come to the small coastal communities, and if someone was deemed "unfit"—in other words, mentally ill—they were taken away on these schooners. The destinations were unknown. Friends and family often never saw the person who left again. Imagine a brother or sister struggling with internal angst and having no way of describing it to another person. Thoughts and feelings so tormenting they might even be considering suicide. Then this person is sent away to a strange place with stranger people. This was all too common in rural Newfoundland and Labrador.

CHILDHOOD ANXIETY

I guess I had a "normal" childhood. I was an above-average student and athlete. I had friends. It's the difficult moments in my life, though, that stand out in my memories. I have trouble remembering being voted valedictorian of my graduating high school class, but I can still vividly recall something that happened to me in grade five on a random Wednesday twenty-three years ago.

I was with classmates in the library doing group work, and we had a small disagreement, nothing to get too upset about. And I didn't get upset. I got sad. So sad, I started feeling the tears welling up in my eyes. I couldn't hold them back. The tears started coming down my face.

Where is this sadness coming from? Why do I feel like this? Is there something wrong with me?

At eleven years old, I didn't know the answers. I wouldn't even have been able to comprehend them at that point in my life.

That's when the anxiety set in. Boys weren't supposed to cry, especially around others. To avoid the embarrassment of crying in front of my classmates, I had to make up a lie. When you struggle to hide your mental illnesses, you become an expert liar—the greatest excuse-maker ever. It's a by-product of not knowing how to deal with anxiety or depression. This was a life-altering moment: the first time I lied to cover up my true feelings.

I muttered the only words I could think of: "I get sore eyes every Wednesday."

What an excuse. Every Wednesday, my eyes get sore to the point tears fall? It would have to do.

The lie worked. Until the next Wednesday.

The girl that had been in my workgroup sat in front of me in our regular classroom. She wasn't a mean person—she was just a kid, too. She turned to me and said: "It's Wednesday, T. J. Where are your sore eyes today?"

Her question caught me completely off guard. Would I have to cry every Wednesday now to hide what happened to me? Would I have to hide the sadness I experienced that day in the library forever?

This was 1997. During the 1990s and early 2000s, there was no visible support for mental health issues in my town. To be honest, I'm not even sure we had a guidance counsellor at St. Anthony Elementary. If we did, I don't remember where their office was located.

ALCOHOL CULTURE

I first thought I might have a mental illness in February 2012. I was watching a documentary on athletes who have struggled with depression. It captivated me. Everything they talked about sounded familiar. It was then I realized that I had the same feelings and thoughts. No, I wasn't a world-class athlete like some of them, but I was a hockey player in Canada, where hockey is king.

It would be four more years before I actually spoke to a doctor about my tantalizing thoughts and fearful feelings. I was living in Nova Scotia when I was diagnosed with severe depression, anxiety, and obsessive compulsive disorder (OCD). It was January 2016, and I had no idea what was happening to me. The feelings and thoughts that I was having had to be abnormal.

I was a year away from finishing up my Bachelor of Commerce from St. Mary's University and about to become a father for the first time in the upcoming spring. So, I did what any 26-year-old male would have done: I hid it all. It was (depending on the day) easy for me to disguise my depression, especially when I was busy and around others. I would wake up daily and put on a mask, smiling to hide the thoughts that kept me up until 4:00 a.m.

I coped by drinking on the weekend with my friends. I was never an alcoholic, but I was most certainly a huge binge drinker. Weekends were a blur from Thursday night to Sunday morning. I knew alcohol wasn't healthy and that it was a depressant, but, for those forty-eight to sixty-four hours, it was my antidepressant. There were no responsibilities and no accountability. I let loose. I didn't drink because my friends did; I did it to open up around other people. To be more relaxed, I guess.

When the binge drinking started to get out of hand, I would often black out and wake up not remembering much, if anything, from the night before. Sometimes I woke up in random places. No idea how I got there or who I was there with. In April 2016, there was a memorable blackout that I do not recall.

This is my friend's account:

We were in Halifax drinking the whole weekend. It was Sunday afternoon. I had just returned from Dartmouth. From a place I didn't know. Dropped off by a woman I didn't know. As you can probably guess, I had blacked out. To be honest, she probably doesn't remember me at all, either.

My friend and I settled into a great pub downtown. Luckily, there was a Toronto Blue Jays game on, ideal for us Jays fans. The bar was quiet, so we sat there with one other guy. He was kind and humble. He turned out to be the drummer from the Canadian band Hedley.

This musician was also a Jays fan, so the three of us hit it off. We talked about the baseball game and then got into deeper conversation about the Blue Jays. Eventually, we found ourselves discussing life and all the wonders that come along with it.

The drummer set aside two tickets for me to his show in Halifax the next day. I didn't get the tickets. I was in the hospital.

That night, I almost jumped off the Macdonald Bridge that connects Halifax and Dartmouth. If it hadn't been for my friend, I would be dead.

We left the bar, and I don't recall what happened the rest of that day or night. I know where we went, but that's about all I can remember. I don't know who I spoke or interacted with.

The alcohol was starting to take control of my decisions. I shouldn't say that—the alcohol was influencing my decisions. All accountability and responsibility ceased to exist. How did I let a great afternoon, in a small, rustic Halifax bar talking sports and life turn into the night I wanted to jump off a bridge?

I would go off-track. A lot. I just didn't want to live. The pain was too much, I thought. But on this day and night, someone, somewhere granted me a second chance. Why? I don't know. I don't need an answer to that. I'm just grateful I am still here. I'm certain if my friend wasn't there I wouldn't be writing these words. That I am sure of. I can't remember the whole debate, and I am too ashamed to ask him what happened. I am fearful of the answer. I don't like hearing about that stuff. I am embarrassed by my alcohol-induced decisions.

That has always been my battle with depression. Things may seem to be going well on the surface, but something inside of me is not well. It's like there is a small flame inside of me. When I pour alcohol on it, it's like gas—the flame becomes a blaze. Fortunately, it has never been a fatal fire. I consider myself one of the lucky ones.

I stopped drinking for over a year after that night.

Why did I share this story? To shed a light on the impact alcohol can have on people, especially if you're dealing with depression. Newfoundlanders and Labradorians are known for many things. Kindness. Accent. Terminology. Another, whether bad or good, is our drinking.

I grew up in a household where there was always a beer in our fridge. I grew up around men who played sports and drank beer afterwards. There was never any pressure to drink, but, on the flip side, there was no one saying it was bad for you, either. My parents did their best to keep it from me as a teenager, but not everyone is like that. I had friends who began to drink as early as twelve and thirteen.

I even knew parents who would allow their teen to host parties in their shed. The reasoning that was communicated to us was those parents felt more comfortable knowing where their son was drinking than not knowing. I get that, to a certain degree. Doesn't make it right. But that was, and still is, a common practice.

Why bring this up? Alcohol is a depressant. Ease of access to it doesn't help if someone is struggling with a mental illness. It doesn't help that drinking is accepted at an early age.

I am not knocking alcohol. If you can use it appropriately, that's great. But in my situation, I fail as a human using it. To help rid rural Newfoundland of this "culture," we need to educate our youth more on alcohol and other drugs or substances. There is a huge chance that a teenager will experiment at least once. This is where sharing information about alcohol and drugs can help. Speaking from experience, mixing alcohol with a mental illness is not that smart. It can lead to a lot of damage. In every meaning of the word.

RURAL STIGMA

I returned to Newfoundland and Labrador in January 2018. It was an important and necessary life move. A month later, a man I have known as long as I can remember took his own life. It was then I decided more needs to be done in our small part of the province.

When I was in a psychiatric unit in Nova Scotia after my first suicide attempt in December 2015, I pledged to share my story about depression. That hadn't been a physical attempt, but I had everything planned out, even the final letters to people. At that point, I decided to share everything that has ever happened to me, no matter how dark it could get. I felt sharing my story would help fight the stigma related to mental illness.

So, in October 2018, a friend and I started a Mental Health Peer Support Group in St. Anthony. Our goal was to provide additional help to the people that struggle in our area. I had so much anxiety built up. I was fearful no one would show up. It was anxiety built upon anxiety.

Six people showed. It went off excellent. My anxiety and fears slowly lost their impact when people started to share their stories of pain and struggle. It's a weekly meeting that we still host. The best part is seeing people share their story with others. Stepping outside of their comfort zones to tell strangers about their struggles.

What we have come to learn in our weekly group sessions is that shame still exists in our small communities. We've decided to coin it "Rural Stigma."

Views and beliefs in rural Newfoundland and Labrador rely heavily on tradition. Information is passed down from generation to generation. It takes a while for new ideas to be accepted.

My parents grew up in towns of fewer than five hundred people during the 1960s and 1970s. There was no education about mental illness. No talk of maintaining good mental health. It wasn't taught in the schools and sure as hell wasn't taught in the church.

Once someone had an opinion about a certain topic—even a topic that they didn't know much about—that belief wasn't changing. When it came to mental illness, how could people's beliefs change? There was no education on the topic. There were no awareness campaigns. No one was there to teach them any different.

Society in the mid to late 1900s in rural Newfoundland and Labrador also had an expectation of what a man should be that did a lot of damage to men's mental health. A man had to be tough. He had to be strong. He had to be able to provide. He couldn't cry. It was impossible to be a man and have a mental illness, because having mental issues was a sign of weakness. If someone died by suicide, it was hidden from the public, as best it could be. Even today, it is harder for adult men in rural parts of the province to talk about their mental illness.

The problem with stigma is people may be afraid to discuss their illness. People are not comfortable going to and being in the hospital. It's viewed as a flaw to go there for help. In reality, it's one of the only places we can go to get help.

To combat the stigma, I keep talking about the difficult topics, such as suicide. It isn't the easiest thing to bring up, but how do we create awareness if we fail to talk about it? It's like it's a fairy tale. Not real. Make-believe.

I also let people know that having a mental illness is not the end of the world. That people can live a meaningful life while having depression. That people can have a purposeful life while having bipolar disorder. People believe that their lives are over because of mental illness. That is not the case.

Trying to preach this message is a hard task, but it can be done. Old views and beliefs can be replaced, but only when what people learned years ago is unlearned today. It is not something that happens overnight. It will take some work. A community, as a whole, needs to help fight the stigma.

MOVING FORWARD

There are resources here in St. Anthony, but they are limited. There are good mental health staff, but they are limited. We don't get the same support as larger communities in Newfoundland and Labrador. It's now halfway through 2020, and our local hospital still does not have a psychiatrist on site. As an advocate for mental health, I believe we deserve the same services in rural Newfoundland and Labrador as they have in urban areas. I've heard every excuse. It's money. It's distance. No doctors want to go to rural areas.

My hospital stays have saved my life. Those stays have kept me alive. My experiences have been great, so I tell people this often: "Hospitals are where we go to get help and live. Not where we go to die."

As a young man who has been hospitalized a few times due to my mental illness, my number one tip to mental health professionals is this: show that you care. Show that our lives matter. The impact that has on a person who views their life as valueless is remarkable. We, people with mental illnesses, come to the hospital for help, because if we didn't want help we would be coming to the hospital in a body bag.

Depression hinders my life. There is no doubt about that. It makes me feel unwanted feelings and have unwanted thoughts. This is my reality. Maybe for the rest of my life.

The key to fighting suicide, however, is finding purpose in life. When I and another community-minded person created our Mental Health Peer Support Group, we didn't realize how much impact it would have. We have seen so many people attend these weekly meetings. It has made a real difference to people in our area.

We're particularly proud that we have remained confidential. No stories or information leak out. We don't hear outside chatter about who attends those meetings at the local Tim Horton's. This is particularly important in a small town.

Growing up in small communities, everyone knows each other. No one is a stranger. This is a great thing. But when it comes to dealing with a mental illness privately, well, that's a hard thing to do. Everyone knows everyone else's business. I encourage people to speak openly about their mental illness, but only when they are ready.

Now, other rural communities are reaching out to us seeking information on starting up their own Peer Support Groups. We are going in the right direction. It will require ongoing education and creating awareness to eliminate stigma. People are starting to accept that having a mental illness doesn't mean you are "crazy" or "insane." We have come a long way. Fighting stigma is a process. Hopefully, someday, the stigma will be completely gone. But for now, we have to keep fighting our battles and living our lives.

Being Jewish in the Land of Cain

by

ROBIN McGRATH

I once asked a rabbi what a good Jew should do if he lives too far from the synagogue to walk to services on Shabbat. He answered that a good Jew wouldn't live so far away from other Jews.

Sometimes, however, circumstances are such that you have little or no choice. Such would have been the case for the first Jewish settlers who came to Canada to participate in the fur trade, and such was the case for Leon Cooper, a Holocaust survivor who helped found the small northern town where I lived for twelve years. Apparently, Mr. Cooper walked off the coastal boat *Kyle* in Happy Valley, Labrador, with a suitcase full of nylons and bandanas and didn't leave until he'd not only sold them all but established a dry goods store, a hotel, a power plant, and a town council.

My own motivation was not one of such desperation, but it was compelling. My husband had survived a bout with cancer, which left him restless and dissatisfied with the job he had been doing for almost thirty years. When he was offered the opportunity to have a significant impact on both the Indigenous and settler communities in Labrador, it wasn't in me to say no. We packed our bags, sold our house, and headed north.

That was fourteen years ago. I knew at the time that there wasn't a synagogue in Goose Bay, or anywhere in Labrador, because when I was a girl the Jewish men and women from the air base there used to fly down to St. John's for the high holidays. I did think there would be some Jews in the area, however, maybe even an informal community. There wasn't. The military had all but left Labrador, so there were no more Jewish servicemen or women, and the Jewish businesses like those owned by Mr. Cooper had moved on. Occasionally a Jewish doctor would come for a few days, or a businessman, but other than a young, transient ecologist who stayed for a few months, I didn't find another Jew living within 500 kilometres of the place.

Two moments in history could have changed the face of Labrador as we know it. Back in 1677, several ships owned by a Dutch Jew named Roderigo Joseph de la Penha touched the coast of Labrador and claimed the territory on behalf of Prince William of Orange, who was soon to reign as William III of England. Twenty years later, de la Penha was supposed to have saved William III's life while he was sailing to Holland in a storm, and in gratitude the monarch granted the whole territory to him. Descendants of de la Penha attempted to proceed with the claim, without success.

In 1977, the original grant instrument was found at the Royal Commonwealth Society and a descendant, Dr. Daniel de la Penha, brought the matter to court on behalf of himself and various other relatives. In his decision in the case *De La Penha v. Newfoundland* (1984), Chief Justice Alex Hickman ruled that the statement of claim "didn't meet the legal requirements necessary for Prince William of Orange to acquire sovereignty over the land in question." De la Penha appealed the case, and eventually it went all the way to the Supreme Court of Canada, where Madam Justice Bertha Wilson denied the appeal.

A second attempt to settle Jews in Labrador came about before World War II, when Frank Banikhin, who owned herring factories all around the country of Newfoundland, proposed to open up Labrador for immigration to German Jewish industrialists attempting to escape the looming Holocaust. Sir John Hope Simpson and the Commission of Government backed the plan, but it did not meet the approval of either the Zionists or the

British Government. Banikhin's son, Flight Sergeant Lawrence Banikhin, was shot down and killed over India in 1942, and a family member told me "the fight went out of the old man," who never fully recovered from the blow. Aside from sojourners like Leon Cooper, who became the first mayor of Happy Valley–Goose Bay, and an occasional doctor or researcher, Labrador failed to attract any Jewish settlers into the twenty-first century.

I knew that I would have to make concessions to my religious life in Labrador, and I thought I was prepared for them. I was aware that keeping kosher was simply not feasible there, not just because of the unavailability of kosher foods, but because of the barrier it would erect between us and the people around us. I'd worked most of my adult life with Indigenous people, and, if you can't eat with them and eat the food they eat, then you can't fully participate in the community.

Curiously, kashrut is compatible with Inuit culture, as Inuit traditionally had a strong taboo against mixing food from the sea with food from the land, but, in my experience, the idea of not mixing milk and meat and, even more so, the refusal to eat meat that had been hunted as opposed to meat that had been raised for ritual slaughter were completely foreign to Innu culture. In Labrador, that would mean no rabbits, no caribou, no moose, no partridge, and no porcupine—in other words, no country food at all. But what I was losing went beyond having a kosher kitchen.

I'm not a particularly spiritual person. I liked being Jewish because it gave structure to my life. The laws, the rules for behaviour, are mostly fairly straightforward. You are expected to study, a little or a lot; to observe the major holy days and holidays of Purim, Passover, Rosh Hashanah, and Yom Kippur and maybe also mark the lesser ones such as Sukkot and Hanukkah; to give your children a basic Jewish education; to remember the Holocaust; to give to the needy; and to treat people with respect. Nobody ever asks you if you believe in God, or an afterlife, or the efficacy of prayer. My form of Judaism filled a social and emotional need rather than a religious or intellectual one.

Jewish observance, as I practised it, was mostly pleasant. I remember making Purim costumes for my children when they were small and attending Purim plays at the *talmud torah*, packing up boxes of *hamantashen* to mail to them when they were in university, and attending readings of the *megillah* Esther at synagogues across Canada. Back in St. John's, our *chazan* and the president of the synagogue would always have a friendly but fierce debate as to the relative merits of *mun* versus prune filling in the pastries, and we would prepare plates of both to take to the few elderly Jewish residents of the local nursing homes.

In Goose Bay, social practices such as these were not available to me. When Purim arrived, I'd read the Book of Esther to myself instead, or invite a friend to supper and tell the story, trying to explain why Vashti was the wicked one when her only crime seems to have been that she refused to dance naked before the court. I made *hamantashen*, which my husband demolished. One year, I brought some to the neighbourhood children and they looked at them as if they were the poisoned cakes from Neverland. I also tried to study a little. It was a poor substitute for the whirling graggers and pounding feet of St. John's, the *shiurim* and shared festivities of our little synagogue. One year, Purim almost slipped by unnoticed. It is all too easy to lose yourself when you have been cut loose from your moorings.

Once, in reading about Purim in Isaac Klein's *A Guide to Jewish Religious Practice*, published in 1992, I came across the words of Dr. Mordechai Kaplan, who wrote that Purim is a good time to consider anew "the difficulties that inhere in our position 'as a people scattered and dispersed among the nations.'" He believed that the fast and the feast of Purim should "make Jews conscious of the spiritual values which their position as a minority group everywhere in the diaspora should lead them to evolve, and of the dangers which they must be prepared to overcome, if they expect to survive as a minority group." Dr. Kaplan was writing on the eve of World War II, just as the full magnitude of the oncoming Holocaust was being manifest. Animosity against Jews is a perennial problem and something he would have been particularly aware of in relation to the accusations Haman was making in the *megillah* Esther. The danger faced by Jews who were isolated, as I was in Labrador, was more benign—it was indifference.

Nobody there cared that I was a Jew. They would ask what church I went to and when I'd say I was Jewish, they'd simply look puzzled and change the subject. In December, they urged me to put up Christmas lights (there is a Christmas competition for the best-decorated street) and expressed surprise that we had no tree in the window or Advent wreaths on the doors.

Only once in twelve years did anyone ask why I had "those funny boxes"—*mezuzot*—nailed on the doorposts instead. If the Holocaust seemed like an impending tornado to Dr. Kaplan, I felt like I was fighting with a puff of wind, a gentle breeze of unconcern. I worried that if a real wind were suddenly to develop, my Jewish practice would collapse before the first gust.

And yet, there was something of value for me in Dr. Kaplan's remarks, something I could see as I looked at the Indigenous community that surrounded me. Goose Bay, once a bustling military base, was rapidly changing and becoming a town dominated by Innu and Inuit. Innu in particular had taken a very strong stand against the mining and hydro developments that were preparing to fill the gap left by the five NATO forces that for the last fifty years had dominated this area.

Nominally Christian, Innu were more like the Marrano Jews of Spain, cherishing their language, their traditions, their spiritual beliefs beneath the surface, and drawing from them the strength and courage to fight for their rights. I found that, while Christian churches stood prominently in the communities of Sheshatshiu and Natuashish, out in the bush, away from prying eyes, were the Sweat Lodges and tents where the *mukashan* ceremonies were still celebrated. Virtually all the adults and children of these communities spoke Innu-aimun, their first language.

Thirty years ago, it looked as if the Innu people were about to disappear off the face of the earth, yet today they are standing strong against government and industry and fighting their way past the impacts of intergenerational trauma to find healing. Where did they find such strength against overwhelming odds? Not at the bottom of a Sugar Pops box; not from reruns of *Three's Company* or *Gilligan's Island*; not even in their Christian churches or their English schools.

Dr. Kaplan would say that their strength came from "the spiritual values which their position as a minority group...[led] them to evolve," and their consciousness of the dangers they had to overcome in order to survive as a minority group. Their strength came from their continued awareness of what they call the Animal Masters, the healing power of the Sweat Lodges, the sound of their sacred drums and songs, their love for their children, and their mastery of their own language—their knowledge that they are People of the Caribou.

So even though I was the only Jew in Goose Bay, possibly the only one in Labrador, I continued to light the Shabbat candles, set the seder table for Pesach, bake *hamantashen*, and read the *megilla* Esther at Purim. And I continued to study as best I could, a community of one with thousands of years of history to support me, for books and beliefs can travel where people cannot. Nevertheless, although I did not make a conscious decision to neglect my spiritual or religious life, bit by bit it faded into the background. My habit of lighting Shabbat candles on Friday night and yahrzeit candles on the anniversaries of my parents' deaths were forgotten as I ran out of the appropriate supplies. My son in Toronto tried mailing me matzahs for Passover our first year there, but all that arrived was a box of crumbs. For a few more years I made matzahs myself, trying to do it within the brief time that is allowed for the process to be kosher, but it was tiresome and not always successful. Eventually I simply avoided bread for the eight days of Pesach. Often my neglect was a result of not having a Jewish calendar, which I was used to getting from a bank on Elizabeth Avenue in St. John's. It's easy enough to print a calendar off from a website, but I lacked motivation.

In retrospect, I realize that it wasn't a lack of calendars or candles or matzah that had made my Judaism fade into the background, but a lack of other Jews with whom to be Jewish. Previously, when Jewish friends visited, it was not unusual for them to touch their fingers to the *mezuza* on our doorpost as they entered the house, or to drop a coin in the *pushke* in the hallway. They might greet me with a *"gut yontev"* or *"shabbat shalom."* These small gestures acknowledging our shared Judaism were so low-key and tiny that they might not even be noticed by others, but they were nudges, reminders that the practice of our shared values had meaning.

I recently read a *shiur* given by Jonathan Sacks in which he explained the famous injunction *na'aseh ve-nishma*. It means "we will do and we will hear," and it was what our ancestors said at Mount Sinai when they accepted the Ten Commandments. My understanding of that phrase has always been that doing leads to belief. Christian religions tend to stress belief as the first step: "If thou canst believe, all things are possible" (Mark 9:17-24). But for Jews, even if you don't or can't believe, following the 613 prescribed laws will lead you to belief. In Labrador, with no other Jews to remind me to "do" first, practice faded and indifference crept up on me.

The sense of belonging I felt in the St. John's Jewish community was something I missed, but over time that emptiness was filled by Labrador friends. I attended the Moravian church occasionally, I went to the Sweat Lodge when I was homesick, attended *mukashans* with the Elders in Sheshatshiu, went to classes in Inuktitut, slept in canvas tents pitched on six feet of snow, baked bread in hot sand, fished for eels, picked berries, checked rabbit snares, mourned at funerals, and celebrated at weddings and baptisms. After a time, I wasn't lonely anymore. After a time, I stopped "doing."

But eventually, our sojourn came to an end. Twelve years after moving to Labrador, my husband retired, and we moved back to the island. A lot had changed, both for us and for the Jewish community in St. John's, while we were gone.

When we had left back in 2006, there was a small but coherent Jewish community centred around Beth El synagogue on Elizabeth Avenue. When we returned, the synagogue building was still there, but the community had divided into factions and the Conservative congregation had shrunk considerably. Two new groups had formed at the extremes of observance: Havurah, which is a loose association of intermarried Jews and Christians, most of whom neither read nor speak Hebrew, and Chabad, led by a strictly orthodox young rabbi who will not lead or attend services unless women are separated from men by a *mechitza* or barrier.

The elders, particularly the Holocaust survivors who had been such an important part of our community, had all died. I missed their guidance, their strength, their determination to go on being Jews in a predominantly non-Jewish society. It was harder to focus on Jewish values without them to remind us of the sacrifices they had made, harder to make sacrifices ourselves.

Keeping kosher in St. John's had become more difficult also. The Dominion store on Stavanger Drive no longer carried kosher chickens or Passover food. The Muslim community had grown enormously, so *halal* meat was available, but, while Muslims can eat kosher chickens and lamb, Jews who keep kosher cannot eat *halal* meat. A return to kosher food practices would require a totally vegetarian diet, which at this stage in our lives didn't hold much appeal, particularly as there was now nobody to share that food with us.

St. John's itself had changed also. The boom in the oil patch had made the city a bigger, more intimidating place than it had been. The traffic alone was alarming. After more than a decade in a tiny, quiet town with exactly two stoplights, the new, busier city did not hold much attraction for me or my husband, and we opted to settle out around the bay, just far enough away to discourage me from attempting regular attendance at Shabbat services, particularly in winter. With prompting from a friend, I did attend Jewish services with both the Havurah and the Beth El congregations, but didn't feel at home with either.

So here I was again, the only Jew in my current community, unmoored and trying to find a place that felt like home. And along came the pandemic, with social isolation for everyone. Curiously enough, it was the coronavirus that led me to begin reestablishing the Jewish observances that were eroded in Labrador. When my husband and I sat down to a Passover seder for two, as we had so often in Labrador, Jews all over the world were doing it also. When neighbours began leaving presents of fresh eggs and salt fish on our doorstep, we reciprocated with homemade jam from the gallons of berries I'd picked in the fall, but I also made challah to leave for a Jewish couple in the next small town on Friday evenings.

When the days of the coronavirus turned into weeks, and I couldn't distinguish Monday from Friday, I began to light the Shabbat candles again to help mark the passage of time. My Hebrew, which I had worked so hard to acquire when I was teaching in Israel, had grown rusty, so I used the Internet to bone up. Then a friend in Toronto sent me a link to the weekly talks of Rabbi Sacks, and, since he was also addressing the issues of the pandemic, it helped me settle in and wait out the duration with patience. I think what I've learned is that it helps to have a community if you are Jewish, but that being Jewish helps when you don't have one.

As I write this, still in the middle of the pandemic, it's been several months since I've been in a library, a bookstore, a swimming pool, or a shop. I haven't seen my sisters or other family members. I haven't visited friends or my next-door neighbours who are both ninety-two years old. I haven't been to a doctor or a hairdresser. I have walked approximately 450 kilometres, fed eight kilos of oat cakes to a neighbour's horse, harvested

122 gallons of seaweed for our garden, and written over 50,000 words of the manuscript of my next book. But I've still had a lot of time to think.

I am now over seventy. My life is not going to change for the better in the coming years unless I find a way to feel more at home in my own skin, and reacquainting myself with my Jewish practices and traditions feels like the route to take. I remember Holocaust survivor Philip Riteman telling me that, after the death camps, "Newfoundland and Newfoundlanders gave me back my humanity." He was talking about the ordinary people he met while peddling "around the bay," people like my neighbours in my new community. Even after all he'd suffered, Philip learned to take solace in his *yiddishkeit*—his Jewish life. He learned to be Jewish by himself, without a community of other Jews to rely on. While Philip was almost destroyed by a storm, I was almost stopped by a breath of wind. He set me an example of how to move forward, and I am doing just that.

In Three Parts

by

IVAN J. WHITE

Differences are plentiful among Canada's Indigenous communities, organizations, companies, and individuals—in language, culture, history, and so much more.

Are we not Mi'kmaq?

Do we not have our own lived history, our own stories? Have we accepted the settler idea of us as our idea of us?

> All Indians are portrayed as living in tipis and wearing feathers, until even some Indians have come to believe this.
>
> —Royal Commission on National Development in the Arts, Letters and Sciences, Ottawa, ON, 1952

Again, are we not Mi'kmaq?

Like the Elders say: "Let me tell you this now."

PART ONE—A NATION DECONSTRUCTED

I know we have people who fear the settler backlash and reprisals. I see it with my own eyes. Those people who still speak about "the Natives" or "the Indians" in the third person. Creating a separate identity from the one that lies deep within their souls at best and sits on the card in their wallets at worst.

The struggle for recognition began anew in 1969 with the elder Trudeau's attempted legislation of the White Paper, which sought to end the special legal relationship between Indigenous Peoples and the Canadian government. Newfoundland Mi'kmaq activists who later came to be known as the Warriors of the Flame were spurred into action. They travelled the island and gathered the Mi'kmaq families. A few hundred at first, then a few thousand. The movement was born in living rooms and on doorsteps in communities dotted across the island. Together they formed the Native Association of Newfoundland and Labrador to represent the rights of all Indigenous people in the province.

The Warriors of the Flame forced the Canadian government to give them a promise: a letter that gave a timeline for recognition of the Mi'kmaq of the island, signed by a cabinet minister. All the leverage was theirs when the Government of Canada came to the negotiation table. In 1987 Ottawa recognized Miawpukek Mi'kamawey Mawi'omi as a Mi'kmaw reserve in Bay d'Espoir, and in 2011 the federal government created the Qalipu Mi'kmaq First Nation, a "landless" Mi'kmaw band, by an order-in-council. But in the process the wrong values were emphasized. The status card would become synonymous with Mi'kmaw identity on the island, and community would no longer be the focus. This has caused a crisis within our communities, a crisis that will certainly recall the days when "Indian" was a dirty word for our Elders and the struggle for recognition was fought by only a handful of people.

We cannot sell the mantra that things like culture, people, and territory exist as brands owned by a corporation. This is incredibly disrespectful to our Elders, our history, and our lands. It trivializes all that was fought for and won; it diminishes the present and future contributions of our people.

Branding in these areas is a falsehood that magnifies the separation of our families, our communities, from the rest of the L'nu (Mi'kmaq) Nation. We do not need to create any more separation—we need to grasp at every spark of unity and breathe life into it. There need to be bridges built and fences mended within and outside of Qalipu First Nation. We need to talk and connect with our families off-island and become part of the greater Nation. Using a name solely like a brand is an indignity to those who came before us and a hindrance for those who come after us.

The name Qalipu, meaning "caribou," is a designation created from the off-reserve concept, a landless band. The name implies that, like caribou, we roam with no permanent domicile, but nothing could be further from the truth. This doesn't mean we do not inhabit territory and act as the protectors of this place. Quite the opposite. We do have permanence in other areas: family and community. Here our connections are strong. Here our connections were solidified and strengthened by the trailblazers of the Indigenous movement in the province.

The name isn't the territory we inhabit. The territory is the ancestral lands of Beothuk and Mi'kmaq. If our words contend that we are on our territory then we need to understand that our territory does not denote ownership—it denotes stewardship and the protection and preservation of our territory for the generations that will follow us.

The name isn't the culture we express. Our culture is built on the history and heritage of the Mi'kmaq, who were dispersed across the Island of Newfoundland over centuries for a multitude of reasons. As the Indigenous group with the distinction of being one of the longest affected by European settlers and colonial ideals, we should be filled to the brim with pride that our people have remained steadfast in their identity.

We cannot have an identity that isn't informed by our past. We cannot be ashamed to be proud of our ancestors and ourselves. My identity is not a brand.

We cannot get out from under government funding programs until we stand up for our rights and title to the lands that we inhabit and protect.

The legitimacy and integrity of the Nation is built on the knowledge and wisdom of the community. There was nothing inherently wrong with the concept of community connection taken at face value. But to insert that into a software matrix, to pull the life out of it and reduce it to a desk job, where there is no heart allowed, was wrong. Paper receipts and posed photography don't substantiate a connection to my home. I know who belongs to my community. I've either grown up around them or heard my community speak of them if they were not around.

Self-determination is one of the pillars found in the United Nations Declaration of Rights of Indigenous People—Article 3 of that document, in fact—and it is immensely important that we exercise those rights and uphold those pillars. We are not a new race: we are Mi'kmaq, L'nu, the Allies, the First People, the People of the Dawn. We were and are all of this and we are more. We are still here.

Opportunists exist. And we should be quite wary of anyone who feels that signing a paper, and that alone, warrants the recognition and rights that this struggle has heralded for our communities. We need to come together to combat the active measures that are being used against us like the notion that there are, or ever will be, one hundred thousand members—the number of applicants who have tried to enrol in the Qalipu First Nation Band. There aren't, and anyone who says there are is actively trying to divide and conquer the Mi'kmaq Nation. They are segregating us from the greater community off-island, and our communities suffer because they are told that that number represents their family. It doesn't. Using that number, which is made up of opportunists and not Mi'kmaq people, is at the heart of our distance from the rest of our Mi'kmaq families.

The sob stories, the ones you stole from my Elders, are transparent when falling out of your mouth. All I see are opportunists, looking to benefit from something they have no connection to. If you were to succeed we would not hear from you again. You are not proud.

Disinformation will break any connection we have to our Nation, people, culture, and history. For the opportunists who continue to prey on people's ignorance and naïveté, or on their willingness to learn, I feel ashamed that you have room to exist. I'm also relieved because in my short time on this earth I have seen you sputter and fail then disappear from the movement. You do not belong so you cannot hold on.

There has been boundless opportunity for people to step forward and share their knowledge and teachings in a good way. Those who have, I thank and applaud you. You should not feel inferior if you come from a community where you were the minority. Your identity, and the identity of your ancestors, is strong and vibrant. We are disconnected by time, place, and a multitude of human interferences. But we are connected through identity, language, and culture. Sit, listen, and learn from those of us who want to share.

The potential for many "newly minted" Indigenous people, through the very rocky enrolment process, colours the public's view of Indigenous people in general. The hype train is currently focused on people rediscovering or finding out about their connection for the first time. But we need constant reminders that there are life-long Indigenous people here as well, and they have lived experience that we can all appreciate in its telling.

We all know that those who came for "benefits" and with their own self-interest at the core of identifying will not show active support for the Nation moving forward. But we can be comfortable with this because we also know that they will not be here long. Those people will drift away from the centre much the same as those who tried and failed to claim Indigenous heritage through the enrolment process.

PART TWO—FAMILY IS COMMUNITY (INTERLUDE)

Our children, my children, will grow up knowing who they are as I did and my parents and grandparents and great-grandparents before them did. We were "the Indians" when very few beyond the boundaries of our community would admit that they, too, shared in our identity. I am absolutely humbled to now have the privilege of being able to say I grew up knowing who I was in Flat Bay and Shallop Cove. Two beautiful Mi'kmaq communities full to the brim with examples of Indigenous activists, leaders, thinkers, and warriors.

To clarify for you, knowing who I was did not mean wearing feathers or stooping in tipis or chanting at the rising sun. I have worn feathers in my adulthood. I have built and slept in tipis in adulthood. I have sung from my heart as the sun rose to caress my face. I was not meant for these things, however. They have never come to me easily, and I struggle heavily to be involved in a way that is meaningful for others as well as myself. But, starting in my teenage years, as I debated and conversed with Elders in the community, I felt a tug. My family and community had a different path for me, you see.

I am a child of loving and wonderful parents; I wish everyone could say the same. I was given everything that they could offer, my upbringing was rich and vibrant, and I wanted for nothing that I can remember besides the written word. I love to read anything that I can get my hands on and head around. I read a lot then, and still do now. I chewed through encyclopedias when I ran out of books and comics. So this "want" wasn't related to our financial standing or class—I was just a black hole that swallowed words instead of light.

I still cannot recall if I realized we were a specific "class," as I wasn't raised with the same ideas of rich and poor as most others. Some people had more things or a larger home but I never felt either of those things created a hierarchy within the community. Instead, there was a true feeling of community built around fairness and generosity; I struggle to find a better word to describe it than "sharing."

I was free and I was cared for—that was the point. I was free to take my bicycle and ride the four-and-a-half kilometres to Big Pond. It was within the boundaries of my community and a place where my parents knew others would watch over me and care for my well-being.

Although the community is isolated through access, with only one road in and out, it was also isolated through the will of others, publicly called a filthy place full of degenerates by outsiders. I've never experienced that. Flat Bay is special. It is the Heart of the Mi'kmaq People on the west coast. Its people are strong-willed and full of heart. There are very few times when I can say I experienced any meetings with someone who was completely unknown to me. We know our people and will defend them to a fault; we will also call you out if you falsely claim the community. We know our people.

PART THREE—UNIQUENESS OF SELF

These are not your stories. I don't want you to take that the wrong way. I just want you to recognize that you cannot read these words and then have them grafted onto your own life experiences. This is who I am, uniquely, as a Mi'kmaw person. If you see some of yourself in these writings then I hope you don't struggle as I do to express these ideas and tell the story you have.

These days I struggle, and swallow hard on my vicious tongue, as I watch people who ignored, ridiculed, and oppressed me and my people now touting their Indigeneity. This is fine: I'm not here to ask for an apology or to stomp on your newfound identity. Keep it close to your heart, though. Shouting about it will certainly cause a bigger fuss than you're ready to handle. Racism is far from dead, and it is not an experience I wish on anyone. I know from experience that allies are few and far between when the "Indigenous card" is on the table.

So, what is a proud, life-long Mi'kmaw man to do? To find my answer I place myself in the hands of those whose knowledge and opinion I trust and value the most: my Elders. I've long been told by my Elders that this situation is our opportunity. Educate others, and, if they are in turn awakened, accept them. There is room for everyone in the circle.

This education is what enables us to connect with our past, understand our present, and empower our future. I find time every day to educate someone about my people, my community, and my person. Even though sometimes that someone is the solitary self called Ivan J. Once you are educated, and this could be true for all people, you should then automatically have the drive to share this with others. There is no other way to go about things for me. It is just how it is. Those willing to accept knowledge without thinking of it as a transaction or a competition have my respect, love, and loyalty.

Come to the fire with humility and your truth, and there you will find acceptance. What a great feeling it is to be accepted for who we are and what we feel. There is no one right way to be Mi'kmaq as long as you legitimately care about the future of the Nation. To some, it might seem like I rarely participate in cultural activities, but this is because I prefer to work in the background. I am a very private person, as is my family, for the most part. I do not feel that my place is to be in the spotlight but rather to coordinate from behind the scenes and to put others centre stage.

If you see me at the fire you might assume I am cold or unfeeling. I do not dispense myself through the presentational aspects of my culture very often. I sing and drum when I am sure that there are others who understand the complex timing and relationship that goes with singing while playing an instrument. I also, and probably selfishly, only sing when I feel the music, when my heart compels me to vibrate the air. I am told that I do have musical talent, but that talent is overshadowed by my shyness. There is also the ever-present thought that, if I get involved and attempt to assist others in understanding the harmony and timing of group singing and drumming, I might be labelled a gate-keeper or misconstrued as someone who thinks there might be people who should not sing or drum because they do not have the ability. I am neither. I do believe that if you are going to put yourself out there to sing and drum that you should do it from your heart and you should have the respect to approach it with dedication and practice.

It is the same with ceremonial practices for me. I will protect you and your ceremony through whatever means I have available to me, but I will seldom take part. I hold you in the utmost respect if you are nourished by ceremony; I am jealous in fact. As a person with a head for administration, I am nourished by paperwork, and I accept this.

As I entered adulthood, if you can call me an adult at my maturity level, I began to recognize that I have been moulded and directed for a purpose by my Elders. There was a reason that I was present at specific times. I was given a fount of knowledge about the people, places, and history of the Native movement on the island. They wished for me to take that knowledge forward. My mission is to insert myself into the settler structures. It will do no good to try and tear them down with passionate pulpit protests. The mechanisms are designed to save themselves at all costs; they do not care for human logic, morals, or emotions. They must be changed from inside. We must make the rules ourselves. Bring what you have learned with you and reshape the world to fit your people.

I recognize many of you as allies, but the strength we could have in numbers remains divided over plastic cards. If you are on edge, and feel discomfort that someone will take your card, then that is just what our foes want. If your identity is questioned and this puts you on edge, then we need to educate you about the movement and help you find pride in your identity beyond a plastic card. The longest battle we have is within, and that is where our foes want us to expend the greatest effort. "Divide and conquer" goes hand-in-hand with "stall and redirect" in their playbook. Make us fight each other and they win. Make us forget—or fail to pass on—the fire of our efforts and they win. Don't fall for it. We can deal with internal issues without interference: every mediation or arbitration we allow is another avenue for those tactics to be used against us.

In the end this is my frame of reference. This is my world view. Love one another and take care of each other through compassion and respect. A plastic ID card does not an Indigenous person make. We know who our people are, and we will stand proudly with each other no matter the circumstances. Come sit by the fire with me if the mood strikes you; I will welcome you with open arms. I'm always ready to listen.

For those of you who are not of the First People I would like to leave you with this:

Consider for a moment that you have baptized yourselves the "Western World" culturally for quite some time. This world is mostly based on skin colour, is split by the great Atlantic Ocean, and is responsible for some of the worst atrocities in human history. If you look to your North, South, East, and West, you will notice that unique and vibrant people have occupied those spaces well into prehistory. And I ask you to consider that you define any time before history as a time when you either don't understand or haven't yet proven, by your own methods and on your own terms, that a people meets your definition of civilized. You say history is written by the victors. But what a hollow victory it is to oppress and have control over a people that welcomed you to your new home.

If you make all the rules you cannot lose.

Rain, Drizzle, and Mental Fog

Growing Up Autistic in a Small Newfoundland Town

by

TORI OLIVER

Warm sunlight slowly sweeps the horizon, its blaze outlining the rugged landscape. Coastal waters glimmer in the morning light before it reaches the foam-lined shores. Sudden winds rattle clusters of evergreen and birch trees, a few of which are just one gale away from exposed roots. Close by, worn dirt paths lead the way to awe and adventure in vast grassy terrain. Some locals are enjoying a morning stroll around a pond-side boardwalk, while more intrepid folks scale the uneven ground leading to a marvellous waterfall. Many a grandmother is making her famous homemade bread or toutons, smelling and tasting so delicious they are unlikely to last past the day they were made. Clotheslines weave and wind between houses as garments of all colours and sizes flutter in the breeze. Gulls spread their wings and dance in a circle, attempting to spot their next meal before plunging into the water below. If someone asked me to describe the ins and outs of life in Gull Island, Newfoundland, this would be the simple, romanticized version. Doesn't this sound like the ideal spot to live out your days? Unfortunately, for some, the quietest of places harbours the loudest of thoughts.

I do not intend to discredit the positive accolades from tourists looking for new perspectives, or returning provincial natives searching for their roots. Even people who have lived here their entire lives feel at ease knowing that anyone in the area will treat them like their own. So, how could I spend the better part of my twenty-three years feeling left out of that proverbial wolf pack? Or any animal's pack *anywhere*, for that matter? Simply put, I am autistic, and for the longest time I stood alone. Fortunately, there are now several "autism families" within the North Shore (a collective colloquial term encompassing my town and several neighbouring areas). And our modern era tends to embrace these individuals with open arms. In the same way that children in kindergarten will play with basically anyone, the younger autistic generation is now an unconditional component of their chosen peer groups. It makes me glad to see that the social barriers I faced growing up are being gradually dismantled. In a closely knit town like ours, it makes sense to instill such inclusive principles early on in a child's life.

My track record of social mishaps began early on, mere months after I was diagnosed. It was mid-1999, not long after my second birthday, and my mother was completing her nursing program in St. John's. At that time, the two of us lived in a cozy basement apartment, still wide enough for a small child to roam despite the limited space. Oh, the nerves she had to take on a youngster and a degree all at once! Fortunately, my nan drove in regularly and even spent a few nights in a row if Mom needed a break or intense study time. We all enjoyed spending time as three generations, and each of us looked out for the others.

They wanted what was best for me in all aspects of life. So when Janeway Child Development recommended socializing me with other kids my age, both of them looked into various daycares in the metro region. Eventually, they came across a place that would enrol me the following week. Things got off to a great start, until some kids decided it would be *awesome* and *hilarious* to cover me head to toe in buckets of sand. They howled in complete amusement as I hid in a corner, trembling and bawling my eyes out. To this day I do not know if they did it out of badness or curiosity. Regardless, my dismay didn't last, and two-year-old me quickly brushed herself off and got back to running around. I felt much more satisfied playing by myself, and soon I was washing the day's events away in some watercolour paints at the craft table. My family didn't exactly share my nonchalance, though, once they learned what had happened. I was promptly picked up by my mother, and that was the last time I went to that daycare.

My mother received her nursing licence in 2001 and moved us back to our hometown after landing a job in Carbonear. There, we would embark on a new chapter in our lives. I spent the next fifteen years in the single-level, sturdy house my grandfather built in the '70s, where Mom had spent her own childhood. It still stands to this day; we returned property rights to my grandmother after we built our own house nearby almost six years ago. Much like that old place, my potential would be built by hand from the bottom up. The secret to the house's endurance was its strong foundation of cement and coarse dirt. I would learn that my own success would depend on keeping myself grounded, by building my mentality with as much care as the home that nurtured it. I really had nothing to lose, with close family by my side and the sea-sweeping winds at my back. The North Shore was my North Star for all my formative years, its natural beauty guiding me away from my troubles without a hitch. It was here I learned that nature truly is best for what ails you.

Many days dawned in clear skies that reflected my inner confidence and satisfaction. Others took me by surprise and threw me into a thick fog, far too expansive to escape. One step into the grey, gloomy unknown could render me MIA for a good spell. Much like physical fog, I found myself shrouded in overwhelming misery and intense rainfall. So heavy it was at times that I found it best to let it wash over me while I waited it out. Eventually, the calm between storms arrived once more. Fierce winds became gentle breezes as the sun beamed through the clouds. Another psychological episode here and gone, made easier by the sight of rainbows and glistening trees. My reflection in the pond became that of a person who could wind rivers to change her fate. And on more days than not, that is exactly what I set out to do. I made it my life mission to let my inner Wonder Woman toss her insecurities aside like a carload of dead weight.

Life in a small town made it difficult to find resources for my conditions. Many therapy sessions I received before kindergarten were done via teleconferencing with specialists outside the province. These usually warranted a day trip into St. John's, since our own rural clinic lacked the equipment for distance treatment. Despite the multitude of virtual encounters with therapists and doctors alike, I can barely recall anything from any of the meetings. All I do know comes from my mother's version of events: sitting in a dim, stuffy observatory anxiously watching my teary eyes as we were instructed to distance ourselves. The intent was to study my "usual" behaviours in an independent context so they could decide which needed improvement. But at what cost? I was obviously distressed, my mother even more so, and our emotional needs were vetoed in the name of behavioural correction. It's a good thing I don't remember this myself, or else it would haunt me. I still get cold shivers down my back thinking of the other poor souls who went in before and after me. If the end result was to make me *look* typical from the outside, I guess it worked out—good for them. Still, one cannot assume from observation that I am without flaws: my inner thought process and spirit are still in the works.

Fortunately, not all therapies are created equal, and more suitable tactics were offered to me as I entered school. I was selected for an autism pilot project in Montreal when I was six, though the details are a little fuzzy in my memory. Not knowing a lick of French at the time didn't help! At night, we stayed in a fancy hotel, and during the day I sorted coloured shape cards and copied block patterns under the guidance of researchers. It never occurred to me at the time to ask exactly *what* I was doing, but I was a pretty compliant kid and it sounded fun, so why not? I did enjoy playing games, after all, and in my mind this was another.

My school revised my Individualized Education Plan (IEP) with similar activities when I returned, in addition to the motor skills and social story training I was already getting. In primary school I was often escorted from my regular classroom to the specialty room during class work. Small-town life meant that school was the closest I was getting to any autism-specific resources. On the other hand, there was plenty of natural space to fulfill my sensory needs. Because I was an only child and didn't have many friends, there was many a day when I had to entertain myself. Giant rocks became the perfect spot to perch and look at my world from a distance. The large, steep hills behind our house were ideal for rolling down on my back without a care. I even made an obstacle course one afternoon from old junk I found behind our shed (and put Mama's blood pressure through the roof while I was at it). What a place to be and a time to be alive. Little did I know, I would never feel as carefree again.

Anxiety, often comorbid with autism, is no laughing matter. I wish I could say it got easier to deal with over time, but that would be far from the truth. Fact is, every stage of my life has presented itself with brand-spanking-new challenges just as I overcame a prior setback. There's a good chance some of you have read this far and think this is a cry for attention: "Oh, *everyone* has problems. That's just life. Deal with it." Think it all you like. I'm used to it by now. If you only knew the reason I ended up like this, starting at just seven years old when I was led down a rabbit hole of self-discovery.

By that time, I was beginning to acknowledge my differences from other children. Though I enjoyed my regular IRT sessions immensely, I started wondering why I was taken out of class so often. It became obvious that this was something my peers did *not* need as much as I did. Being as shy as I was during childhood, simply asking if a friend could visit did not come easily to me. Thus, my only source of companionship came from attending school, with the occasional kind invite to a classmate's humble abode. How much of this was out of generosity as opposed to obligation? I will never know. Still, this was not exactly a place where one could be picky with playmates. Even back then, when there were kids by the dozen living in my area, I only felt close enough to two of them to warrant a get-together.

I do know one thing: that I never could properly fit in with anyone. By the time the 2000s came around, people were beginning to understand the mechanics behind autism and its presentation along all parts of the spectrum. Of course, girls were still diagnosed less, and being the only autistic female in my rinky-dink elementary school proved no easy feat. As hard as I tried to keep up the act of "masking" my struggles, I would eventually burn out and make a fool of myself. Some children were legitimately concerned and attempted to console me. Others, however, shoved me into a metaphorical corner to fend for myself. The inconsistent cycle of sympathy mixed with confusion was not the relationship I wanted to have with my peers. I wished to be treated as an equal, not to be tormented or infantilized. From then on, it became clear that I was an easy target.

I agonized over how to fix myself well into the third grade, seeking ways to ease my frustration without necessarily thinking of consequences. For instance, I began binge eating every snack I could find in our cupboards. I felt comforted at the time—food instantly drowned my sorrows— but my indulgence only created horrible habits that still follow me today. What should have been a time of childlike wonder took a dark turn towards self-doubt and shattered confidence. Many a night I lay in bed, struggling to find answers to daunting questions no primary schooler should have to ask themselves: *Why am I like this? Why doesn't my brain work? Why can't I behave like I should, though I know how to?* Some would simply dismiss it as a behavioural problem that had to be "disciplined out of me." I knew it to be much more, yet I was left at the hands of experts and laypeople who had differing opinions on how to handle me. Regardless, I faced the rising tides of my identity, sailing an emotional steamship without a loyal crew.

That is, until a new student entered my class the following school year. She had moved to Western Bay that past summer to be closer to family. Looking back, every kid in the room was like family because we grew up together—for sure and certain some of us were literally related to each other through so-and-so's aunt, grandparents, or distant relative. Our group of kids was also smaller than the average class, making one-on-one time among students and teachers a possibility. Much of my class had relied upon others at one point or another. Tight finances from seasonal work at the crab plant periodically made their food supplies plummet, and some families could barely survive even on unemployment assistance. Other households were on welfare or disability accommodations. Kind people often provided spare resources, despite controversial targeting of people who "worked the system." These children knew how it felt to be left out. Even beloved family members would get too political and distance themselves over opinionated squabbles. So the young girl who just walked in with a nervous smile and a brown-rimmed pair of glasses was a welcome, fresh face for all of us.

Well, most of us, anyway. Not even two hours after the poor thing made her entrance, a few boys claimed their territory as she walked past their lockers at recess to get to her own. These were the "hard tickets" of the class who were known to make their rounds to the detention room at least twice a week. They eventually grew to enjoy the negative attention they often received. Having a newcomer amongst us didn't make this any different, and I soon caught them sneaking around me to snatch her snug woollen hat in one fell swoop. Even *laughing* as they did it, too! Well, I wasn't having *any* of it. When I questioned them in my angriest voice through gritted teeth, these fools decided to play dumb with me. I tried to back one into a corner myself as the new girl backed herself against the wall. I was determined to give that cap to its rightful—now terrified—owner if it was the last thing I ever did. Despite my best efforts, though, the boys' teamwork prevailed and the hat got swiftly flicked into the nearest waste bin. They ran like mad bulls toward the school's main doors before I could say anything else.

Luckily, I didn't have to dig too far into the trash. I handed the white furry hat over to my newfound friend, who appeared relieved to have someone stand up for her. She asked me to walk alongside her to the playground. We made our way through the gravel parking lot and onto a set of swings, where we had a heart-to-heart chat. Apparently, what had just happened was no different than what she had suffered through in her old class. She didn't quite interact with others in the usual way, and people picked on her for being weird and reclusive. I had felt the same way for a long time. At long last I had found someone who shared my struggles.

It became clear that I was not alone in my own experiences, and, as the first month progressed, I already noticed a lot of myself in her. One October day in particular changed my self-conception forever. This was when I found out I was autistic. Had I not been curious about her presence in the same IRT session, I probably would not have found out for years. It felt strange that I never found out before, but I couldn't complain—I now had a concrete reason for my quirks. I guess people had some reservation in differentiating me from the crowd any more than they had to. In some ways, that was a good thing: it meant I was otherwise on equal footing with peers and allowed to become somebody in the same way. But what made anyone think a word like "autism" could baffle me? I was at a high school reading level pronouncing things far more complicated! Either way, I was relieved that there was a name for what I was and how I behaved.

My family and community also provided a great support system throughout the years. That in itself made the rest of my youth more manageable. Teachers took the time to identify my individual interests, and my mom and nan encouraged me to pursue them. I became motivated to write out my thoughts as a form of expression, much like this literary piece. So far, it has worked like a charm. When it comes to my life's journey, the pen has indeed become mightier than the sword. I wrote myself to a high school diploma and a bachelor's degree, despite lifelong and recent challenges. Had I grown up in a more urban landscape, there may have been more opportunities, but my life in the sticks taught me to hang tight to my roots and make the most of what I have. Even if all there is to comfort me some days is my own company.

I have accepted over the years that I run under a different operating system than most people. I could liken the inner mechanics of my brain to a smartphone: everything works how it should until there are too many "tasks" open at once. At that point, the battery drains faster and lag is inevitable. Navigating social nuances has always been similar to those unskippable mobile ads that pop up in the middle of a game or online video. They're a given if you're surfing the web (or in my case, the sea of neurotypical faces), and, annoying as they are, you eventually acclimate to them. In writing this, I hope all who share my conditions feel connected to me, and that everyone else is inspired to create a network of acceptance for every person who thinks or acts a little bit differently from "normal."

Assumptions

by

MICHELLE KEEP

"Many people in the sex industry have trauma."

My stomach turned, twisted to a knot. I stared across the table at my therapist. A container of scratchy tissues sat between us, and their mere presence reinforced the idea that to be vulnerable was to experience pain.

But at that moment, I wasn't vulnerable.

My heart raced, my hands clenched.

Years had been spent finding and re-finding therapists, and this one was new. Replacing a kind, understanding human that I had spent months building trust with. I was still in grief that I was having to repeat the process over again, baring my soul to a stranger, and then she uttered those words.

Sex industry. Trauma.

I went numb. It wasn't that she was speaking a truth, one that hit too close to home. Just the opposite. She had so catastrophically misunderstood me that all hope for a relationship was shattered in that one sentence. She had dismissed every single thing I had said about what brought me happiness and pleasure, and what was the cause of my unhealed wounds.

She had ignored and even defended my actual abusers, and tried to shift blame to something unrelated and important to me.

The body has its own lie detector tests for when we're lying to ourselves. You may tell yourself you love being with the people who hurt you, but a knot in your stomach whenever they're near says otherwise. Hearing a certain song or smelling a familiar fragrance rips us out of our current time and space, exposing our deepest and darkest secrets. It conjures up feelings, emotions, experiences so vividly that you're forced to confront it and what it means for you.

In the years since I left my job at the strip club, I often find myself yanked back there. One of the songs I used to dance to comes on the radio. A perfume reminds me of the soft, silky-smooth skin of another dancer as she brushed past me. An email ad for impractically high heels that I momentarily lust for.

Trauma? No. Trauma never came into play. No matter how many times I flash back to my time on the stage, there's a flood of emotions, but, most of all, joy.

I was never a conventional stripper, as if there were such a thing. I'd never even been in a strip club before my audition.

What was I thinking?

I was told to change in the bathroom, the little stall closing in upon me, my elbows bumping off the metal as I turned and twisted to get into my lingerie. I couldn't breathe. Perfume invaded my nostrils, my mouth going dry, my legs trembling.

And then I strutted out towards the stage, the music curling around my form like a protective blanket. The beat reverberated through me, syncing up with my heart. The cold metal of the pole met my clammy hand as I began to move to the rhythm.

Four other dancers watched me, judging me along with the manager, but it was a rush. I felt powerful. It was *exciting*. I'd been dreaming of this moment for years and working towards it for months. It was even better than I had imagined.

I got the job, and I rushed to call my partner and tell him the good news. "You did it?!" he asked, pride in every syllable.

"I did!" I squealed breathlessly.

I'd asked my partner months prior if he thought I had what it took to be a stripper. My job contract was coming up on expiry, and I was feeling bored and restless in office work. I wanted a change, and he wanted me to be happy—whatever that meant.

We had started seeing each other in high school. Seeing each other isn't the right term. He was in Newfoundland, and I was in Ontario. One night, he was cleaning up his computer and decided to do one last search on AOL Instant Messenger. He searched for someone interested in "Books"—AIM didn't have great search parameters—and I was the only Canadian on the list.

The odds against our online meeting were phenomenal, and at times I think that perhaps fate is what brought us together. That our souls were searching for each other without even realizing it.

At the same time, there's a special type of romance to the belief that it was all chance. The random chaos of the universe, throwing us together at the perfect moment in our lives. He needed someone to save, and I needed to be saved.

Three days after I graduated high school, I boarded a plane by myself for the first time. I flew 3,000 kilometres away from everything and every-one I had ever known except for him. I watched as the neat rectangles of farmland faded and were replaced by rocky, uneven terrain. I saw the cliffs that met the Atlantic Ocean, and I fell in love not just with him, but with St. John's.

Our first years together were marred by poverty and strife. My parents had not prepared me for what it was to be an adult. To pay bills and rent, to understand taxes and savings. How to find a doctor, how to negotiate wages, how to cook. There was so much knowledge I'd been denied, and, once I moved out, they made it clear that I was on my own.

I found a minimum-wage retail job, and I worked hard but could never get ahead. I wanted full-time hours, but it was better for the company if they scheduled me for five three-hour shifts and then had me desperate for additional hours. I took every shift I could get, but even then it was rare that I could cobble together thirty hours a week.

My first cheque was for thirty-seven dollars and I wept. I spent so much time working and couldn't even afford dinner at a restaurant. I didn't realize that the cheque was for the week prior and that I didn't get paid up to the day, as it had worked when I was a babysitter. Another piece of knowledge I was denied.

But at $5.75 an hour, even a full-time job would barely pay my share of the rent and bills.

I didn't know about stripping, then. Or, rather, I did, but thought it was for other people. Beautiful people. Women with confidence beyond their years. Ethereal and graceful and perfect. That wasn't me.

For one thing, I'm short. For another, I have soft, curvy thighs, decorated with stretch marks.

Of course, those things never mattered, but, in my young mind, they were disqualifying. And if not those, then I would have found other unforgivable flaws on my body or within my personality. I was an expert at that.

Years passed, and more struggles followed. Moving from one job to another, the wounds of poverty and abusive bosses building onto scar tissue that I wasn't capable of acknowledging. There were days, so many days, when my self-hatred felt like a boiling vat of oil threatening to spill over. My confidence was shattered, time after time.

I felt unworthy of the unconditional love my partner afforded me. He was living off scholarships and student loans but always put me first. When the last Harry Potter book came out, he used his birthday money to buy me a hardcover copy so that the ending wouldn't be spoiled for me. When I would cry over nothing, he would hold me, and, when I would cry over something big, he would make things all right.

I fell in love with him over and over. I would try to push him away, and he would just hold on tighter. He was my rock, my world, my everything.

And slowly, together, we pushed forward. We found stability. We shaped our life into something to be proud of, and I still remember the first time we had one hundred dollars in a savings account with no outstanding bills, no rent, no nothing. It was just one hundred dollars, but it was ours. For the first time, there was a light at the end of the tunnel.

The confidence that came with that was unreal.

That was the point I started thinking about stripping.

———

"How did it go?" Concern laced his tone as he held the door open for me after my first night at the strip club.

I feigned a frown, going to the kitchen table. I opened the small wristlet, colourful and bright, just like my cheerfully pink eye shadow and lipstick. It was three in the morning on a Monday, and I'd smudged my mascara rubbing my eyes in the cab on the way home.

Bills spilled out of the wristlet onto the table, and I began counting out twenties, putting them in neat little stacks. I'd learned how to count cash pretty fast in my retail jobs, but this was different. This was mine.

I lined up the stacks and beamed at my partner.

"That's how it went," I gushed, and threw myself into his arms. He ran me a bath and made me a slice of toast topped with peanut butter as I told him all about my night.

It was a Sunday shift, and it started early. There were no other dancers when I arrived, and it gave me time to nervously fix my makeup and hair.

"I want to see some of the other girls on stage before I go on," I told the manager who was also the DJ who was also the bouncer who was also the bartender.

"Of course," he said.

And then the American military invaded, as they are wont to do. Still no other girls showed up.

"I'm really sorry, but there's no one else, and we need to give them a show," he said. "Do you think you can go on stage?"

"Sure," I said, though I was the opposite of sure.

I told him the three songs I wanted to dance to. I can't remember when, precisely, the regret hit me, but I imagine it was around one minute into my first song.

Layla. Eric Clapton. Album version.

Seven minutes and eight seconds long.

I didn't know any fancy pole tricks and, admittedly, my ability to gracefully get down on the ground and roll around was lacking. I stood, clinging to the stripper pole to keep my balance, and rocked my hips from side to side. I touched my skin.

I prayed for the song to end.

Finally, it did, and a wave of relief washed over me, until my next chosen song started.

Angel. Aerosmith.

Five minutes and eight seconds long.

I always remembered the song as a nice, high energy rock anthem. I didn't realize, until I was onstage in very little clothes, that it takes three minutes and ten seconds for the high energy part to start, and three minutes is an eternity on stage.

I can't remember my final song. I may have tranced out by that point. The crowd was all incredibly polite and well mannered, clapping appropriately as I clumsily made my way off the stage, covered in sweat and shaking from the sheer rush of it all.

I don't get nervous doing public speaking anymore. There is nothing that can compare to over fifteen minutes of being onstage in various states of undress, swaying and spinning to the slowest rock songs I could think of.

It was seven or eight in the evening before other girls came to work. I'd been there for three hours at that point and hadn't made a dollar. I'd spent hours researching the art of the hustle, researching love language, researching how to ask for a dance, but I wanted a mentor. Someone to push me forward.

I was nervous about meeting the other dancers. I'd heard about strippers' competitiveness, their cattiness. And there was still the lingering feeling that I was an imposter, a fraud in a short skirt and a sparkly bra who needed chunky heels because stilettos were a death trap.

"Just go over and ask," a blonde told me, looking up from the pages of *Twilight*. "The worst they can say is no."

That was all it took. I stood up, took a deep breath, and smiled at the young serviceman near me.

The rest of the night was a beautiful blur. It was such a rush, and I quickly got in the zone. By the time I returned home to my partner, I was glowing.

"That's how it went," I told him, and he beamed back at me, pride and delight twinkling in his eyes.

⁓

"Sex work did not traumatize me, and there are people with trauma in all industries. If the sex industry has a higher rate of people with trauma, it is because it is a flexible career that offers a good income."

My therapist stared back at me, doubt and pity in her gaze. I could hear her internal thought process. I was in denial. I just didn't realize what it had done to me.

I walked home after the session, anger fuelling each step.

The sex industry freed me. It was where I found my confidence, my unique spark, my business acumen. The skills I learned on the floor helped me every day, and when I launched a writing career with my partner—now husband—you better believe that learning to sell dances helped me sell books.

My trauma came from neglect. The knowledge my parents denied me about life went deeper, into every facet of my being. My undiagnosed ADHD, my untreated depression, my unrecognized needs and wants, that's my trauma.

Stripping was me *healing* from trauma. Stripping taught me autonomy. It made me learn how to stand up for myself, to put myself out there, to ask for what I want. It gave me confidence in myself and my skills. It taught me persistence and patience and acceptance. The things I would later go on to learn about in therapy—personal rights, boundaries, radical acceptance, breathing exercises, physical activity, musical therapy—I practised every night in the club.

Stripping gave me community. I saw the way the girls looked out for each other even though everyone told us we were in competition. The way we all rallied around the new girls to give them the lay of the land and help them learn their hustle. When people feel on the outskirts of society, there's a strange sense of bonding, even between people who hate each other. It was a family, with all the good and bad that comes with it.

I still think about going back. To feel the thrum of the music in my rib cage. To be able to lie down at night and still sense the beat in my skull, the lights burned into my eyelids. To experience the rush of a good night when you feel like a goddess and the entire room is dedicated to you. To revel in the thrill of going onstage and hearing people cheer, seeing them beam up at you.

Even the bad days of sitting around and waiting for customers, leaving at two in the morning with barely more than minimum wage in my wristlet, waiting an hour for a cab in a snowstorm. The times that customers tried to rip me off, or when a girl yelled at me for moving her bag. The times I had to go to the bathroom for a quick cry because there were twenty-five dancers and two customers and it was almost midnight.

Even the bad days.

Even the bad days weren't traumatic. They were just bad days, like in any other job.

"Many people in the sex industry have trauma."

It still boils my blood to hear those words in my head, an awful echo of trust being shattered. How many people in retail have trauma? And how does poverty contribute to that trauma? Because it wasn't until I had one hundred dollars in my bank account that didn't have to go to bills or rent that I was able to start moving past my trauma. It wasn't until I started stripping that I was able to exercise my personal rights and boundaries. It wasn't until I started stripping that I was able to afford therapy and medication.

The sex industry is filled with people on the outskirts of society, not because of the work, but because we live in a world that demonizes, stigmatizes, and harms sex workers. Any trauma being done within the sex industry can be lessened by real, meaningful efforts to recognize erotic labourers as workers.

In our capitalist world, human needs have a price tag on them. We all need a place to live and food to eat. In the past forty years, the cost of goods and services has soared while wages have stagnated. Whether you love your job or hate it, you work at it in part because you have needs that require you to pay for them.

The real trauma in our society is that in Canada it takes four generations for those born in a low-income family to approach the mean income. The real trauma in our society is that the worst-performing rich student at university has a better chance of graduating than the smartest poor student. The real trauma in our society is low-wage work capitalizing on desperate workers.

Our society urges us at every turn to pull ourselves up by our bootstraps. We blame sex work when we should blame capitalism. Sex work is filled with people who come from the lower classes. The people who had to work hard to never get ahead, the people who had to decide between food and bills, the people who never knew what having one hundred dollars in their bank account felt like. The trauma of poverty.

Sex work offered me a way to get ahead in my life and in my finances. Sex work helped pull me out of the trauma of poverty. Sex work was the solution, not the cause.

My therapist had biases about sex work, and, in voicing those biases, she was reinforcing that stigma.

But the body has built-in lie detector tests, and the sensations you get when you're yanked back into the past can't be faked.

On the Way to Hopedale

by

ALEX SAUNDERS

"What did you say was pinned to the door of that abandoned house, Uncle?" my mother said to our grizzled visitor at Old Davis Inlet. We had just shared a big meal of fresh codfish that the man we called "Uncle" had brought from his summer place at Ailliak further to the south. Pipes were lit as Mother cleared away the supper dishes, chatting gaily with our visitor who was very well known for his love of the spoken word.

"Yes, Maggie," he said to Mother. "I should have looked closer, but I was young and in a real hurry to see why there was a flag flying from a house that had been empty for years. My, 'twas terrible, and I got the fright of my life upon entering and finding three dead men inside. It seems they died of starvation, but they left things behind that gave evidence as to what happened to them. They had come to Labrador to start a sawmill for the new military base being built at Goose Bay, but they went astray and eventually ran out of fuel in their plane, forcing them to land near that old house."

The quiet evening idled away as our ancient visitor related the tragedy that was to haunt me in short order. He had a gift for tales and seemed to savour his spotlight in our one-house community sitting by the water's edge under the towering mountains to the north.

I had my own little place about ten miles to the east of Old Davis Inlet, and, when the elderly gentleman had completed his grisly tale of dead men with their faces eaten away by mice and weasels, I prepared to leave by boat to go home. I intended to leave from my place early the next morning for a week's partying in Hopedale, as we had finished up our summer's fishery and I had a pocket full of money that I planned to squander on the opposite sex and good times.

My Old Man walked me down to the landwash, chatting about the route I should take in order to get to Hopedale safely. I had never travelled that route by myself, but, being young and overconfident and very headstrong, I wasn't at all concerned about any mishap. He told me what to look for, what direction to take from my place, shapes of hills and colours of stone markings, shoals and breakers to avoid. I listened half-heartedly, as I was thinking about a girl I had met on the coastal steamer earlier in the season and was anxious to see her again.

So early the next morning I was on my way to Hopedale, all excited and full of plans, and hoping for some fun after a long summer of back-breaking work. Now my time to play was upon me!

Well, what now? I had entered the waterway my Old Man told me to follow with a prominent black head to the southwest, but I was in a narrow channel with high hills surrounding me on all sides and the tide hissing and throwing up white foam. Ocean swells were rolling through the narrow opening with great force, and my little boat was being thrown around like a rubber ball in a bathtub. I felt danger and near panic as I turned the boat around to go back the way I had come. A storm had arisen that would change my plans and change the way I saw my world.

I had just gotten away from that dangerous place and was steaming by an island when the motor quit on me. I had oars, so I rowed the boat ashore on the island to try to see what the problem might be. I knew next to nothing about small engine repair and didn't know what to do, so I walked up the bank to look at the island. There was a large pond to the east, a small abutment to the southwest, and only one small, stunted copse of spruce trees about two-and-a-half-feet tall, growing in a small indentation in the middle of the island. Little did I know they would offer shelter, solace, safety, and a sense of home for me for the next nine days!

Fine, fickle, I didn't know where I was or where to go. I had no radio or other means of communicating, no food other than one chocolate bar and a tin of soft drink. I was dressed in good rain gear with warm socks, gloves, and woollen cap. I had a gun, some shells, and a tomahawk. But what I didn't know at the time was that I was also blessed with Inuit ingenuity and survival skills as old as those towering hills. Somehow they kicked in and helped keep me alive until I got off that barren, desolate island.

I dragged driftwood up from the west end of the island to my new home and made a fireplace near the trees that offered protection from the northwest to the northeast, then took stock of my surroundings. There were blackberries growing profusely all over, some plants that I knew had edible roots, different kinds of low growth for tea, beachy birds flitting around, and sunshine. And there were waves roaring on the shoreline, kicked up by the increasing northwest wind that didn't stop for nine whole days.

The day passed slowly. I prepared to spend the night under the stars and those close-knit boughs of the little trees. Darkness came, and along with it came fear, near panic, self-loathing, and tremendous doubt. It was terrible trying to sleep on the cold, hard ground; my feet had sweated in my rubber boots during the day and were damp and cold all night. I sat up, took my boots and socks off, and tried to dry them by the fire but was afraid of burning them, so I spent a sleepless night until the raucous gulls started their wake-up calls in the grey of pre-dawn. Then I pictured Mother's clothes flapping away on her clothesline, and it hit me: let the wind dry my boots and socks! I did and started my first day on that island with warm feet, at least.

I picked and ate huge handfuls of blackberries, some leaves from a small waxy plant that I knew was good to eat, and found a bean tin on the beach that I brewed tea in. I was quite content sitting by my fire by those life-saving little trees. At low tide I took my tomahawk and went to the beach to forage for mussels and clams and some seaweed, and found an abundance from Mother Nature's larder, which I ate raw. I also shot four little beachy birds that I cleaned while eating raw livers, hearts, and little gizzards, and took the birds back to my fire to roast them over the hot coals.

That first afternoon I went to the prominent head to build a signal pyre. I had just finished making it when I looked up and saw a black boat about four or five miles to the south, steaming away from me. I started firing my shotgun in volleys of threes, which was a stupid thing to do as they were too far away to hear and I shot all but one of my shells. Well, my attempt at rescue only added to my dilemma: how would I get any of the meat that all Natives depend on?

I went back to my non-existent shelter, feeling very dejected and more uncertain than before. I knew that I had not yet achieved complete Northern status and that I had a lot to learn. I had to learn to survive on this island with its harsh environment or succumb to the elements. I was twenty-seven years old with lots of life ahead, so I resolved to live.

I cut heather sods and reinforced the boughs to stop the wind from blowing freely into my shelter. Then I built up my bed, even made a sod pillow, dragged up firewood, picked mounds of berries and stored them in my shelter. I got beach stones and made a fireplace that would deflect heat into my space. I fashioned willows into a dome over my feet, filling the space with dry grass and recreating the comforts of home.

A couple of days later I was sitting in a little vale that was covered with tall, dry standing grass. I fell asleep in the warm sunshine, and, when I awoke hours later, confused and drained, bathed in sweat from the effects of the hot sunlight on my rain gear, I knew real panic. The sun was low in the west, and I knew I had about three hours of daylight left. If I had to spend the night in these damp clothes it could spell disaster for me.

Quick action was definitely required, so I stripped naked and hung everything on the low trees, then trudged barefoot down to the beach to drag up firewood for the night. It was blowing a gale from the northwest, and I knew that wind could keep up for days, weeks even. Goose pimples covered my body as did scrapes and cuts from carrying up the wood. My feet were bleeding also, but I never faltered, as I knew heat was essential for survival and, at the end of September, nights in the North could get pretty cold. By dark my clothes had dried in the sun and wind, and, after eating a meal of berries, roots, and some mussels, I hunkered down for another night. Noisy gulls and the ever-present loud moaning of the wind woke me just before dawn, and I was surprised at how long I had slept under the stars.

On the third day I saw another boat steaming away from me with the wind on her aft quarter, so I lit my signal fire only to see the dark, billowing smoke driven by strong winds across the tops of the waves low to the water. I knew the boat would not see my signal. Good lesson learned: do things right! That day, however, I was cooking some mussels in my bean tin when I drank the water from the tin and was immediately jolted by my reaction from the effects of the broth. It must have been the salt or the nutrients, or God knows what, but I was instantly rejuvenated and filled with renewed vigour and energy. Another lesson learned.

I wandered that island looking out for rescue all the time, but knowing in my heart that it wasn't going to happen. The old folk must have been thinking that I was really enjoying my time in Hopedale. They would be land-bound with this high wind also, so this sort of settled my mind knowing that I would have to wait out the fall gales.

I found an old stone wall that the ancient Inuit must have built up to make a smooth sleeping platform for their igloo or skin tent. At one place I saw something gleaming between the rocks, and I picked away at this place until I found a small, smooth rock hidden in the crevice, oddly shaped and almost transparent. When I held it in my hand I immediately got strange tingling sensations running up my arm, and, when I turned the rock over to see the other side, my breath caught in my throat. The top of the rock was formed to look like a wide forehead, the contours moulded into high cheekbones ending in a sharp chin. It was the eyes and the mouth that took my breath away, downward-slanting evil eyes, and the corners of the mouth turned so sharply that I knew this was a powerful amulet from some ancient shaman.

I carried that rock for a couple of days, always getting unpleasant feelings when I took it out of my pocket. The hairs on the back of my neck and on my arms would stand straight up until I got so scared of it that I threw it into the ocean. The ocean has secrets, and this stone was destined to become another for it to keep.

The wind had been up for days, and the waves were crashing and roaring on the north side of my little island. I was fully dressed in my sturdy, warm oilskins, so I wandered right down to the seaside and sat at the water's edge behind large boulders that trembled from the power of the wave action. I was so close to the wild waves that the salt spray flew over my head and ran down my face and into my mouth.

I was so mesmerized by the rolling, crashing water and the roar of the surf that all else around me ceased to exist. I sat there for a long time, just feeling the power of the sea, completely immersed in the moment and fully alive, and trembling along with the land that was smothered in spray and foam. It was an uplifting and exciting time and made me realize again how wonderful the ocean can be if we open our hearts and souls to its gifts. Longings are awakened in us as the great ocean sends pulses surging through the body to thrill the soul.

On the fifth day I set wire snares for Arctic lemmings, as there were numerous runs between my copse of trees and the willows that grew by the side of the pond. I knew those plump little fellows became as tame as house pets in no time, and I could imagine the delicious odour as I roasted them over the hot coals. I set six little snares amongst the underbrush and checked them about a dozen times that first day, always coming up empty-handed. I didn't know what size the snares should be, how high off the ground to set them, or how to camouflage them for success. This new venture proved to be quite the experiment, and I filled that day with attempts to improve my methods.

While sitting by the comforting fire, slipping in and out of sleep and lost in the glow of the coals and a dream world of people, voices, and noise, I was jarred awake by a sudden rushing energy that pulsed through the night air. I felt something big just over my head, some force that flew down close to the earth and rose again to the night sky. I listened intently, feeling with all my senses and tingling all over at something unexplained. Then I noticed the Northern Lights. They were alive and undulating across a starry sky, made brighter by a harvest moon. They moved with a sinuous, wave-like action, displaying a smooth rising-and-falling, side-to-side motion as they sped across the Arctic sky.

I meandered out onto the heather and lay on the ground looking up at all this wonder, listening to the noises the lights were making. I could smell the earth and the low fragrant plants that grow in the Arctic. The night air was cool but sweet and pure. I felt as if I had been doing this all my life as a secure sensation enveloped my being and bestowed on me a feeling of belonging in this land.

The colour display was amazing, mostly pale green with purple tinges, laced with blue hues outlining the body of the cosmic energy moving in the heavens. Different intensities came and went as fading bodies of light sped north, only to be magically replaced with newer and brighter bursts of colour. I lay on the ground for a while wondering if this was a survival endeavour or an awakening of self-realization—a coming of age for a Native son.

I think I was blessed to have witnessed such a spectacular display by Mother Nature, and a warmth filled my being as I sipped a last tin of herbal tea before going to sleep. I found contentment and peace on that barren island and a sense of identity that I hadn't been aware of before. It was so surreal that I thought to myself: *I am dreaming the land and the land is inside me.* We were dreaming each other and creating new heights of human awareness and feelings that seemed to transport my soul to another sphere. I learned what silence was, patience and acceptance, and an understanding of a part of a whole that was the Earth and me.

The next day my lemming snares were empty again, so I placed smooth stones in little pits I dug in their runs and camouflaged the openings. At the end of the afternoon I had caught eight of those fat rodents, which I quickly dispatched. How I enjoyed the aroma of roasting meat, so tantalizing, fat dripping onto the hot coals! My resolve to eat only a few quickly dissipated into a desire to devour them all. Meat is the essence of life for all Native people, bolstering our well-being to allow us to continue on and to face the adversity that is part of subsistence living.

On the eighth day I lay on my pallet thinking about Uncle's tale of the mice and weasels—not a good idea while looking mournfully at a silvery moon and listening to the North Wind whistle around my precarious shelter. The wind was still up, no rescue in sight, wet snow in the rain, and wind moaning in the dark night when I heard someone say, "I see his fire over there." I heard the sounds of an approaching boat, oars rattling on the gunwale. The prow hit the beach, and I grabbed my flashlight and ran out into the dark, wet, windy night to meet my rescuers.

I ran to the beach where my boat was, but there was silence. No sign. So I ran west. No sign. East, nothing. What was happening? I felt lost, defeated, and panicky, and knew I had been hallucinating. Enough! I resolved right then and there to get off this island. It was either drown rowing to the mainland or die here from all manner of afflictions.

Before daylight on the ninth day I managed to shove my boat out into the water and row westward to what I now knew to be the most travelled route in that area. It was still blowing hard, and the tops of the waves were blown into my boat. Rowing was difficult, but after four strenuous hours I made an eastward turn that brought me into more sheltered and calmer waters, where I landed on a beach. I found an abandoned tent with nothing but one old, dried-up tea bag in it. Hours later, a single-engine float plane flew over my head, dropping an airsickness bag containing a chocolate bar and a note saying that someone would come to get me.

At dusk, while lying in the warm tent with the wood stove going, I heard a swarm of bees. Bees at the end of September? I don't think so! I ran from the tent down to the water to see my father—Jim Saunders—and Ralph Webber haul up in his speedboat asking if I was all partied out! Father had been trapped by the same storm and had only realized when he contacted Hopedale that I had never arrived. He asked the pilots of Labrador Airways to fly the inside route between Hopedale and Old Davis Inlet, and that was how I was located on the evening of the ninth day, as the great storm subsided.

When I finally got to Hopedale, the girl I was hoping to see had gone south on the last boat—so much for romance! We went on home to Old Davis Inlet; when I walked up to the house and saw Mother standing on the flagstones by the door with her apron wrapped around her middle, the sun shining on her face, and the wind blowing her salt-and-pepper hair, I almost faltered. Her brusque and practical manner saved me from falling. All she said was: "Thank your lucky stars you're alive."

And I did.

You're Not "Disabled"-Disabled

by

MICHELLE BUTLER HALLETT

All I wanted was a coffee.

A few years ago, my husband and I stopped off at the Jumping Bean on Military Road on my way to work. Most days I could get into the coffee shop okay, not always a given when one uses forearm crutches, when one's spine, sacroiliacs, hips, knees, ankles, and feet are stiff. I could get in okay if someone else held the door, though I could not simply step up like an able-bodied person. The entrance, raised a crucial several centimetres from the sidewalk, required a hop and swing-through.

Another customer on his way out, an expensively suited man probably in his late twenties, saw me approaching the door alongside my husband. The narrow porch would not allow all three of us to stand there, so I started to move aside to make room for the young man to leave. He made eye contact with me, nodded, then walked straight into me, either deluding himself that I could and would, as was his apparent due, just step out of the way, or deluding himself that I did not exist at all.

I could not move out of the way quickly enough to appease him, so he plowed into me.

Startled, as though unable to conceive that I really did exist, that I really could not just step aside at high speed and let him pass, he stared at me a moment, blinked, then held open the door and addressed my husband.

Sure, we can debate whether he really did see me—he did—and we can debate if he meant to be so callous. I will listen to the counter-arguments, and I can only respond with how often this happens, how many people have made eye contact with me and then behaved as though I was nothing more than a hallucination, one that will not react when walked into, jostled, or left to contend with a door closing in her face.

I can only respond with how often strangers treat me as though I'm invisible. As though I don't exist.

This never happened when I was able-bodied.

Sometimes, however, I am not invisible. Sometimes I must be examined and judged. This happens a lot when I park in a blue spot. I resisted getting a parking permit for years. My reasoning: we have so few blue spots that I should leave them for others who need them more. (Generally, the number of blue parking spots has increased in the last few years, and so have the fines for parking in them without a permit.) Then, a doctor hearing my difficulties with walking and pain levels got me one without listening to any more nonsense from me. I use my permit on bad days, when I know saving a few steps will make a big difference to pain and fatigue levels later in the day. Far too often, when I am driving my own car and getting out of it in a blue spot, people watch me. This does not happen when I get out of the passenger door. It's as though my being able to drive while hanging a disabled parking permit in my car is deeply offensive. Sometimes people have started to march up to me, obviously indignant, only to turn away when they see my crutches. Sometimes they just glare until they notice my crutches, which are black and often blend into the dark clothes I like to wear. I am being judged. I am being policed. I must prove, regardless of my permit, that I am Disabled Enough to use a blue spot.

I mentioned one such incident to an acquaintance. He told me he inspected people using blue spots as well, to make sure they're "really disabled." He framed this activity as somehow helpful to me and was confused that I showed no gratitude.

I walked away.

Well, limped away.

When I first visited Rheumatology on a lower floor of St. Clare's Mercy Hospital, I couldn't believe the department was in the dampest and draftiest part of the building. Then again, I could believe it. Those unaffected by rheumatic disease don't have to think of the pain-inducing effects of dampness. After all, rheumatic disease is often dismissed as "just arthritis," and rheumatologists in Newfoundland and Labrador lost their few hospital patient beds in the early 2000s.

Then I noticed the high chairs—not the sort babies sit in, but adult-sized chairs with raised seats. Instead of bending to sit down, a motion that caused me severe pain, I could back into a chair, prop myself against it, then sort of slide onto the seat. It felt so much better.

So, this "just arthritis" I have? First, let me start with the term "arthritis." It's become a catch-all word for over one hundred distinct diseases and conditions, but really all "arthritis" means is "swollen joint." Arthritis is not a disease but a symptom, sometimes of the wear-and-tear condition osteoarthritis, in which joint cartilage breaks down, perhaps leaving bone to rub on bone, and sometimes of a more serious, life-altering rheumatic disease.

As painful and disabling as osteoarthritis can get, it is not a systemic disease that can affect multiple joints and multiple organs, and cause debilitating fatigue and fevers, like the autoimmune and immune-mediated autoinflammatory rheumatic diseases. As we currently understand them, autoimmune and immune-mediated autoinflammatory diseases are the result of the body's immune system trying to destroy a pathogen. Maybe there is a pathogen we haven't discovered yet. Or maybe the autoimmune system has been hacked or tricked into attacking the body. Some of these diseases, like rheumatoid arthritis, systemic lupus erythematosus, Crohn's disease, and ulcerative colitis, are relatively well known. A family of diseases called the spondyloarthropathies—diseases that cause arthritis in the spine—are not as well known. That said, many patients with ulcerative colitis or Crohn's also have a tagalong spondyloarthropathy. Psoriasis patients can develop a spondyloarthropathy called psoriatic arthritis, which mostly affects the spine and small joints of the fingers and toes. New technologies and revised diagnostic criteria—long overdue—have led to some huge changes and a new understanding of spondyloarthropathies as existing on a spectrum, not in a binary. For far too long, the diagnosis of my specific spondyloarthropathy depended on X-ray evidence. We now understand that X-ray evidence of a spondyloarthropathy can take a decade or more to show up. Ten years or more. Patients might be left in a diagnostic limbo, genuinely and seriously ill yet disbelieved and untreated because of the limits of medical imaging technology. Now, rheumatologists recognize, diagnose, and treat a condition called non-radiographic axial spondyloarthritis. That means symptoms are present, other diagnoses are excluded by testing, and some spinal changes may be visible via much more sensitive MRI scans.

What sort of changes?

Bone erosion. Calcification of facet joints and ligaments. New and deranged bone growth. Spinal fusion.

At the other end of the spondyloarthropathy spectrum lies a condition still called by its old name, ankylosing spondylitis. This is my diagnosis. In ankylosing spondylitis, now considered a progression of non-radiographic axial spondyloarthritis, bone changes do show up on X-ray. Ankylosing spondylitis—ank spond for short—is still erroneously described on otherwise reliable medical sites as mostly affecting young males. We now know that females are susceptible to ank spond, too, but they often present symptoms out of alignment with the old diagnostic criteria, which were in turn derived from observing and treating male patients. Medicine has a sexism problem.

So what does ankylosing spondylitis do? It inflames and calcifies the spine. It inflames any and possibly all other joints, especially the sacroiliacs and the hips. Common complications attack the eyes, mouth, gut, and rib cage—and thereby lung capacity. Less common complications affect the heart and lungs. Even without complications, non-radiographic axial spondyloarthritis and ankylosing spondylitis can utterly disable a patient with fatigue, fevers, a stiffened spine and other joints, and deep, rotten, excruciating pain. For years, I could only function by taking corticosteroids long term—never a good idea—along with heavy painkillers and non-steroidal anti-inflammatory drugs that came with warnings about causing heart attack and stroke. In 2012, I tried a biologic, one of a relatively new class of medications for severe disease. Usually given by injection or intravenous infusion, biologics target inflammatory markers in the blood and thereby reduce symptoms. Some patients even enjoy remission.

I reacted badly. For the first few months, the biologic worked well, giving me much better symptom control. I could walk without crutches, and I came off my pain meds. Then I developed a rare side effect mentioned in the biologic's black box warning: nerve demyelination. Specifically, my right optic nerve. For several weeks, I was functionally blind in that eye, and the eye itself, inflamed and swollen, hurt like hell. I had to patch the eye to keep out the light. Worst of all, I had to stop taking the biologic immediately, and I could not try any other biologic because they all came with the same risk of nerve demyelination. I received a massive dose of corticosteroid intravenously to treat my optic nerve, and that somewhat cushioned the fall from the biologic. Pain, fatigue, and stiffness returned— somehow, even worse than before. I struggled to function as a mother, a wife, a novelist, an employee. I rarely saw plays, concerts, or movies. I rarely saw my friends.

And it was around that time I heard the phrase, "But you're not 'disabled'-disabled."

The speaker meant it as a compliment.

In her view, because I was not using a wheelchair—or, to use the ableist terminology, was not "confined" to a wheelchair—because I did not match the commonly used disability icon, I was not truly disabled.

The worst part: initially, I agreed.

I'd considered disability on a binary, an either/or, a false digital clarity of 0 and 1. A tax specialist preparing my return suggested I apply for the federal disability tax credit; I declined, saying "But I can still work." That's not the point of the disability tax credit, which goes some way towards offsetting the many disability-related out-of-pocket expenses, and that's not the point of my condition. Whether I can work or not, I am disabled. The severity of my symptoms can vary greatly. On a sunny Monday, I might park at the far end of a lot because I want and need the exercise. On a rainy Tuesday, I might need to park in a blue spot because walking is now difficult, exhausting, and deeply painful. On two really awful days, I've used a wheelchair.

As my spine continues to fuse, movement is crucial. The more I move, the longer I can delay—but not stop—the fusion. Wheelchair or forearm crutches, I am disabled. If I stand before you without obvious mobility aids and tell you I am disabled, I am still disabled. I am Disabled Enough to use a blue spot and do not need policing. Neither do I need internal policing, the grating little voice in my head that would ask "Are you really that sick?" or "Do you really need that accommodation? After all, other people have it worse." Many people do "have it worse," but disability is not a competition, and most of all, disability is not a binary. Like the spondyloarthropathies, disability exists on a spectrum as something more complex than a limited category. I can't possibly satisfy the self-appointed guardians of blue spot morality who decide they have the right to pronounce that I am not "disabled"-disabled.

Why is this so problematic? Why can I not shrug and say, "Oh, well, that person just doesn't understand"? Because that person's lack of understanding contributes to systemic ableism and bias against disabled people. Because that person's lack of understanding can lead to unnecessary hostility towards disabled people. Because that person—and I have been that person—must try to understand, must make even a minimal attempt at empathy and connection.

Consider the term "Newfie." Some Newfoundlanders don't mind it, and I'm not about to argue with them. I object to it, but I always try to parse the context in which it's said and then start a low-key discussion on the term's loaded history. For me, the problem with "Newfie" is its history as a slur and how it functions as an identity imposed from the outside. If CBC were to call us "Newfies" in a news broadcast, the move would likely be seen as rather informal for journalism at best, grossly insulting at worst. Either way, an identity has been imposed from without, and it functions as a binary: Newfie / non-Newfie. Newfie / Canadian. Newfie / smart person with a work ethic.

Consider the word "Newfoundlander," which remains problematic when applied willy-nilly to Labradorians, but which can serve the islanders. "Newfoundlander" is more formal, and it does not carry the same slur baggage as "Newfie." If we define "Newfoundlander" as someone born in Newfoundland, it seems easy. That definition functions as a binary: Newfoundlander / non-Newfoundlander. What if we expand the definition to include someone like my son, born in Ontario but raised in Newfoundland since infancy? He considers himself a Newfoundlander. Other Canadians and international immigrants who make a home here: at what point can they be called Newfoundlanders? Can they call themselves that? When do they become Newfoundlanders?

I argue: whenever they say they do. Why? Because the identity of Newfoundlander is a spectrum, a range, not a binary. Human behaviour, including migration, is far too complex for the linguistic and imaginative limits of strict and static definitions.

So, here I am, a disabled Newfoundlander. What have I learned? That my disability and my identity as a disabled person exist on a spectrum, not a binary. I am valid as a disabled person, as a Newfoundlander, and as a disabled Newfoundlander. I've also learned that our self-serving cultural myth of the Friendly Newfoundlander needs a good hard look. Many of us are friendly, perhaps to the point of pathological nosiness. Some of us aren't. Newfoundlanders, like any other grouping of humans, are not homogeneous, and disability is one place our friendliness can fail. The behaviour of the twenty-something man who pretended not to see me at the coffee shop was no anomaly. Those who inspect people who park in blue spots with permits and make sure they're somehow Disabled Enough are hardly being friendly: they're indulging in a weird power-trip, one that at least acknowledges the existence of disabled people but in turn belittles and compartmentalizes us.

The COVID-19 pandemic has disabled me in a whole new way. The second-generation biologic I take treats my ankylosing spondylitis in part by suppressing my immune system. This leaves me especially vulnerable to infection and complications. I started my preventive self-isolation on March 16, 2020. This means no double-bubble, no visiting friends, no leaving the house except for short walks—and doing that alone or only with my husband. I cannot safely go to a pharmacy or grocery store. This situation puts additional pressure on my husband, who is now responsible for fetching all the food and medicine. I've no idea when this situation might change.

When I hear resentful discussion of pandemic restrictions, one line of talk really unsettles me, and it's eugenics. Few people use that word, but eugenics, which was accepted and commonly practised in Canada well into the 1970s—and still is, in the case of involuntary sterilization of First Nations women—informs much of our thinking and vernacular. We can hear it in utterances like "I come from good stock, so I won't get sick," or "Just let the vulnerable people stay at home. The virus will only kill people who are already infirm," or even "Let the elderly and disabled die where they will. Nothing we can do about that."

Eugenics led to the murder of millions by the Nazis. The disabled were specifically targeted. Eugenics, with its absurdly simplistic understanding of genetics and heredity, with its base in binary thinking, quickly erodes compassion and empathy. Strong / weak. Fit / unfit. Healthy / sick. Economic contributor / economic drain, or, to use the even harsher Nazi slogan, "Life unworthy of life." The binary thinking of eugenics allows one to more easily dehumanize others, to negate their inherent worth as human beings, and to require the dehumanized to somehow measure up to a mysterious and impossible standard controlled by the more powerful. The parallels to the blight of white supremacy, which intellectually relies on eugenics, are clear.

Even here in peaceful, reasonably friendly, yet still flawed Newfoundland and Labrador, others police and judge me. Am I disabled enough to merit a blue spot? Am I human enough not to shove aside? Am I still somewhat fit for human society if I'm "not 'disabled'-disabled"?

Am I human enough?

I am disabled. In or out of a wheelchair. On or off my crutches. Writing a novel or burning with a fever. I have endured ordeals of sickness and pain— and will do so again—and I know who I am. No one else can negate that.

The larger question is: why do we even try to negate others' identities?

All I wanted was a coffee.

Black Motherhood and Womanhood

Resistance and Resilience

by

DELORES V. MULLINGS

BLACK MOTHERHOOD

When my daughter and I arrived in St. John's, Newfoundland, in August 2009, I was in the middle of a forbidden love affair with...wait, hold on for a moment. I will come back with the juice later. First, let me do something that I love to do, and that is to share my experience of being a Black mother and an anti-Black racism and anti-racist academic activist living on the Rock!

My young daughter and I left a large extended family, well-established Black communities, and friends in pursuit of a new life filled with adventures, knowledge, and lessons in St. John's. We landed on "the Rock" in the middle of August on what should have been a bright, sunny day. Nature, however, had indeed greeted us with a foreshadowing of what the weather and the general human connections would be like for the next nine years—frigid. Some days it seems as if I have lived in the province for fifty years and other times it seems like I arrived only yesterday. The most challenging part of my life in St. John's has been my role as a Black mother trying to guide a young Black woman to understand her place in society.

I live in the skin of a Black Mother
A Warrior Mama who asks questions
That challenge the stereotyping of Black children
Hanging out on the Rock, the nicest place on earth,
Failed to bring relief from the idea that
My Black child was inferior
So, I had to fight even harder
To remind her of her greatness

Living in Newfoundland as a Black woman parenting a Black youth coming of age was daunting. As women and mothers, we are socialized to believe that we must be everything to our children; we are expected to show perfection in parenting our children, to support, love, nurture, and guide them in order to create miniature adults that reflect success based on the prescribed notion of what success looks like. All our children are unique and need different types of parenting and resources to help them reach their full potential. In addition to these, Black parents must adopt alternative strategies for Black children to support their growth as they move into adulthood. Regardless of how hard we work, the strategies we employ, and how much we advocate with and for our children, we sometimes feel like failures as mothers. During our first year in Newfoundland and Labrador, I came face to face with that ugly feeling of being an ineffective parent. My heart broke for my daughter as I could only watch and listen while what Philomena Este calls everyday racism—and what we know is actually anti-Black racism (ABR)—affected her. Most of her friends were wonderful, ambitious, and friendly young people, keen to participate in the usual coming-of-age activities in most young people's lives with the unique twist of growing up on the Rock. In spite of my daughter's flourishing social life, impressive extracurricular activity involvement, and seemingly successful adjustment to our new home, she failed to thrive. Black children need to see themselves positively reflected in their surroundings, books, education, teachers, and in the media.

Although she was born in Canada and is fluent in both English and French, Canada's official languages, she was presumed to not only be an immigrant but one that was not proficient in English, the dominant language spoken in St. John's. Her Blackness motivated students at Holy Heart secondary school to refer to her as an "ESL kid." This derogatory and discriminatory term is used primarily to describe racialized immigrant students at Holy Heart. The characterization robs racialized students of their humanity and excludes them from the fabric of Newfoundland society. It also stripped my daughter of her Canadian identity at a time when she was already struggling to find a place to call her own in Newfoundland. These subtle types of ABR made her move and settlement much more challenging despite her having class, language, and health privilege as well as a vibrant social life and close friends.

As I was writing this piece, I talked with my daughter, and we reminisced about some of our experiences. My daughter said, "I was made to feel as if I needed to represent your entire race, so you have to prove that Black people can be smart, we don't have to be 'ghetto'—with parents especially. Some people who live around the bay have never seen Black people. Teenagers have to blend in when we are around white people, some who don't see Black people or who are not around other people of colour. I felt my identity slowly being stripped away. I didn't know it or really understand it until after I left. That was hard. I could never live there again."

I watched as my daughter's self-confidence eroded to rubble. Her interest in school dipped, and then she said the words that every Black parent dreads: "Mom, I'm not smart" and "I can't be a lawyer because I'm not smart enough." This is the child that I raised to know that she *is* smart and who used to recite words including "I'm brilliant" and "I'm smart" daily. How did she get this idea, and where did it come from? How did this seed germinate and grow into a full plant inside this brilliant Black child who knew that she wanted to be a veterinarian before the age of eight, or at least wanted to do something in the field of biology? The teachers' low expectations of my daughter compounded the situation as she was complimented for being awarded grades that were not acceptable in our home and that were, at times, far below her established capabilities. As Black parents, we strive to instill certain values and ideas in our children, like self-confidence, a sense of cultural identity, and pride in their heritage. We also want them to chart their own course and not be limited by other people's ideas of who they are or what they can accomplish. This is important because they are socially conditioned through stereotypes in popular culture and through experiences in schools and daycare and other institutions to believe that they are less than all other groups, that they are not smart, and that they do not belong. As African-Canadians in Newfoundland and Labrador, we are also regularly accosted about aspects of our Blackness, including our hair.

STOP TOUCHING OUR HAIR

Have you seen strangers walk up to pregnant women and touch their bellies without asking? What about rubbing cancer survivors' bald heads? Have you seen or experienced that? Unwanted touching happens to a lot of Black people, too. As African-Canadians, our bodies are constantly invaded as Newfoundlanders reach out to touch, grab, squeeze, pat, tousle, and rub our hair. We are made to feel like exotic animals being petted in a zoo. My daughter and I were—and I am still—under constant surveillance and are forced to be responsible for educating people about our hair. We are regularly harassed and accosted with questions about it:

"Why is your hair that texture?"

"Is your hair real?"

"Do you wear extensions?"

"Can you shampoo and condition your hair?"

"How do you sleep on your hair?"

When we change our hairstyles, we are asked if our hair grew overnight or if we cut our hair. We are expected to be a walking tutorial for mostly white people's curiosity about aspects of our Blackness. Do they have similar questions about Selena Gomez's, Britney Spears's, or Kim Kardashian's hair? People just assume that Black people cannot have long hair and that if we have long hair it must be extensions. I have long locs, and it is interesting how so many individuals assume that my hair could not be real. The underlying assumption is that Black people's hair cannot grow past a certain length. Hair is an important aspect of women's and girls' identities, all the more so of Black womanhood and Black identity, and it is burdensome to face a barrage of questions that suggest that our hair does not fit the expected mould of what constitutes "good hair."

Black women and girls wear their hair in multiple ways. Some introduce chemicals into their hair regimen and others have what is called natural hair, which means the hair does not have any form of chemical treatment that changes its texture or length. Both types of hair can be long or short, and women and girls with either type may wear their hair in braids (e.g., cornrows) or may introduce weaves, extensions, jewellery, colouring, or headwraps. Hairstyles can tell stories about the age, class, and status of women, youth, and girls, along with women's skills, creativity, courage, and independence. There is a special bond between mother and daughter, grandmother and granddaughter, auntie and niece, or other close and trusted women during hair care and grooming where socialization is done; stories are shared, problems are discussed, and strategies of various kinds are devised to deal with life stressors. These rituals are rooted in the racial and cultural values and practices of African womanhood. Families may carry on hair-styling traditions as well.

Continental Africans and Africans in the diaspora have a long history of hair grooming, styling, and presentation, and, for those whose ancestors were brutalized in the Transatlantic Slave Trade, these values and norms are vital. Not only were enslaved people of African descent forbidden from continuing with their hair-care practices, they also did not have access to their traditional hair products, styling tools, or relationships with kinswomen who could help them with hair-care rituals. As a result, the women relied on each other, which took on fundamentally new shapes and meanings of group bonding at a time when Black families and communities in the Americas were violated, terrorized, separated from each other, and dismantled.

Black hair products, beauty stores, and hairdressers are not readily available in Newfoundland and Labrador, and this limits Black Newfoundlanders' opportunities to build their traditional hair communities. The hair industry has historically inferiorized and excluded Black hair products by either rendering them invisible or storing them in small, designated "ethnic" spaces, thereby sending the message that Black hair is abnormal and needs to be segregated. Black hair is versatile: it straightens, shrinks, stands up, bounces, rolls, or lies flat, depending on what we choose to do with it. Black people are extremely creative in what they do with their hair, which is why someone may sport a do-up, headwrap, braids, ponytail, or bun all within a week. Our hair is a personal expression of who we are and can represent acts of activism, political statements, reclaiming power, and expressing resistance against colonialism and white norms that mark tightly curled, kinky Black hair as bad or inferior to straighter, flaxen hair.

In short, please stop asking Black women if we cut our hair or if it grew overnight, if you can touch our hair, if our hair is real or if all of it is ours, how we wash our hair, and why we wear extensions. These are intrusive questions; they are complicated and nuanced and sometimes we actually don't know the answer to some of your questions. If you want to know if your Black hair questions are appropriate, substitute the words "breasts" or "teeth" and see how that goes.

MY FORBIDDEN LOVE AFFAIR WITH A ROCKSTAR

"Dr. Mullings is the worst professor I have ever had."

My daughter endured racist presumptions from her teachers and classmates, and we have both faced unwelcome, ignorant nosiness about our bodies from strangers. But I haven't been any more safe from anti-Black racism in my professional life at the university, the ivory tower where people are supposed to be judged on the basis of their ideas, where students and faculty are supposed to be more aware of how bigotry unwittingly informs our thinking. To flourish here, I have looked to the landscape for inspiration and have come to rely on my own sense of self-worth.

The beauty of the landscape leaves me breathless,
Gives me hope and fuels my soul
Under the watchful eyes of trees that whisper

Unabashed howling winds and mountains of snow
I have experienced great success,
Profound isolation and loneliness
And monumental challenges
That helped to shape a Rockstar

I live in the skin of a Black woman, born and raised on the beautiful island of Jamaica. Newfoundland sold salted cod to Jamaica and in return, Jamaica sold rum to Newfoundland. Since both are islands, I frequently joke that Newfoundland is Jamaica's cousin. So why did a Black woman of Caribbean descent choose to live and work in Newfoundland?

When I finished my PhD in my late forties and was looking to embark on a third career, Newfoundland was an easy pick for me after I got over the idea that I would be without Black friends, family, and neighbours. I wondered who would want to hire a forty-something Black woman in academe when everyone wanted young people who could serve the institutions for forty years. Why would they hire me? I'd seen the news articles of the mass exodus of middle-aged, mostly white men and women professionals who had worked for thirty, forty, and fifty years in one company and who had suddenly been pushed out of their jobs and careers for younger contract workers.

The words "Dr. Mullings is the worst professor I have ever had" jumped off the page among the many comments that students offered. Although some feedback was positive, the negative comments felt more prominent, primarily given their personal nature. As I read the words written by undergraduate students who had been beaming from ear to ear at me the very day that they wrote those comments a few months ago, I could not help but feel sad—devastated, actually—for that student. When I read those words, they brought me back to the reality and pitfalls of teaching while Black, focused on what I call facilitating transformational decolonized education. Many students, administrators, and colleagues alike marked my body as hostile, harsh, monstrous, bitchy, rude, uncollegial, and uncooperative. I brought discussions of anti-Black racism, whiteness, and colonization into the classrooms of Memorial University's School of Social Work (MUN SSW). I introduced an anti-Black racism and anti-racism agenda long before police publicly executed George Floyd and killed Chantel Moore in a wellness check. The backlash was swift and almost deadly.

I endured aggressive and unhelpful criticism, a poisoned work environment, hostility, and personal attacks. I was typecast as the "bad Black woman teacher," much like almost all Black teachers in the movies. Questions arose about my hair, competence, qualifications, clothes, mannerisms, the way I talk, and my right to be here. I was constantly being "tone policed" as Layla Saad calls it—I was asked to adjust the tone of my voice so that white people could feel comfortable when I speak. One MUN alumnus wrote to one of the SSW deans to air concerns about my teaching methods, saying, "This kind of professor is not what we need in Newfoundland...she doesn't belong here." A student commented that I "should not be allowed to teach social work." In response to the attacks, I have made some adjustments, because it is more important to me that the message I am transmitting is heard and that the agenda of uprooting ABR and decolonizing is successful. I coached myself using mirrors that were strategically placed in my home to practise smiling conservatively and adjusting my facial expressions in what I understood to be the acceptable white standard. I also worked with my voice to make it softer-sounding and higher in pitch. While I am still direct in my arguments, the change in tone and pitch helps to reduce white fright. These qualities I understood to be less intimidating and authoritarian and more acceptable by white standards. Now, I am complimented on how different I sound and how much easier it is for white people to hear what I have to say about ABR, anti-racism, and colonization without being offended.

In the scholarly area, in my eleven-plus years at MUN, not one white academic staff member has invited me to collaborate or partner with them on any aspect of scholarship, even though I have invited and submitted grant applications with at least fifteen of them. One former SSW senior administrator described me as "a one-trick pony" for my intersectional ABR and anti-racism scholarship, and graduate students were regularly discouraged from working with me even in my research areas, like settlement. So, while I am encouraged to take risks, I suffer the consequences of being institutionally excluded as my colleagues choose other Black and racialized academics who speak in what is considered a less offensive manner and who are seen as working towards the better good of the province using the outmoded multicultural lens or a more palatable brand of ABR and anti-racism work. I agree with bell hooks (1992), who encourages Black feminist scholars to take an "oppositional gaze" at the Black women stereotypes because there are so few positive representations of who we are. In essence, I challenge the stereotypes placed on me as a Black woman by engaging in the type of work that helps to change the narrative of Black women teachers. For example, I introduce course content like Gloria Ladson-Billings's article "Who You Callin' Nappy-Headed?" that explains racism and sexism against Black women teachers. For me, it is also important to name, make visible, and narrate my experiences of violence and brutality in academe. I tell my story in my own words and challenge the one-dimensional stories told by white students, administrators, and other colleagues.

In my travels around the world, I have heard people describe Newfoundland and Labrador residents as "the nicest people in the world." Although I have lived in the province for more than eleven years, I have never felt that niceness beyond a surface salutation or talk about the weather. This was imprinted in my brain in 2016 when my daughter and I had Thanksgiving supper alone in a restaurant. We have a large extended family in Ontario and, like Newfoundlanders and Labradorians, many Black families, including ours, don't need an occasion to gather around the kitchen table and connect. Here in Newfoundland, family seems to extend only to those who are blood relatives. When I mentioned that to the women in my yoga class, five of them asked me why I had not told them that we were not invited anywhere as they would have had us over for supper.

Now, in 2020, I have: a handful of friends, so I don't need to eat alone unless I want to; many students and colleagues who see the value in my work; and administrators who have warmed up to the idea that my brand of academic activism is needed in the ivory tower. My activism is here to stay. St. John's, Newfoundland, is one of my homes. I am contributing to our province in ways to ensure that it is better than when I arrived. It will take time—after all, Africa was not destroyed in a day—but I am resilient and committed. I stand on the shoulders and rest on the backs of a long line of my African ancestors, so my continued success is certain.

How did I persist here in the province for all these years in the face of ABR, disrespect, and loneliness? Love is one of the things that keeps me going. I moved here because of a love affair with a Rockstar, and I've only fallen more deeply for this person the longer I've lived here. That person is myself. I believe in me and my ability to contribute to the Newfoundland and Labrador communities where I travel and live.

Under the harsh gaze of white students and administrators
Who would stereotype me as the worst
While questioning my worth and value as a teacher
I need to maintain my love affair with myself
In so doing, I thrive beyond measure
I am the original #Rockstarsocialworkteacher
Come to learn and grow or move downwind
And if you don't like it
Cum tes mi noh!

Les Franco-Terre-Neuviens

Ces mémoires, aussi, sont les miennes

by

MARCELLA CORMIER

Je suis Marcella à Mark, à Charlie, à Johnny Alfred, à Johnny Victor Cormier, originaire des Îles-de-la-Madeleine, installé à Cap Saint-Georges.

Je ne suis pas Québécoise, ni Acadienne.

Je suis Franco-Terre-Neuvienne.

I am a fifth-generation Franco-Newfoundlander, proudly born and raised on the province's majestic Port-au-Port Peninsula, a *carrefour* for French, Anglo-Saxon, and Mi'kmaw cultures and languages. While the history of the French presence in our province seems widely known, I am met with pure surprise 100 per cent of the time I introduce myself as a Franco-Newfoundlander. And not only by Newfoundlanders and Labradorians, but also by other Franco-Canadians. This should come as no shock to me. I am a part of the smallest francophone minority of Canada, constituting just under one per cent of the total population of the province. Despite this fact, our tiny but colourful Franco-Newfoundlander and Franco-Labradorian population is another beautiful piece of Newfoundland and Labrador's diversity. Growing up as part of a linguistic minority in our province came with its challenges, but stubbornly holding on to my birthright has been the beacon that has guided me on my life's voyage thus far.

If you are a Franco-Newfoundlander, you get used to the screening questions with new acquaintances. You know what I'm talking about:

"You mean, you are pure French? You speak French? But your parents must be from New Brunswick or Quebec? They aren't? Really? But your English is perfect...*Mais, tu n'as pas d'accent, comment ça?*"

Well, actually, I can thank an American Army Base and an Irish grandmother for that. Even though the Bay St. George area was densely populated by Acadian, French, and Mi'kmaq communities at the turn of the twentieth century, the arrival of the Americans and the promise of economic prosperity during World War II in pre-Confederation Newfoundland and Labrador nearly sealed the fate of the French language on the province's west coast. Officially, there should no longer have even been clusters of French and Acadian descendants on the west coast, since France's fishing rights had been revoked in 1904.

That's where my Irish Newfoundlander grandmother arrives on scene. The young teacher moved to the west coast from Ferryland. She then married a young, handsome man of Acadian origin who worked at "the Base," but who didn't speak a word of French. His father had decided that the youngest of the siblings would only speak English, to improve his prospects of finding employment outside of the fishery. Consequently, my mother—their daughter—grew up in a French community without understanding a word of French until she met my father and his family. At the time, it was a true advantage for her, especially at school. That's right; you read that correctly.

My father's experience was different. He was the thirteenth-born of a third-generation French (Renouf, Leroux) and Acadian (Chaisson, Cormier) couple at Ti-Jardin, on the end of Cap Saint-Georges. French was spoken in the home and in the community. Although my paternal grandparents had little formal education to speak of, they were able to teach my father, one of their youngest children, some English before he ever sat on a school bench. Once he arrived at school, it was forbidden to speak French.

Instruction was offered by both clerical and laic staff whose mission was to bring up good English-speaking children of God. Unfortunately, he saw many of his friends take severe punishments, including strappings, if they spoke French. It goes without saying that many who experienced this treatment left school early, struggled with poverty, and the scars of their trauma trickled down through generations.

French was to be spoken in private; it was certainly not to be cultivated. It was the language of the poor, the dirty, and the ignorant. It was to be forgotten. I vividly remember walking into Ozzie's General Store, also known as *"la boutique,"* and hearing the cashier and customer switch to English until they knew I was *"la fille à Mark."* Unknown to our people, this was also the experience of other minority francophone populations not only in Canada, but also in the United States. Paired with the economy, church and school were major assimilatory forces.

My father later became a teacher, a principal, a professional musician, a leader, an advocate, and an activist for French Newfoundlanders and Labradorians. He joined the movements to demand minority language rights, along with many other Franco-Newfoundlanders and Labradorians in the 1970s. He finished his 31-year career as a teaching principal at École Notre-Dame-du-Cap, one of the French First-Language schools in our province, and continues to work and volunteer in education and the arts today. My mother raised two Franco-Newfoundlander children who attended French First-Language schools. She took French "alphabétisation" classes at night, kept up traditional crafts, and volunteered in the community. My parents are now "Granny B." and "Grand-père" to two beautiful francophone grandchildren who are bilingual and thriving. My brother and sister-in-law both speak of our histories with the children, and, even at their young age, they understand and are proud of who they are.

How things have changed...

But have they?

In 2020, in a world of growing polarities between education, tolerance, and acceptance, paralleled with deep-rooted racism, hate, ignorance, and intolerance, I find myself both excited about sharing my story as one of many experiences of being francophone in Newfoundland and Labrador and wanting to simply hide it, because I could, with the greatest of ease.

Even though I grew up with every privilege and freedom that generations before me did not have—notably, a French First-Language education—I still struggle with so many doubts when dealing with my identity. I also witness it among my peers. As we know, identity can be fluid and can change over the course of a lifetime. Individuals not only base their identities on physical traits, but also on systems of belief, or language. They may identify as being part of a community based on a number of commonalities. This being said, all too often, native speakers may experience a certain subtractive bilingualism resulting from being a minority, especially if they are unable to receive formal instruction in their first language. An insecurity emerges, and some may identify as a speaker of their second language based on their perception that they are incompetent in their first. Would you identify as an athlete if you were terrible at sports? Probably not. It is far easier to say that you are a competent bench warmer.

We also see ourselves too often through the eyes of others. Adding to linguistic insecurity are comments from everyone who feels the need to tell us how great or poor we are at speaking French. If you're good, you're promoted to "A+ francophone" in their books. If you have traces of a different accent, or if you have the misfortune of using colloquialisms, then you get to be an "anglophone." I should mention that none are more guilty of this than other francophones. I will never forget an anecdote that my cooperating teacher shared with me during my internship when I felt insecure, when I felt like an "ait" pronounced "é" would make me less francophone. Growing up, I spoke the French I learned in my community, a two-hundred-year-old hybrid between Acadian French and France French. Although she had been born and raised in France, once my colleague arrived in Canada, she was asked if she was an anglophone from Montreal. I still chuckle about it from time to time.

"Are you pure French?" I mean, how does one answer that? Was the person asking about my genetic composition or about my competency in French? I am the product of exogamy—marriages between my French-speaking ancestors and cultural outsiders—therefore I guess I am not. I don't need one of those spit-in-a-tube genealogy kits to determine that. I suppose that technically I have two primary languages, and I would go as far as to say two mother tongues. Yes, ladies and gentlemen, I was a bilingual baby before it was cool. But language is not blood. It can be lost within a generation, or even less—remember what I mentioned about members of linguistic minorities identifying with the majority based on their perceived competency in their first language? But genetics remain, you say. Well, my dark skin, dark hair, prominent cheekbones, and family history suggest that I am also of Indigenous descent, not just Acadian, Irish, and French. Unfortunately, I have no linguistic or cultural connection that makes me able to confidently self-identify as Indigenous. Today, I recognize that this is a part of my linguistic and cultural identity that has been lost because historical context made it so my ancestors decided it was best to hide. At the time, it may very well have been to survive.

I am decidedly fortunate to be able to openly and proudly identify as a Franco-Newfoundlander, though I have to admit that I have tried on other labels. French Canadian, you know, to be part of a bigger minority. I then tried Acadian because I learned through travel that my spoken language is closest to theirs. There was no way I could get away with being French or Québécoise. Trying to pass for an Irish Newfoundlander was funny—I mean, I do have a few freckles on my golden-brown skin, and I swear my natural hair colour turns reddish during the summer! In the end, however, the only name that fits is *Franco-Terre-Neuvienne*. Generations before me stubbornly held on and got loud so that I could proudly speak my language and practise my culture today. Even though it grates on my nerves, I do take time to explain, in a thirty-second-speedy-social-media-video fashion, who I am and where I am from to those who will listen.

There are days when I am simply a Newfoundlander. It fits. I eat my Jiggs' Dinner with a "good heart" while I listen to that local radio station, I'm always up for a good laugh, I love my mountains and the sea like everyone else. Until I open my mouth. Don't get me wrong: I don't have a thick Pepé Le Pew French accent. It's my syntax and idiomatic expressions that give me away. The perfect conversation opener is and always will be the weather. That's where I get caught. "It marks for good weather this week," to which I get "It what?" Saying "I'm heartsick" gets good reactions too. We anglicized "*J'ai mal au coeur*," which means "I feel nauseated," not "I feel dejected." Starting sentences with "Me, I..." gives it away if nothing else does. Busted. And then come the screening questions and the thirty-second video. No hiding this time.

I grew up in DeGrau, in the municipality of Cap Saint-Georges, population one thousand. It is the only officially bilingual municipality in Newfoundland and Labrador. I attended French First-Language schools and, subsequently, universities in New Brunswick and Québec. Every paycheque I have earned has been from a job that I have done in French. I have been a teacher and administrator in the *Conseil scolaire francophone provincial*'s schools since 2003. I occasionally freelance at writing and editing. I have dabbled in journalism. For years, I was also a small business owner for that Latin-inspired dance fitness class that your moms love. Music, reading, dancing, travelling, and cooking are my favourite pastimes.

A year ago, I moved near the province's capital. I love living here. I could not have more easily moved anywhere else; this is also home. There are wonderful differences, and I love discovering them every day, because they also highlight my own uniqueness. I have grown accustomed to being different. For instance, I don't bother saying my name to clerks anymore: I simply offer to spell it. I see gratitude and relief in their eyes when they see the finished product.

I refuse to anglicize my name. Unbeknownst to many, numerous west coast families anglicized their names, or changed the spelling to appear English. Some did it intentionally; others had their names changed for them by the church or the government. How do you contest that when you are illiterate, because you did not attend school, because you were punished for speaking a different language? Though simple, my refusal to anglicize my name is important. I will never forget being at a cash register at a grocery store in Stephenville with my mother. For some reason, she was asked her name. She responded "Cormier." The cashier gave a snicker and said: "Oh, pardon me, you're a Corm-ier and not a Corm-yer. You must be from the Peninsula." I gaped, and my anglophone mother said: "Yes, that is correct, and that is how you correctly pronounce our name." My anglophone mother stood up for our name. She realizes the importance of pronouncing it in French.

Yes, there are times when ignorance of our province's diversity also rears its dirty head, even in the most "educated" of environments, not only in the news comments section on social media sites or in grocery stores. A few years ago, in a professional setting no less, a colleague and I were interrupted in the middle of a conversation to be invited to a social, but the person extending the invitation spoke only to my co-worker, saying with a chuckle: "You can bring the jackatar with you if you want." He was referring to me. I was the only person sitting in the room who was very obviously of mixed French and Mi'kmaw descent, and everyone knew. I don't anglicize my name, remember?

As silence cloaked the room and I did nothing but gape, another colleague leapt to her feet and blasted: "Tell me you did not just say that! Do you know what that means? Do you know the history behind that slur? I saw my French Catholic Nan from the Peninsula excluded from the family dinner table because she was the dirty jackatar, the mixed-breed, that my grandfather had married." She went on to reveal that she, too, was of Franco-Newfoundlander origin, but that part of her family history was buried deep due to the stigma attached.

I will be forever grateful to her for standing up for me and her grandmother that day when I was so taken aback that I would not have been able to say a word to defend myself without choking on it. Please know that in no context is it ever appropriate to use the word "jackatar." I will not laugh or shrug it off. It is a word that appeared in the province's lexicon generations ago that is at its very root pejorative, racist, and discriminatory, akin to other words no one would dare say today.

Because of the rights, privileges, and freedoms I enjoyed, I cannot pretend to have shared the experience of the generations before me; however, it is important that I be cognizant of their experience. It is the reason that I speak what we call the "old French." One time, when I was home visiting from university, one of my uncles spoke to me in English. I nearly cried. He said that his French was not good enough, that he was embarrassed. I have not, to this day, forgotten that moment, and never has a family member spoken to me in English since.

I consider that culturally, linguistically, I grew up in a rich environment where I had permission to thrive. I was not entirely sheltered from discrimination and ignorance, but I had licence to be myself, with programming, legislation, infrastructure, and, most importantly, recognition. I offer my hand and heart to our diverse population so that other individuals and communities may grow similarly.

I invite you to spend time on the Port-au-Port peninsula for the views, the people, the music, the food, the language. You will hear French that is hundreds of years old, English that sounds French, French with English words. It is a treat for linguists. You will hear *"Tantine"* and *"Nonque"* instead of "Aunt" and "Uncle"; even families who have lost their French use *"Maman et Dadda"* as well as other epithets to express affection. What happens when we get angry, you ask? We get mad and cuss in English. It is that much more transgressive.

While some families have lost the French language through the forces of assimilation, most have held on to oral tradition, music, and culinary arts. The accordion and fiddle are present in many households. Songs and jigs have been passed down for generations. So it is in my family. My father learned to play guitar to accompany his older brothers, who began playing the accordion by ear before they celebrated their tenth birthdays. Our musical heritage is still alive and well with the newest generation of French Newfoundlanders who are learning from a well-known artist-in-residence in the peninsula's two French First-Language schools. The community supports its artists by organizing festivals, garden parties, and other events that place French Newfoundland traditional music in the spotlight.

My contribution to the arts is what I shall call my "accidental writing." I studied French (*quelle surprise!*) and history in university. As a high school student, I gobbled up any book or website that spoke of Franco-Newfoundlanders. Most were documentaries, or folklore journals. No literature was to be found. No songs, poems, or plays were written in French about Franco-Newfoundlanders until later. A few years ago, I was approached by the *Association régionale de la côte Ouest* to work on a narrative about the late fiddler Émile Benoît to mark his centennial. That project led to the authoring of three children's books.

My favourite text, however, is a poem that I wrote when I was sixteen. My school held a poetry contest when I was in grade twelve, and I placed. My father saw the text. When I was in university, he asked my permission to compose a song with it. Indifferent, I said *"Ouaip, vas-y"* and assumed that would be the end of it. A few years later, I was substitute-teaching at my old school on the day the students went to perform at the Rotary Music Festival in Stephenville. My father was the choir director. The curtains opened, and the children began to sing. I quickly recognized the words from my poem from my school days. They sang with beaming smiles—they even made up a little dance to it, which is not something one would expect to see at that particular event. I sobbed like a baby. They had a song to sing about themselves, about their community. When I began teaching, I made a point of presenting the song and text to my students, and I encouraged them to write, to position themselves, to tell their story as well. For as long as I can remember, on May 30, on provincial Francophonie Day, we sang together "*Les Franco-Terre-Neuviens, ces mémoires, aussi, sont les miennes. Pêcher, jaser et danser, que c'est beau de voir le passé,*" dance and all. I unwittingly gave them words and a song to tell their story. Our story.

While family and community are pivotal in developing and maintaining a Franco-Newfoundland identity, education is paramount. For a little over a generation, cohorts of students, not only on the peninsula, but all over the province, have proudly held on to their French culture and heritage, regardless of their origins. We have grown up with a quality education, with pride, with hope. So many have gone on to live harmoniously in their communities, to be leaders and great contributors to society. I have even had the privilege of having my former students drop their children off for their first day of kindergarten.

For the next generation, I am hopeful.

I am aware that there are other stories, other realities experienced by my neighbours. Some are shared, some are not. I tell these in particular, because they are mine. My sixteen-year-old self knew that when I wrote "*ces mémoires, aussi, sont les miennes.*" They guide my actions. They make up who I am. I am not only a teacher, an administrator, a leader, an artist—I am a member of my Franco-Newfoundland and Labradorian community at large. I am also an ally for my community. Early on, I knew that the best way to help my people grow was through education. My upbringing gave me a strong sense of self, but learning about and connecting with the wider world helped me reaffirm my identity. As with many oppressed populations or populations dealing with intergenerational trauma, education empowers us to create a future where we, as Franco-Newfoundlanders and

Labradorians, are respected and understood. Where we are recognized as valuable, contributing citizens of a global society. We do not need to "go away," or disappear. Assimilation is not an option.

Why bother? Why continue to speak French in our province? A language is so much more than words. It is another way of seeing the world.

My story is not only mine—it is the story of generations, of a community, of other francophone communities in Canada. I am sure that my Acadian ancestors were aware of this in their way of identifying a person. I will always be *Marcella à Mark, à Charlie, à Johnny Alfred, à Johnny Victor Cormier.*

Franco-Terre-Neuviennement,
Marcella Cormier

Man of Many Faces

by

STEPHEN MILLER

Like so many Newfoundlanders before him, my father made his living on the water. I was born in 1987, recently enough that I've been able to keep up with technology but long enough ago that I can remember having to say prayers in school. It was a different Newfoundland than the one my father grew up in. For me Newfoundland was part of a much bigger world, full of possibilities and cultures. There were options. But I always felt this odd sense of guilt for not being drawn to or emotionally invested in things that supposedly defined the Newfoundland identity. Despite being born here, raised here, and deeply in love with the place, I felt like a phony. Whether or not they were merely the machinations of my mind, I had inadvertently created a different identity for myself: the outsider.

Perhaps it was the role I was born to play. From day one I've been stubborn, forcibly removed from my mother with forceps after more than twenty-four hours of excruciating labour. I like to do things my way, even when it leaves me bloodied and bruised. It's not a personality trait I either hate or adore—it has served me and hamstrung me. I've just never seen the appeal of the preordained, of following a path set out for me, even if it was mapped with the best of intentions. I've always wanted to be free to make my own choices and deal with the consequences. And boy, did I ever. Some of those choices led me to love and personal growth and prosperity. Some of them led me to prison. Funnily enough, those choices are why you, dear reader, are seeing my work in this collection. Because, aside from what I suspect is a touch of undiagnosed PTSD, prison gave me a unique perspective. It's always the facet of my existence that seems to interest the law-abiding types the most. And in my aspirations of being the world's most approachable ex-con I am happy to acquiesce.

Firstly, I want to make clear that my trajectory towards prison was not the result of unfortunate circumstances or events. It was my doing. I had every opportunity afforded to me. Stable home, attentive and loving parents, no abuse...unless you count being forced to attend church every Sunday until my teenage years. I had it good. We weren't wealthy—no cars as gifts or designer clothes—but I have never known what it is like to go to bed hungry. Many of the men I did time with were not so lucky. The cards were stacked against them, born into cycles of abuse and poverty with prison all but a guaranteed outcome. This is not to say that those men don't have agency or that their actions deserved to go unpunished. I'm just saying we are all, to varying degrees, products of our environments. I refuse to blindly condemn people for not living up to an example that was never set for them.

So now that we all understand that A: I'm only a victim of myself and B: My parents are not to blame, I'll do my best to share something insightful.

As a boy, I remember trying to wrap my head around what it would mean to be a man. I had a good example to look to. My father has always put his own needs last. He never complained about his months away from home as part of the coast guard or later as a fisheries observer. My mother was no different in terms of selflessness, but my father was a man, something I was told I would be one day. My dad was strong and stoic; he provided. I wondered if someday I would feel capable of that. I wondered how to get there.

Growing up, trying to figure out what separates men from boys, I often worried that my lack of interest in the ocean was indicative of my lack of worth as a man. This might seem absurd, and surely it is, but anyone born 'round the bay (anywhere on the island outside St. John's) knows exactly what I'm talking about. My particular bay community was Marystown on the Burin Peninsula. Now not every "bayman" makes his living on the water, but I was the odd man out in just about every behaviour and interest common to my peers. I liked the outdoors, but it was because I just appreciated spending time in nature. I never had any interest in snowmobiles or all-terrain vehicles. I had no moral opposition to hunting provided it was done responsibly, but I also had no interest in participating. The handful of times I've fished with a rod or jigged a squid I enjoyed myself, but it felt like more of a novelty than a passion.

The lack of shared interests caused me to miss out on a lot of bonding experiences. I was a chubby kid who liked to read and write his own little stories, and, even though my own preferences contributed to how much time I spent alone, I grew a bit resentful. I might have always liked to call my own shots, but the desire to fit in with your peers is particularly potent during this period. Eventually I became guilty of what I perceived to be their sin. Instead of admitting that I was longing to be included, I mocked them. Poked fun at their brand-name Ski-Doo racing jackets, their taste in music, and their obsession with major league sports. I fancied myself intellectually superior. I see now that it was my ego trying desperately to protect itself.

Ironically, it was during my "fuck these people" stage that I made the most friends. A quick wit and a sharp tongue got me a lot of laughs, especially when they were weaponized against someone. I finally fit in, and all it took was giving up. The outsider was now the comedian.

Back when I was in grade school, grades seven to twelve all attended Marystown Central High School (MCHS). I was twelve years old when I started grade seven. Some of the boys in grade twelve, and those who had been held back, looked very much like men to me. They drove cars and had moustaches, had sex and drank alcohol. Decidedly adult things. They always intimidated the hell out of me and the other boys my age, but mostly ignored our existence.

I ended up doing grades eight and nine in a different school, when the educational system was reorganized so that MCHS became grades ten through twelve only. By the time I returned there for grade ten, I was much more confident in myself. Teenage angst of unknown origin had turned my father from idol to oppressor. My parents were suddenly embarrassing and a distraction from my super cool friends who I was certain I would remain close to for my entire life. Now my male role models were kids with moustaches who liked to smoke and get in fights. I knew a man was strong, but I'd yet to realize that it was how he wields that strength that is to be admired or admonished. I was too young and naïve to see the difference between respect and fear. Someday I wanted to be cool enough to date girls much younger than me and drive a Z-28 Camaro. Yeah, I know, I know.

My first foray into crime would come as I tried to ingratiate myself to these moustachioed man-children. Once I started stealing booze and condoms I was suddenly cool enough to hang with them. At first it felt like an achievement, but, as Gord Downie put it, "even babies raised by wolves they know exactly when they've been used." Now this is not to say I stopped stealing, far from it...I just started making a profit. I only stole from big businesses and never people—it was wrong but not as wrong. I had a natural talent for it, or maybe I just didn't fit the profile.

Employees kept an eye on the kids from the "wrong" part of town, but smiling, well-spoken Stephen was always above suspicion.

I hung out with the wrong crowd until I met a nice girl from "town," a.k.a. St. John's. She wasn't interested in that scene, and her many charms quickly convinced me to become the kind of guy she wouldn't mind introducing her parents to. I appreciated her for a while, but eventually we parted ways. I still had wild oats to sow. We ended up breaking up before my first year of university.

I had no idea what I wanted to do; I only attended university because I had the grades and no other plan. I wanted to be in the city, and the rest I'd figure out. After a year in St. John's my grandmother passed. It would take several books to express the depths of my adoration for that woman. So let's just say her loss devastated me. For a while grief and pain was all I knew. I did not deal with it well. I didn't deal with it at all. Suddenly nothing mattered but escaping that pain. It was during this time that I was first exposed to opiates. And the pain became profound emptiness. I cared for nothing and no one, least of all myself. The comedian was now the nihilist.

I didn't know it at the time, but I had just begun an addiction that would last a decade. It was a decade of loss and alienation. I pushed away those who cared, to surround myself with those who enabled. It was a very toxic existence. Eventually everyone I knew outside of my immediate family was in a similar situation to me. Those who tried to save me always ended up disappointed. Most gave up. I sure don't blame them.

I managed to stay out of prison for the first three years or so of my addiction. Each day was a rat race of trying to stay high and avoid withdrawals. My life became one of crime and violence, and I was eventually handed my first sentence. I got six months for theft, for assaulting someone who tried to prevent me from fleeing the scene of the crime, and for skipping out on court.

My first few stints at Her Majesty's Penitentiary (HMP) in St. John's were relatively quiet on account of my placement within the prison. I wasn't in protective custody or anything—where prisoners who needed protection from other inmates, such as sex offenders or those with "good" meds were sent. I just wasn't in "the jungle," the name they have given units 3A and 3B. It's where they put the hard tickets. It was still awful in terms of isolation, but there were relatively low amounts of sociopathic behaviour and violence.

The third time I went to prison I was placed on 3A. Suddenly I was living amongst alleged and convicted murderers. These were mostly lifers, their names and their deeds well known throughout the law enforcement community and, in some cases, the community at large. My first day there, a simple misunderstanding led to me being brutally savaged by a group of prisoners—the misunderstanding being that I thought my medication was for me. I was on anti-psychotics and anti-anxiety meds at the time— although I was being tapered off both at a rate much faster than recommended. I was not special in this regard: the prison psychiatrist's main function, in my opinion, was to cut inmates off any medication they could survive without as soon as they were placed in his care.

There are about twenty inmates, give or take, on any given range. Most cells house two inmates, but some are single occupancy and you become entitled to them based on your length of time incarcerated. If you were charged with any sort of institutional offence, you would lose your place, among other privileges. One of the cells was a bit bigger—the one where they gave me a beating that left my nose broken and bruises in places I didn't think were possible—was designed with wheelchair accessibility in mind. But no classification officer was crazy enough to put a person with a physical disability amongst violent criminals with very little interest in "fair" fights.

I would later learn that inmates on this range refer to the cell colloquially as "the octagon" because that's where the fights often went down. Lots of room, no cameras, and a code of silence made it the perfect venue for the sort of barbarism that would absolutely shock polite society. I was a lamb to the slaughter. I'm a big, strong guy, but there were five other men in the cell with me. At least four of them took turns stomping me when I fell to the ground after being struck in the head unexpectedly by a convicted killer. They stomped me while educating me on how things worked around here.

The odds were stacked against me. This was a range run by the most infamous criminals in St. John's, and I was some bayman no one knew. It's kind of funny, but those were the lines the almost entirely Caucasian prison divided itself along. Townie versus bayman. Making matters worse, two of my assailants had just received bad news on the day I arrived. Their partners on the outside had realized, as is common, that waiting isn't as easy as it sounds.

Prison culture is in many ways the opposite of polite society. Kindness is not a strength. Mercy is not a virtue. Brutality is the official language. My first day was very informative. I was the perfect target because all the hate that built up on the range could be safely unleashed against the new guy: there was no fear of retribution from one of the range's other "cliques." I was expected to "check off" (leave the range out of fear, to be placed elsewhere), which would earn the unit a ten-day lockdown. For the range's inmates, this would mean a loss of visitation rights and only one hour outside their cells each day. Everyone knew that this was the penalty for violence. This is a cycle that plays itself out at HMP over and over. Despite the consequences, though, long-time inmates still target the new guys. It's their way of letting a little pressure off to keep things from boiling over.

My stubborn ass decided to stick it out, too proud to leave a clearly dangerous environment. My beating was obvious to anyone, and I was hauled off the range and interviewed by various guards, nurses, etc. I never named names and maintained my injuries were sustained prior to my incarceration. They knew this was absurd, as I'd been in custody for months at this point. But eventually they stopped trying to rescue me from myself, and I was sent back to 3A. There were no lockdowns, no nothing. This caused my stock to rise dramatically. Suddenly I was "solid," to be trusted. I was instantly in on all the various rackets and given access to drugs that most new guys wouldn't have a chance in hell of getting their hands on.

I wish I could say my experience made me want to protect the ones that came after me from similar fates, but to be honest I was just happy the target wasn't on my back. I could tell you that I didn't engage in any of the strong-arming or bullying...but I don't want to lie to you.

Aside from a few fist fights over exceedingly stupid issues, like card games or what to watch on television, I never felt that target on my back again. I came close, when inmates noticed the journals I kept writing in while in my cell. A group of them confronted me, convinced I was taking notes for the "white shirts"—what we called the higher-ranking correctional officers. Once they realized it was just my own writing, they did a full 180. In short order, I was reading my work to an eager audience as soon as it was finished. I monetized my literary skills on the range, writing children's stories for inmates with kids. I had many occasions to help inmates who struggled with literacy correspond with loved ones. I was finding my place in this new world.

As for the guards, some were absolute tyrants, but they were the exception. Regardless, the dynamic was adversarial by nature. Their job was to enforce the rules we sought to break. I never personally had much problem with them. My only real trouble came from being caught with contraband and the like.

My time in prison solidified the idea in my mind that I was no longer a part of the same society most inhabit. Hell, I'd been forcibly removed from it. I never saw a way of being accepted back into the world I once knew. I still carried all the pain I never processed and then some. My escape was drugs. There were plenty on the inside and on the outside. My probation conditions were to abstain from drugs and alcohol, so, as an addict, it was just enough rope to hang myself with. I couldn't even go to the bars that "normal" people went to. The underworld was the only one that would have me. The police were much more likely to catch me breaking conditions in a bar than when I was hidden away in drug dens. So began the cycle of in and out, in and out.

There was a woman who meant a lot to me on the outside. We were both addicts, meeting due to our similar interests. I think we both saw the good in each other, but all of it came second to the monkey on our backs. She always intended to wait for me when I did a stint in prison but never did for long. Yet I kept returning. I felt I deserved as much. She was just doing what she had to do to get by.

She died in 2015. Her body simply couldn't take it anymore. Months earlier I had lost another ex in a car accident. She had left me on account of my addiction but never stopped caring about my well-being. Once again, I was swallowed whole by enormous loss. I'm sure it was accurate to say I was suicidal, or perhaps indifferent to the prospect of my own death. I ended up in custody just a week later when a "wellness check" from the local RCMP turned into an arrest for breaching my conditions.

I was sent back to prison to do my grieving. It was cruel and came close to breaking me, but my stubbornness saved my life. I decided to do the opposite of what was expected of me. I decided that the deaths of two of the women I cared for most would not be in vain.

Here in 2020 things look a lot different. I'm a published author: I contribute regularly to the CBC since completing my journalism program. I have a very healthy relationship with a woman I adore and respect. She's a pharmacist, irony being a recurring theme in my existence. I'm not sure where my path leads, but I feel competent enough to overcome whatever obstacles I meet.

There's still work to be done, and there always will be, human nature being the way that it is. I'm still slowly trying to let go of the idea of stoicism and considering other options to deal with my trauma. I've been around long enough to know that just because all fury feels righteous doesn't mean it is. I have surrounded myself with people that want what's best for me and have no qualms about telling me when I'm out of line. I feel like every passing day I move further away from the brute I was in prison, and it's a damn good feeling.

One thing I know for sure is I want to help who I can and hinder none. I hope, dear reader, my words can help in some small way, even if all I do is convince you that people can change for the better. After all, you now know an optimist who used to be a nihilist. I now occasionally report on crimes instead of constantly committing them. I went from unironically referring to myself as a "thug" to unironically referring to myself as a "cat dad." People can change for the better. I hope you encourage it whenever you can.

Popcorn for the Blind

by

ANNE MALONE

I can't remember a time when I wasn't aware that there was something wrong with my eyes. I started wearing eyeglasses before I was two years old. My parents noticed that I held objects very close to my face to examine them and that I was tripping over or bumping into things a *lot*, even for a toddler.

Some of my earliest memories are of visits to my ophthalmologist. Even as a tiny child, I sensed the gravity that surrounded these appointments in a dim room where I sat on my mother's lap and stared at a bright screen and tried to see the bunnies hopping in different directions. Sometimes I could see them, but more often I could not. Even then I could sense both my mother's and the doctor's disappointment when I could not. I remember the inadequacy and confusion I felt when I failed to see the bunnies, so sometimes I would pretend to see them even when I couldn't. It was many years later that I realized this kind of pretending had become a pattern in my life. I was diagnosed with congenital high myopia. I was very, very nearsighted.

My baby glasses had round pink plastic frames that held lenses so thick and heavy they hurt my ears and the bridge of my nose. If I looked down, their weight made them fall off. The gravity problem was solved by the addition of a band of elastic that gripped the back of my head in an angry pinch.

In family photographs, my baby-self squints up at the camera and into the future, my heart-shaped face all but obscured by glare from sunlight or a camera flash. I looked for all the world like a tiny, begoggled Amelia Earhart, feisty and adorable in a mildly comical way. It was a kind of cute that had a short shelf life though, and, somewhere between playpen and playground, the thick glasses that shrank my eyes to small blue beads and reduced the world to Lilliputian proportions became the bane of my girlish existence.

On the playground, if someone yelled "Hey, Four-Eyes!" or "Helen! Helen Keller!" they were calling me. When they began to say things like "You're blind! Blind as a bat!" their taunts were bloated with contempt and accusation. I felt shamed and confused. "Blind" meant that you couldn't see *anything*, not even a little bit, didn't it? But I *could* see, I protested as the heat of shame scorched my cheeks, and tied my tongue, and crowded the voice right out of my throat.

Back then, in that schoolyard, I could not name or understand the source of my tormentors' contempt or of my humiliation, but I felt the crushing constraint of it rising to engulf me. What I *did* know was that if I could just ditch the glasses—the only evidence of my poor eyesight, I thought—I would, like the plain, bespectacled women in the movies, reveal myself to be a beautiful butterfly freed from her Coke-bottle-bottomed chrysalis. While other children around me had wishes galore for birthday candles or falling stars, I had only one: I wished those glasses gone.

No adult ever talked to me about my eyesight, and I never wondered in any organized way whether I should be worried that my glasses got bulkier every year. At some point, though, I noticed that even though the lenses were thicker they were not as good at helping me see.

Something you need to know about visual impairment is this. The child who is visually impaired may not know it. She may think everyone sees things more or less like she does. She doesn't know that everyone else can actually see the sums on the blackboard in arithmetic class; she thinks they have to listen very carefully and puzzle out the blackboard mysteries for themselves, like she does. She doesn't understand why she fails arithmetic;

she believes herself to be careless, because her teachers don't know either and write "careless mistakes" in red ink on her tests. She will sometimes not realize that her teacher is asking *her* a question because she can't see who the teacher is looking at, and she may have to write "I will pay attention in class" one hundred times on the blackboard after school. She may believe, because no one has told her otherwise, that she can see as well as anybody because she has glasses and because she always sits in the front row. She doesn't know that she only has a six-foot radius of reliable visual information and that if she makes a mistake she will live inside that mistake until someone else corrects her. When a teacher commands once, twice, three times "Look at me!", she may stand there, paralyzed with panic, never daring to scream "I can't *see* you!" Instead, she will obediently hold out her hands to be strapped for disrespect.

In the fall of 1969, I turned thirteen and started grade nine in a new school. American television and teen magazines of the era were filled with tips on how to be popular, how to attract a boy, what different clothing styles said about you, and how to apply eyeliner. I had already taken dozens of teen personality quizzes and knew that the style that matched my personality was "bohemian" or "hippie." I spent hours planning how I would accessorize my school uniform, a Newfoundland tartan jumper over a perma-press white blouse, to reflect my bohemian nature. My image of hippies was informed by photographs of college students in warm American cities, and even I knew that Indian cotton tunics, flowing sequinned skirts, and beaded headbands would be impossible to find in the shops on Water Street, much less in the tea-stained pages of the current Sears catalogue.

I had long since outgrown the pink baby goggles, and my current glasses looked like a couple of chunks of optical glass jammed into red plastic frames. Looking through them was like looking through the wrong end of binoculars. They made the world a lot less blurry, but everything appeared much smaller and further away than it really was. When I looked at a printed page, the letters were clearer, but so small I had to hold the book within a few inches of my face to read it.

My annual eye check-up was a few weeks away, and I had my heart set on blue-tinted granny glasses with silver frames, just like the ones I'd seen Goldie Hawn wear on TV. I thought the blue tint might make them look more like ordinary glasses, and they were the coolest glasses I'd ever seen. These glasses could change a girl's life.

On the day of my eye checkup I sat in the waiting room with my mother, fidgety and impatient. I couldn't wait until the ophthalmologist handed her the new prescription so we could go to Cabot Optical and pick out the glasses of my dreams.

Finally it was my turn. Every appointment was exactly the same. I tried to read letters on a chart and started getting them wrong at the third line. The doctor began humming fragments of random songs, releasing the scent of Juicy Fruit gum as he leaned towards me to put drops in my eyes. He looked into them with a light that blazed across my retina like a blowtorch. I flinched. His chair was on wheels, and he glided around the room on it, first to flip through the pages of my chart, back to me for another look into my eyes, then spinning away to face my mother.

"She needs a much stronger prescription, but we've done all we can with eyeglasses." He glided back in my direction, and, for the first time in nearly thirteen years of appointments, he spoke directly to me. "I think you will have a much better result with contact lenses. They will take a little while to get used to, but I think they will be much better than glasses."

I was speechless. Contact lenses! Did ordinary people wear contact lenses? Weren't they very, very expensive?

And so it was, on a hot September afternoon, my most fervent wish came true. I was ditching those damned glasses. A few weeks later I was seated at a mirrored table positioned in front of a mirrored wall. The optometrist opened a small plastic case that held two small plastic discs. To my amazement, they were tinted blue.

"Like your eyes," the optometrist said. "They'll be easier to find when you drop one."

Then he showed me how to pick up a wet lens with my fingertip and insert it in my eye, first the right and then the left, while I looked down into the mirrored surface of the table. Immediately the world expanded and glowed with light. My fingertip, still poised close to my eye, looked huge. I blinked and blinked my watering eyes, lifted my head to face the mirrored wall, and, for the first time in my life, I clearly saw my own face, freckles and all.

It took a few days to adapt to contact lenses and my enhanced, true-to-size view of the world. I tripped over steps, over-reached for things, and marvelled that I could read with ease. I occupied the single bathroom in our house, just staring into the mirror while one of my seven siblings banged on the door to be let in. I'd walk the beach close by, watching small fishing boats bobbing in the distance, gulls riding the frigid gusts of wind. Everywhere I went, I looked and looked and looked. My eyes were hungry.

My experience at school changed dramatically. Things that had been hard became easy. I had always loved reading; now I visited the library two or three times a week. I quickly worked my way through the whole juvenile fiction section and moved on to the adult section, assuring the librarian that yes, my parents allowed me to read anything I wanted. When, at the end of grade nine, I wrote a book report on Percy Janes's newly published *House of Hate*, the teacher did not believe I had read the book and written the report myself. My father was furious, and, though I still don't know what he said to her on the phone when I told him, I got an A+. The teacher was mollified, my father was proud, and I felt vindicated and victorious.

Best of all, I was no longer the four-eyed curiosity who laughed gamely with my peers when they ridiculed me. I joined the drama club, the debate team, and was elected to the student council. I had a flair for public speaking and won a provincial award for my school. Four-Eyes was gone. I was enjoying my first taste of how it feels to be perceived as "normal," and I loved it. I was free.

Although the contact lenses greatly improved my ability to see, even when I wore them, my vision was 140/20, meaning that what a person with excellent eyesight could see at 140 feet, I could see at 20 feet. The lenses did not give me perfect eyesight, or even kind-of-okay eyesight—in medical terms, I was still visually impaired. When I was nineteen I began to notice that I had a foggy white spot in my field of vision in one eye. If I looked at something with my right eye, there was no central vision. I could only see what was peripheral to what I was focusing on. An eye exam revealed that the myopia, which was still progressing, was causing my retina to deteriorate. There had been multiple tiny, painless hemorrhages that had left scars I could not see through. The damage was permanent and progressive. I was, over time and in tiny increments, losing my vision.

I was not afraid. I had lived with poor vision my whole life and had always found ways to adapt and compensate. I had become so proficient at this that very few people discerned that I could not see well, and I was determined to keep it that way. I could never forget the profound difference in how others perceived and related to me after my thick glasses had been replaced by contact lenses, thus removing any visible sign of my visual impairment. The stigma I had felt as a child was far more painful and difficult to navigate than visual impairment had ever been. It would be years before I would hear the phrase, but what I was doing had a name. I was "passing as sighted."

Growing up, I had never met or even seen anyone who used a white cane or a guide dog. Not in school, not anywhere. I thought blindness was a rarity. Until the 1980s, children from Newfoundland and Labrador who were blind or whose visual impairment required that they learn Braille and other skills were not educated in the public school system. Instead, they attended a boarding school, the Halifax School for the Blind, which closed in 1983. Upon finishing school, people who were blind had very limited choices for employment and were offered training in a narrow variety of occupations including crafts such as basket-weaving and broom-making.

It was not uncommon for blind adults to live in institutional residential settings, and, in many ways, these people were conditioned to be dependent upon well-intentioned institutions that assumed a kind of custodial oversight of the visually impaired/blind community. Many of these organizations were formed after World War I, when tens of thousands of soldiers worldwide were blinded by mustard gas on the battlefield. The Canadian National Institute for the Blind was founded in 1918 as a result of the Halifax explosion of 1917, when a ship holding ammunition exploded in Halifax Harbour, decimating the Richmond district of the city, killing two thousand people, and blinding scores of others who sustained injuries from flash burns and flying debris. At first, the vast majority of the people served by these institutions were, in addition to being blind, recovering from other injuries and trauma and did indeed require multiple therapeutic and rehabilitative services that addressed their catastrophic injuries. As time went on, future generations continued to be treated as if they were much more incapacitated and limited by blindness than they actually were, absent of the injuries and trauma experienced by the victims of the war and the explosion.

This approach to blindness as a devastating "handicap" resulted in generations of visually impaired and blind people who were groomed and conditioned to view themselves as being significantly disabled, and the institutional system led to a form of social isolation and marginalization that is unique to this community. This exaggerated view of the limitations caused by blindness continues to resonate in the twenty-first century and manifests itself in an unemployment rate among blind people that ranges from 70 per cent to 99 per cent in Canada, a devastating reality that has been static since the 1990s despite research that confirms that there is very little difference in academic achievement between the visually impaired/ blind community and the general population.

My own life experience has borne this out. For over twenty years, as my vision deteriorated, I was able to adapt and learn to compensate for my visual deficits in ways that made it possible to conceal my vision loss and pursue a career in arts administration and cultural management. When my sight finally reached a point where I had no choice but to disclose my visual impairment, I experienced chronic unemployment for the first time in my life, and the realization that I, like many others, was held hostage by false beliefs about my abilities as a visually impaired person was traumatic—emotionally, socially, and economically. The undeniable truth is that visually impaired and blind people in Canada are, even today, hindered by assumptions, superstitions, and biases that can be traced to sources that are thousands of years old.

Consider representations of blindness in fairy tales, literature, mythology, and folklore around the world. Universally it has been viewed as a curse or a punishment for some immoral act. It is associated with darkness, a consequence of moral failure, a retribution. Often, a blind character will be in possession of some compensatory gift, a sixth sense that infuses blindness with a mystical quality that can be used to supernaturally activate good or evil. Historically, blind people have been perceived and portrayed as being dangerous and unpredictable. In these tales, blind characters whose sight is restored are deemed to have received a redemptive gift, one that frees them from darkness and the penalties of their imagined malicious intentions towards the sighted world.

Themes of blindness also arise in contemporary popular culture, where blindness emerges in a new role as the embodiment of vulnerability. Blind characters are often shown in situations where their blindness is exploited and they are depicted as unable to detect the harm lurking just a few feet away. The comedic version of blindness is characterized as clumsiness and has a distinctive slapstick aspect—in contrast to blindness as melodrama, where, in a modernized version of the redemption tales, a beautiful, fragile girl or woman has a sight-restoring surgery that culminates in a lengthy, emotional removal of bandages and full recovery of eyesight.

Even our language stereotypes and stigmatizes blindness. The word "blind" is used to describe naivety or gullibility, as in "blind faith" and "love is blind." A phrase like "blind ambition" links blindness to ruthlessness and exploitation. Isn't it interesting how the ways in which we use blindness as an adjective most often link it to negative character traits? "Vision," on the other hand, is frequently used to describe creative imagination, and sight is used as a metaphor for heightened awareness as in "insight" or "I see."

Could the historical wariness of blindness inform systems and practices that treat people who can't see and other people with disabilities as a problem to be solved? I believe that it does, that the social shunning of people who are blind manifests in our contemporary world as socio-economic inequality and social isolation arising from the inaccessible environments we often live in. Which raises the question: Why is it that governments often approach accessibility accommodations as an add-on, something to invest in only when budgets allow? Is it possible that they don't recognize that they unconsciously hold the belief that we aren't worth it? Is it possible that they erroneously believe that allocating funds to accessibility creates scarcity of funds for the majority of people who are not disabled? Do they balk at imposing undue hardship on the larger community without consideration of the hardship that has been imposed upon us from the dawn of recorded history?

When my vision finally deteriorated to a degree where I could no longer hide it, I began to observe and interrogate my own life experience in order to understand my childhood shame and my pattern of keeping my visual impairment secret. As I researched representations of blindness in the arts and the experience of blind people across time and cultures, I concluded that all of us have been influenced by these misbeliefs. They are deeply embedded in our collective consciousness and are held not only by sighted people but, most disastrously, by many blind people themselves, who have marinated in exactly the same flawed belief system.

That was the source of my childhood shame. *That* was the secret behind my secret. The otherness that I felt in my childhood, the unnameable "it" that I felt as a suffocating constraint. I was burdened with thousands of years of unconscious, implicit bias born of superstition and the projection of sighted people's anxieties about the unknown onto those who appeared to be the very embodiment of those fears. Digging deep into myself, I uncovered my own ableism, my own complicated and conflicted view of myself.

A few months ago I visited my neighbourhood supermarket and was met by the aroma of freshly popped corn. It caught my attention, and I peered around, looking to see where the enticing buttery vapour was coming from. As I followed my nose, I found a man popping corn at a bright red cart. I decided I would come back and buy some on my way out of the supermarket. As I walked by, I heard him call out: "Popcorn for the blind! Popcorn for the blind!" An organization was fundraising for a program that supports people who live with sight loss.

His plea for donations to support "the blind" ignited my imagination in a flash of recognition. Echoes of other voices from a distant time and place—fourteenth-century Europe.

In the aftermath of the Black Plague epidemics that ravaged Europe, reducing the population by at least twenty-five million souls, people who were blind were often shunned by their communities because it was believed that their very existence had caused the epidemic. They were forced to join other marginalized people to eke out an existence by begging "beyond the pale" (outside the walls and fences that marked the borders of cities, towns, and villages), where they forged a subsistence by scrounging for food from respectable travellers with whom they shared the roads and byways that connected surrounding communities. These people existed in great numbers, and magistrates were authorized to hold court events in which people who were blind were expected to prove to the magistrate that they were indeed blind, and not "undeserving of charity." The beliefs that informed these proceedings were complex, but among them was the idea that a sighted person might feign blindness to extort money from potential donors. If a person's blindness could be verified in court, the person who was blind was given a licence that hung around their neck, signifying that they were "legally blind" and therefore entitled to charity.

Hundreds of years later, "legally blind" is a term that is still in common use to describe a person who is partially sighted.

As I hurried my guide dog past the enticing promise of a buttery treat, I could hear within myself the voices of generations of people who were marginalized and impoverished not by their blindness, but by what their sighted contemporaries *believed* about blindness, and therein lies a profound truth—that despite the passage of time, the advances of science and cultures and civilizations, we must carefully investigate the origins of our beliefs, to ensure that the artifacts of the past do not continue to cause harm in the present.

I have never felt my poor eyesight to be a burden, but I do feel burdened by the necessity to speak and write my truth, the truth that is shared by all people who have disabilities—that it is not me that is the problem, but rather the unchallenged beliefs of a world that seems able in every sense, save the ability to value and include us, just as we are.

My Family's Battle with Residential School and Its Everlasting Effects

by

TYLER MUGFORD

Both of my grandmothers, along with an estimated 150,000 other Indigenous children, are victims of residential schools. If people had never begun opening their eyes to the horrors of assimilation, I could have easily been added to that list, which is a haunting thought. Did you know that the last residential school that closed down in Canada was in Saskatchewan in 1996? Just three years before I was born. The last one to close down in this province was Yale School in North West River in 1980. 1980! The year the much-anticipated sequel to George Lucas's *Star Wars* released in theatres, the year former Beatle John Lennon was shot to death outside of his apartment in New York City, and the year the Rubik's Cube debuted to confuse the shit out of kids everywhere was the same year the last residential school in Newfoundland and Labrador, built on "killing the Indian within the child," shut its doors. Unbelievable, isn't it? If you're unaware of what the residential school system is or what life was like for the children that attended these schools, let me tell you my family's story and how even to this day the residential school is still affecting us. I was in high school when I learned what my grandmothers went through; my class of eight briefly covered residential schools during our grade ten history class. I clearly remember learning about it—years of torture, abuse, and racism described in a few paragraphs. If only it were that simple.

My grandmother on my mom's side of the family is Ann Noseworthy. At seven years old she was sent from her home in Spotted Islands, just outside Black Tickle, to the Lockwood School in Cartwright, a place she stayed until she was fourteen. She told me very little of her experience, but from what she did share I could tell her seven years at the Lockwood School had taken their toll. Growing up I always knew there was something wrong with my Nan Noseworthy. I, my older sister, and my cousins were accustomed to her anxiety, especially in the car, her sudden outbursts of anger over things that seemed so little, her mood swings, and her constant worrying; we all knew that something wasn't right, but the reason why was never spoken about. It was a strange silence, a silence I'm sure many people here in Newfoundland and Labrador can relate to, but I blame the residential school for that silence in my family.

It was only a few years ago when Nan finally began opening up about her experience there. She was in a rough spot, depressed and filled to the brim with anxiety. To add to the flames, her doctor put her on the wrong meds, which completely messed her up. I'll spare you the details, but she could barely function. It was scary to see her in such a state. The whole ordeal brought our family together, and we began to open up, especially about mental health and well-being. It's now something we all take seriously. Back in May of 2020 I completely broke down. I wanted to die. I remember I was nervous about opening up to not just my nan but my entire family about what I was going through mentally. It was a huge step, one I'm glad I took. Everyone was so supportive and showed me so much love, especially Nan. She completely understood what I was going through, which at the time was so helpful, but also equally heartbreaking knowing that she probably felt the same as me for so long.

Nan was both physically and emotionally abused in residential school. No wonder she referred to her seven years there as a "nightmare." Bugs in her food...she even told me her younger brother got kicked in the face by a teacher. He was scrubbing the stairs, and the next thing he knew his tooth was chipped. To say I was shocked would be an understatement. I had no idea just how much she went through in that seven years, and I think what she told me was only scratching the surface. The pain in her voice when she recounted her experience was haunting, and to know she still carries those memories around even after fifty-seven years of being out of residential school makes me sick.

My mom and I talk about residential school and its effects on our family a lot. Once we were on the phone speaking about Orange Shirt Day, about the importance of remembering residential school, when out of nowhere she began talking about her childhood. She told me growing up was tough: Nan didn't know how to raise a kid, all she knew was her experience in Lockwood, that was her "normal." Mom spared me the details, but Nan took a lot of pent-up anger and trauma out on her for a long time.

"There was a lot of resentment and pain inside her when I was young, and I didn't know where it came from. As a kid you think you're the problem," she said over the phone, "but I know now where that resentment came from."

I often think about how strong my mother is. Intergenerational trauma is something that's spoken about a lot these days, especially within Indigenous families. If you're unaware, intergenerational trauma is when untreated trauma-related stress is passed down to other generations in the same family. That untreated trauma could easily lead to mental illness, addiction, and violence. Everything but violence was something my family had dealt with, and by all means Mom was a perfect candidate: her mother, my nan, was a victim of unspeakable trauma and showed her very little love. When mom had me, she could have taken the trauma she had built up and lashed out at my sister and I, but that never happened. She broke a vicious cycle that destroys Indigenous families across Canada, and that in itself is very, very amazing. I don't blame my nan for what she did to Mom as a kid, and Mom feels the same—we all know now what kind of monster Nan was facing, all alone. But it's not all bad. Nan has been doing really well this year. Sure, every day is a battle with depression and anxiety. She was at some really low points recently, but, despite everything she's been through, she's still able to smile and laugh. Mom can't stand when I torment Nan with my witty and, most of the time, silly jokes, but I just can't help it. It's wonderful to see her smile and probably does me more good than her. I love her so much that words can't describe it—I'm beyond grateful to be able to call her my nan.

My other nan on my father's side, Mary Mugford, was born just outside of Rigolet in 1921, in a place called John's Point. I don't know much about her childhood, but I would assume it was one of hardship and hard work. What I do know is that, in the spring of 1928, my Nan Mugford's life was changed forever. Her two brothers were out on the ice to ice-fish. Before they realized what was happening, the ice they were on broke off and began drifting away from land. Nan's mother and a few others were back on the shore at John's Point and decided to take an old hunting boat that had clearly seen better days. They launched it and made way to try and reach the boys. The rescue mission was doomed from the start. The boat was riddled with holes and quickly began to fill with icy cold water. Everyone perished.

My nan was at the Yale School in North West River when everything happened. Her two brothers and mother had drowned in the icy waters miles away, and there was nothing she could do about it. Details are sparse, but Nan was only seven at the time so I'm sure the tragedy hit her hard. Since it was in the spring of the year in the late 1920s, transportation to and from North West River would have been pretty close to impossible. I later found out that Yale School was labelled the worst residential school in Labrador. Stories I read from survivors painted a horrifying picture in my head. Sexual, mental, and physical abuse were all common for the students who attended, and I can't imagine what my Nan Mugford experienced there on top of her grief. Almost all the memories I have of Nan Mugford are very cloudy. She passed away in 2008 when I was only eight years old, but I remember her as a woman who preferred solitude over anything. She looked grumpy, her face full of wrinkles, always wore these flowery gowns, and I hardly ever saw her smile. But as I learned more about her after her passing, it began to make sense why people thought she was a sullen woman. Everything was taken away from her at such a young age—it's tragic.

One of the fondest memories I have of Nan Mugford is her gorgeous grasswork, a traditional Inuit craft that is so unbelievably tedious and time-consuming that even Bob Ross would have trouble doing it! In layman's terms, grasswork is the process of sewing split blades of grass that you would normally find down along the landwash into beautiful dishes, jars, bowls, and so on. The amount of craftsmanship put into one piece is stunning, and the finished product, with simplistic, colourful patterns, is mesmerizing. I remember her love for grasswork, her old eyeglasses and strands of grass going in every direction as she was sewing. I think she used grasswork as a way to escape, to distance herself from reality even if it were only for a little while. Though Nan Mugford's resentment and pain wasn't as visible as my Nan Noseworthy's, I'm sure she still felt the same way, but she never shared her experience at Yale School with anyone—not her family, her friends, or her only son, my dad.

"She didn't tell me much, b'y. Kept it all to herself," my father said over the phone. My father spent his childhood living off the land. Fishing, hunting, trapping—you name it, he did it. He remembers his mom as a quiet woman who, like many others, was cross at times, but he had a normal childhood doing what any kid would be doing at that time. During many of our conversations about the past, he did share one thing that never fails to warm my heart. Nan was in awe when she held me for the first time; she couldn't believe she was holding her own grandson at seventy-eight years old. She cherished me and spoiled me. I remember one Christmas she saved up her money to buy this music box; I'll never forget when she came out holding it, proud as could be. I can't imagine the strength it took in order to overcome all that trauma she carried. Despite the grief, the hatred she endured, she came out the other end and able to love her son and even her grandson.

For me, it's crazy to think that in an age where everything is at our fingertips, where we can look up anything at any time, the residential school system is something not many people know about. Maybe they know that it happened, but they don't know personal stories like my grandmothers' and how even today in 2020, the spectre of residential school still has its claws dug into Indigenous families. I'm glad, however, that it's something that's being spoken about more and more. In late November of 2017, Prime Minister Justin Trudeau came to Happy Valley–Goose Bay to apologize to the residential school survivors in Newfoundland and Labrador. It was a huge step forward for reconciliation in this province and extremely important to the victims of residential schools. Sadly, Nan Mugford didn't live to hear it, and Nan Noseworthy lives on the Island so she wasn't able to attend in person. I was also on the Island for college, but I remember listening to it live on the radio. It was bittersweet, knowing that victims like my grandmothers have finally gotten the recognition they deserve, but I clearly remember the feeling of hatred, that something like this should never have happened. The anger is still there; it will always be there.

The year 2017 was also the start of my career as a journalist. It was my first few weeks in College of the North Atlantic in St. John's, and Jonathan Crowe, my teacher, had asked me to speak about my grandmothers to my classmates, who, at the time, were complete strangers. It was nerve-racking, but I did it anyway. They were stunned. Stunned that something so horrifying happened in this province. It was an eye-opening experience for me, too, as I realized then how many people are ignorant of us Indigenous people—what we went through and what we continue to go through. It was then that I made a promise to myself that I would take any chance that I could to educate people about residential school. I feel as if I owe my family that much.

It's terrifying to think how long these schools stood. The first to open its doors in Canada was the Mohawk Institute in Brantford, Ontario, in 1831, and they lasted all the way up to 1996. Back in September of this year, the Lockwood School in Cartwright was finally flattened down to the earth. Gone with it are the horrible memories, but for many survivors like my nan their experiences at that school will haunt them until they take their last breath. From 1831 to 1996—165 years of torturing 150,000 innocent children who were only guilty of looking and acting differently from the white settlers who saw them as savages to be purified. Residential school is not "a dark chapter in this nation's history;" it is in fact living, breathing trauma. Although mostly unseen, residential school has its claws dug deep into thousands of families. This is not history. My grandparents and my family are a testament to that.

If there's anything that I would like you to take away from this chapter, it's an appreciation for our resilience. Both sides of my family faced unimaginable evil just because of who they were. No matter how many years pass, the trauma caused by residential school will always be there. It's something that not only my family but many other Indigenous families across Canada have to face. But despite it all, we're still here and always will be.

Out of Oceanic Time

Trans Women's Lives at the Edge of a Dying World

by

DAZE JEFFERIES

Six years after the new millennium, I had just finished the sixth grade, and the pedagogy of splitting students in two to learn about binary sex stayed with me for the wrong reasons. The words I did not know and the questions I could not ask about my own gender and sexual diversity weighed on my hurting heart. While the warmth of late June had its way with my light blonde hair and chubby, freckled face, I wondered how I might feel joy during my last summer before junior high. Whereas my peers were excited to get into trouble one way or another, I stood in fragments at sunset, just a step away from a cliff's fraying edge above the Bay of Exploits in Beothuk territory. Staring out at Farmers Island as the blood-orange sun sank into the water, I dreamt about my future in a different world beneath the aquatic surface—wishing so badly to jump from that ledge—and I wasn't sure why.

As a child, my northeast rural hometown was shaped by gentle economic, social, and technological sea changes. Spectres of out-migration and the cod moratorium haunted everyday life, and high-speed Internet wasn't available until the fall of 2006. Before then, I spent most of my time training my piano fingers, writing poems, or riding bikes with my mom. A very sensitive and *artistic* (queer) little kid, I didn't know that the weight of bullying would soon try to shatter my soft difference. Punished by my peers for failing at boyhood, I started pulling away from my handful of friends to be alone with my feelings. Eventually, the coves and cliffs of my hometown became safe havens where I could dream another future into being. Becoming allied with cold Atlantic waters made my fishy displacement all the more sensitive. In a world of my own, I came to be fascinated by mermaids and sea life: there was something surreal and magical about fishy beings that I saw in myself. Imagining these oceanic others as kin—embracing an ecofeminist ethic of my own making, like a poet who didn't know it—I started to learn more about surviving the pains of my childhood. If I had it my way, I would have lived the rest of my young days underwater.

Back then I didn't speak the language that could help me write this story. I only knew that something about my embodiment was out of balance with the world around me. How could my youth be stolen by bullies? Who could understand my queer desires? Why did I want to dive into the water from such a great height? I wasn't happy anymore, and there were deep wounds in places I didn't know and couldn't understand. Keeping my innocence was a losing game as my betraying body transformed itself in strangely painful ways. Surrounded by fisherwomen with short messy hair and tattered work clothes, I didn't have to think about restrictive gender roles. Everyone told me I acted like a girl, but how could I know what it meant to be one? I was just a delicate child whose secrecy from the rest of the world forced me to see relationality (confronting self with other) as a kind of unthinkable difference. Maybe I was too far away from the life I needed, trying to survive in an impossible place. Maybe the mermaids were helping me form an escape. They wanted me to know myself.

For months, I had been unsettled by my gender pains, but I felt peace at those special beachy borders between life and death. So I kept going back. I was swallowed by an oceanic dreamscape; the water called me, and

I wanted an out. There I stood: an eleven-year-old kid who was loved to the ends of the earth and deep into the Atlantic. It was never enough to keep me safe from the violence of becoming other. The more I reflect on this moment of felt knowledge in my life as a hurting child, I think about how my longings for better—another body, another world—were entangled with the emergency of my yearning to transition from male to female. These desires appeared to be so far removed from the culture that had raised me as a young baygirl. Within my coastal home, the language of gender and sexual diversity was a well-kept secret that made my pubescent punishment all the more complex. But one evening in mid-March 2008 while my family and I were watching NTV News, the world around me ruptured to make trans women's lives visible for the first time.

WHEN THOSE FISHY FINGERS TOUCH MY SKIN STRETCHED OVER SILICONE, THE SECRETS OF YOUR ABSENCE START TO CAPTURE MY LOVE / LEAVING POISONS IN ITS PLACE, THEY OPEN ME UP TO A CRUEL BLUE DARKNESS / YOU ALWAYS SAID THAT BREAKING THE SURFACE WAS NEVER ENOUGH TO SURVIVE / NOW I PICTURE YOU RETURNING TO THESE WOUNDED WATERS / MAKING A WORLD THIS VERY MOMENT / SINKING INTO MUD, YOU ARE BORN AGAIN INTO A BODY LIKE YOUR OWN / COME BACK TO ME AS THE NOTRE DAME BAY / ALWAYS ALREADY A HOLE / PULL ME IN AND SHOW ME YOU ARE MORE THAN JUST SOME MISSUS WHO VANISHED IN THE 70S / EVERYTHING AND NOTHING AS THE ARCHIVES THAT HOLD YOU FREEZE AND FOG OVER / WE GO MISSING AT SEA, BEATING HEART / LOSING BLOOD AND SPLITTING INTO THOUSANDS OF REMAINS / IN ANOTHER LIFE, SOMEONE WILL PUT US BACK TOGETHER / WITH NO OTHER WAY TO WEATHER EARTHLY CRISIS / FROM THE FICTIONS WE INSCRIBE UPON THE LIMITS OF OUR BODIES TO THE FROTHING OF OUR TENDER MOUTHS / WE HOPE FOR NEW LIVES THAT CAN MAKE IT THROUGH THE MADNESS / BUT WE HOLD BACK AS THE PAST WE KNOW DRIFTS FURTHER OUT.

In many ways, my womanhood was unimaginable until I witnessed that touching news segment, *When Boy Meets Girl*, which followed the life of transsexual Come-From-Away Jennifer McCreath. A world apart from my own embodied fictions that I struggled to understand, her story was both awe-inspiring and fearsome—the kind of visibility that put my sheltered little life into disarray. At first, I didn't see myself in her narrative, and I was certainly afraid to make sense of my reality with the scattered few words that I had learned. As much as I tried to fight my feelings, I knew that my boy body caused me pain but that I also wanted to be touched and loved by one. Struggling to understand the difference between my gender and sexuality, I turned to the Internet for help. By this point, I had been spend-ing countless hours each day online— searching for music, knowledge, and community—and as my gender curiosities and desires grew more intense, I understood that there was no going back.

At the time, I had already started to grow out my dirty blonde hair, and it only took a short while before I began to colour my bang with orange and brown box dye from Dollarama. Soon after getting my hands on some skinny jeans, eyeliner, and mascara—coupled with more hair experiments involving bleach kits and food colouring—I was creating a distinct gender expression for myself as a rural teen. I was a "scene queen" at heart, and these beauty tools offered me an escape from the dead boring strictures of cisnormative boyhood. Those two years taught me how to live in better relation with my body—they also helped me find newfound freedom as I crossed the threshold of my adolescence and imagined a livable future for myself with queer aesthetics. Unbeknownst to me, I wasn't the only fish out of water in the bay using hair and makeup as an opening into unknowable womanhood. An analogous lived experience is chronicled by my trans sister and kindred spirit Violet Drake in her haunting poem "Gendersynthesis" from Breakwater Books' recent anthology *transVersing* (2018). She writes:

> whereas most boys my
> age spent their summer
> fulfilling their father's hunting pacts,
> i made my own with the mirror

they set snares
as i set powder,
both of us bonded
in execution

Her painful imagery of becoming anew resonates with the struggles of my youth in profound ways. As my own hunt for imagined authenticity progressed, I quickly abandoned my scene queen embodiment to experiment with my gender in new ways. I was lucky to have parents who supported my gender play, but there were reasonable limits to their understanding. Outside of my lonely bubble, there were arguments and frustrations and lots of silence. Sometimes, pieces of my wardrobe that I had curated from thrift stores, like leopard print tights and simple dresses, would suddenly go missing. As I reflect on my gender expression as a fifteen-year-old rural Newfoundlander who rocked ripped tights and heels and faux fur coats, with black lipstick, heavy eyeshadow, and a platinum blonde mullet, I recognize how my parents wanted to keep me safe from harm. But having agency over my appearance became an act of resistance as I tried to negotiate with being an incredibly misunderstood youth, one whose social location in the Bay of Exploits disconnected me from the possibilities of forming kinship bonds with other queer weirdos who were searching to belong in a world that didn't want us.

Lacking critical education and transition support beyond the digital realm, I kept so many of my true feelings hidden from even my closest friends. Although I had abandoned boyhood with great pleasure, *woman* was an uncertain orientation that still seemed impossible to touch. Feeling like *neither/nor* at the time, following the poetics of Mikhail Ravalia—my queer darling from Twillingate—I was deeply lost in my confusing thoughts. Pushed and pulled between senseless logics of binary gender, I started to call myself a ghost as the spectral tribulations of my difference were made all the more complex by my isolation in the bay. Trying to make peace with my solitude simply wasn't working, and, despite being connected via Facebook and Myspace to so many alternative teens from across the province, I didn't know anyone else who was struggling with the same internal questions that troubled my everyday life.

Hoping to meet other gender ghosts in the real world—and convincing my parents that they would finally see other people who dressed like me—I fiercely made my way to St. John's on a short family trip in the summer of 2010. Neither of them liked the city of sin, but they knew that I really needed an escape. We stayed at the old Battery Hotel in a room overlooking the harbour. With Marilyn Manson's "If I Was Your Vampire" thundering through my earbuds, I gazed upon the architecture at the water's edge and wondered if I might really stumble upon anyone else like me over our few short days in town. I didn't know anything about the queer, trans, and sex-working geographies of Duckworth and Water that stretched back into the historical past for countless decades—I was just looking to feel less alone. Being this close to St. John's Harbour felt much different than sitting beside the ocean all alone in my hometown. Nothing peaceful about it, I saw emptiness and slimy conquest, although I didn't have a name for it then. I didn't know about the mermaids—our great ocean-keepers—that had visited the harbour for centuries (as illustrated by Theodor de Bry). Without such sacred knowledge, I was only searching impossibly to find my place.

Over the next few days, we travelled all around the city, searching for fishy beings who were missing from our rural world. But as much as I needed to connect with others on that trip, the rare encounter I had imagined many times simply did not materialize. Who and where were these women? Why was I still so alone? Each of us, my parents and I, went back to the bay with shared but contrasting frustrations. They couldn't understand their child's pain, and I couldn't continue to live through my loneliness without taking action. As a matter of course, I continued to spend sentimental time with water, but I had forgotten the magic of mermaids. How could I survive those next two years without the hope that buoyed me as a child? I soon chose to make sense of my displacement in creative ways. In the silence and safety of my bedroom, I wrote countless poems and short stories, composed an unsettling experiment of a dark electronic album (nidificating by fo//ic/e), and focused on my studies. Believing naively that others wouldn't make claims over my body or gender when I got out of my hometown, in my last year of high school I promised my seventeen-year-old self that I would start living as a woman when I moved to St. John's during the summer of 2012.

EVERY ONCE IN A WHILE WHEN THE BEACH FLIES SETTLE, I DIG FOR ANOTHER UNKNOWN SOUL IN FROZEN SAND / TOGETHER, WE ARE GREEN-GREY AND SMELL OF SOFT DECAY THAT LINGERS THROUGH THE EVENTIDE / HERE ON THE BROKEN COAST, I HAVE NO COMPANION TO KEEP ME SAFE FROM HARM / SOMETHING WANTS ME TO STAY A LITTLE LONGER, BUT THE MORE I WAIT I BEGIN TO SHUT DOWN / MANY A NIGHT I IMAGINE MY NIPPLES TURNING BLACK FROM THE COLD AND FALLING OFF / MY BODY-MIND FINALLY KNOWING RELEASE / BEFORE SOFT WAVES BREAK OPEN, I'VE GIVEN A LUSTRUM AND SOME YEARS OF MY LOVE TO THE GHOSTS OF ST. JOHN'S / THE CAGE I LAST CALLED HOME, A ROTTING TOWNHOUSE AT THE MOUTH OF THE WATERFORD RIVER / WHERE FUTURES ARE SHAPED BY TRADE AND EXCHANGE AS WE INCH CLOSER TO THE DIRTY WATER / PEERING INTO THIS MOONLIT VOID WE CALL THE NARROWS, I FEEL CENTURIES OF MISSING WOMEN BUBBLE DEEP BELOW / REMEMBER KNOWLEDGES STOLEN BY VIOLENT ARRIVALS / NOW OUR GREAT OCEAN-KEEPER DIVES TO THE BOTTOM, NOT THEN COVERED WITH LAYERS OF SHIT / TAKING SO MUCH OF OUR HISTORY WITH HER / WITH NOTHING LEFT TO SAY, WE HOLD ON AMONG THESE MANY ENDS OF LIFE / I DREAM MY WAY TO YOU ACROSS A SEASCAPE OF LOSS AND NEED YOU TO LOVE ME MORE THAN HALFWAY.

I was a wild child during my first season in the city, and it made me feel even more empty. As my eighteen-year-old body began to bloom in social transition, I subsequently sought belonging, community, and access to medico-legal care as ways to hold on just a little more tightly to the world I needed. St. John's, however, turned out to be so different from the liberatory dreamland I once foolishly imagined. Like many other kids from the bay, I was never alone in wanting more than the quiet stillness of outport life, but I would come to find out that this city is a difficult place for young trans women to survive. Strangling my ability to live and love the truth of my womanhood, being visible here has left scars and cuts all over my body. Intimately shaped by loss and trauma—as well as a confusing network of simultaneous sexual desirability and social disposability—the past eight years of my life have forced me to grapple with incredibly complex forms of displacement, survival sex, and precarity. I am lucky to have found a fiercely loving family of queer, trans, non-binary, Two-Spirit, and sex-working kin who help pull me through this island world abounding with rough waves of violent transmisogyny.

At present—with more tools and connections than I could have ever dreamt of as a child—I continue to seek and follow the lives of trans women from this oceanic place. Searching through archives and connecting with elders, feeling my way through Newfoundland and Labrador's historical record and encountering waves of trans women's in/visibility that drift in and out of reach between the early 1970s and our contemporary moment has touched me deeply. By listening to the oral histories of other trans women islanders, I have learned that media—books, newspapers, radio, television, and even course material from university-level psychology classes—have informed our transitions for several decades. Always already lifelines to another world, glimpses of women like us have offered healing and hope. As these narratives lead me back toward an origin story that is shaped by slippery movements through the water-world we have come to know as a troubled home, I have also learned there's no escaping the shared hurt in our histories. Such have been the struggles of coming into our truths before, during, and beyond the heavily critiqued and historically ignorant "tipping point" of trans visibility (see the powerful 2017 anthology *Trap Door: Trans Cultural Production and the Politics of Visibility*). But for all of the uncertainty in these fishy times—captured by devils and flooded with loss—how might we continue to both remember and reach for pleasure, release, and joy?

Revisiting these moments of my life narrative helps me situate so many of my longings as a gender-creative youth alongside my positionality as a wounded but resilient young adult, within changing trans geographies in Atlantic Canada. From my childhood affinities with the North Atlantic, to the unsettled secrets and fluid movements of out-migration, through to the violent sexualization of mermaids and other fishy women for so much of our historical past, there are hauntings all around us that begin and end with water. Amid the thousand breathless spaces that have taken so much away, I have never abandoned my dreams for better futures. All the emotional textures of being fetishized and iconized by strangers and peers alike, all the hundreds of hands and lips that have touched my skin over five years of survival sex, every man who has thrown me to the sharks while wanting to consume my flesh for their own pleasure, every hope that has been ruptured by a multitude of pain—let my body in crisis and catharsis be carried out to open ocean as I drift through the wavering tides of my young life.

Lipstick

by

LEILA BEAUDOIN

PART 1—FAT AND PLUMP

When I heard it, I knew it was for me. Although my head was down, busy piling books into my backpack, I knew that name was for me. I looked up and saw their faces; the hustle and bustle of after-school chaos was as still and silent as a photograph that will forever be imprinted in my brain.

When I was in junior high, kids called me a name that stuck. It was racially inaccurate and concerned my lips. Smack dab in the middle of my face—I couldn't get rid of them. That first time was my first day of grade seven. A girl rushing by with a group of friends called "it" out to me.

That night I went home and took a long, hard look in the mirror at my lips. Fat and plump. Unlike the thin slip that most people in the rural fishing village where I grew up had. Port Saunders is a white town. I remember touching my lips. Hating them. Hating myself.

It (alongside some other racial unmentionables) eventually went away, only to resurface again in grade ten economics. During class one day, I made the mistake of correcting a girl who remembered that name. She turned around and got me back in the best way that she knew how.

The slur stung like it had so many times in the years before. Like an open, bleeding wound that everyone could see. I wanted to be like all the other girls: thin, blonde, and blue-eyed. Small-lipped.

I didn't realize when I was little that my lips were a feature I inherited from my father. As were my eyes and what a cameraman once told me was my "olive-coloured skin." My father is North African.

PART 2—A COLLISION OF ROCKS

My parents' short-lived love story reminds me of the Tablelands in Gros Morne. A beautiful stretch of rocks and formations that came to be when plates from ancient continents collided. According to some geologists, the Mars-like rock is the result of a collision between earth from North Africa and North America. Thousands of years in the making.

The '80s rush out West was the force that drew my parents together. My father, Adel Latrous, ran away from his Tunisian home to explore a career in cooking. Western Canada ate him up shortly after he graduated from a culinary school in Germany. Patricia Goodman, my mother, like many rural Newfoundlanders, grew up to go away. She completed a cooking diploma in Stephenville and headed to Alberta with a suitcase in one hand and a ticket in the other.

They found themselves cooking in the same kitchen, and the rest is a couscous-meets-salt-beef love story. Both newcomers in the Alberta world, they found solace in each other's company, trying to make a living as foreigners. But being united in their differences was not enough to keep them together. It was—in the end—the same thing that pushed them apart. Their relationship turned sour not long after I was born.

Like the Tablelands, I am the aftermath. The in-between. The collision of worlds. A different colour. With different features. That are my own.

Something people will, from time to time and place to place, guess at. Like my ethnicity is a question on *Jeopardy*.

"Are you Spanish?"

"No."

"French?"

"No. I'm from Newfoundland."

"You're a Newfie? But...*how?*"

PART 3—A BROWN BABY IN THE WHITE SNOW

There were a lot of questions when my mother came back to her home on the Northern Peninsula with a brown baby and no husband. But like so many before her, she didn't hesitate to return to those rugged, unforgiving shores. To this day she clings to rural Newfoundland as Wordsworth did to the Lake District. It is that geographical first love that never leaves us despite how far we stray from the land where we came from.

For the first couple years of my life, it was just Mom and me. My nan, my mother's mother, cast a net of caring around us, but love isn't enough to keep food on the table. To make things work, Mom started cooking at the local hospital and wore a white uniform. Always smiling and always making me feel like we were the luckiest people in the world. I didn't know then how hard life was for my mom. Like all daughters do, we grow up and see them more clearly as we experience life as a woman.

My favourite memory of her was watching her put her makeup on. Often looking up at her from her bed. Me in my pyjamas and Mom in her white uniform. Smiling back at me in the mirror, she would start with a little eyeliner, a tiny brush of blush, and then the best part: a carefully lined and painted lip. To this day my mom wears an icy mauve better than any movie star.

I remember looking up at her and thinking, *My mother is magic.* Not realizing that, each time she put on that brave, beautiful face, she was getting ready to go out into the world to work for me. For our little life in tiny, sometimes racist, kind, and beautiful rural Newfoundland.

Around that time my mother escaped an abusive relationship while putting up with gossip from the local church, whose praying wives were like wolves in the night.

Port Saunders, like many rural communities, is entrenched in religious politics. It has gotten better, but there was a time when marriages between Catholics and Protestants were forbidden. When gay boys were sent to church camp so that their "gayness" could be prayed away. My mother's narrative did not go over well with the dutiful churchgoers. Moving home, unmarried, with a brown baby.

So when she found herself victim to an abusive relationship—a relationship she only escaped when she was brave enough to press charges in the town that loved their boys, but did not see their faults—there was a night when the women from the local church got together for tea, and the topic of discussion was my mother and how she deserved to be beaten. A meeting, of sorts, that got back to my mother. Their mutual agreement that my mother deserved what she got. Things so violent I will never forget. Like when he broke his way into our home and threw my mother across the room. Holding her at knifepoint. Hearing her screams as she fought for her life. Violence that did not stop until the police arrived.

One of the ladies who was at the house during the tea where they tore apart my mother and praised her abuser later apologized to my grandmother. Finally feeling the shame of what they had done.

PART 4—DIFFERENT SHADES

Being a Tunisian-Newfoundlander feels different wherever I am in the world. Today I am living and reporting in St. John's, and you would think after years of being on television and reporting out West this would be easy for me. *Coming home.* Considering it's half of where I come from. But it is not. In Newfoundland, I feel like I am constantly battling for both of my identities. My father's and my mother's.

It's not uncommon for people in "town" to refer to the part of the island where my mother comes from as if it were a rotting, dying, decaying limb. Sometimes when people in the city realize I grew up "around the Bay," as settlers call it, I watch as their confusion with my face melts into a smug sort of "gotcha." It's a subtle sort of colonialism unique to island people that looks down on rural life. Ironically, outside of the province, all "Newfies" are treated the same.

There's no space for my brownness in the common narrative either. A communications person once told me they didn't like my name as much as the English version "Layla." A colleague said I didn't look "that" Arab, and I could pass as white. As if he were bestowing a blanket of white grace over me.

I, much like you, want to be seen. I want to be a part of the conversation that embraces differences—to say it out loud. In this moment, and as I write this, I identify with both halves of me. Realizing I have struggled more than some. Realizing my privilege is greater than others'.

As a reporter I make it my job to create space for BIPOC people, having lived that experience.

You aren't supposed to "feel" the news, but I do. Especially considering the lack of representation of non-white people in this province. Without contextualized reporting we aren't telling the real story. Unearthing privileges, giving weight to the invisible challenges silencing marginalized communities.

The year 2020 opened things up. A global outcry against anti-Black racism when we watched George Floyd plead for his life in broad daylight on the streets of Minneapolis. An event so painful, an event so awful that people everywhere rallied.

Following those eight minutes and forty-six seconds I upped my game to amplify the voices of the Black community in Newfoundland and Labrador, where many argue racism doesn't exist. A lie I experienced. A lie I witnessed. Two of my Memorial University friends were pushed out of this province for being Black. You can't see it, but they felt the ugly underbelly, when employers didn't give them a call back because they could not pronounce their African names.

My privilege here is my mother's whiteness. I know that. And I recognize it. But there are layers, like what that whiteness means depending on where you were born in the province, and I think it is time they come undone. I want to be on the right side of that undoing. I believe this beautiful land of ours has some courageous healing to do and real grace to acquire. Reconciliation for the Indigenous Peoples whose land was colonized and who continue to fight for Nation-to-Nation relations, missing and murdered Indigenous women, and truth and reconciliation.

Globally, we've learned from great thinkers like Ava DuVernay that creating space changes the game. I want to be on that team. Space creators. I know if someone in my youth, my high school, could have done that for me things would have been different. I could have loved myself more.

PART 5—A KARDASHIAN RENAISSANCE

Around the time I went to journalism school, I would like to thank what I will call "a Kardashian Renaissance" for the acceptance of my features.

For the first time in my life my face became okay. Not my face exactly. But brown girl faces and brown girl features. Brown eyes, big lips. Darkness.

Big-lip beauty was in. Cosmetics companies earned a fortune by making a whole new set of women feel inadequate—this time, some of the same thin-lipped girls who once called me racist names.

Just recently I was shopping and a woman behind the cash asked me, "Where did you get your lips done?"

"DNA," I said, laughing.

But she didn't get the joke and asked, "Where is that?"

I couldn't help but reply: "Between Northern Africa and Northern Newfoundland."

Today my lips continue to define me. Not because of those racist names I was called as a child but because I love lipstick. I am drawn to the bright, vibrant colours. Pinks, rosey mauves, plums, wine-coloured reds; they warm my heart and make me happy. I grew up with art and colour on top of those other things, and, besides being a Tunisian-Newfoundlander, I am an expressionist.

Putting on lipstick is a ritual that will always connect me with my mom. In that moment I feel her. Her story. Our story. Mom in her white uniform and me, peering up at her as she taught me at a young age that the art of perseverance is empowered by a good shade.

A viewer wrote me an email once to say my lips were too big to wear bright lipstick. She very politely told me I was a good reporter but should stick with neutral shades. To not distract the audience.

I wrote her a two-page reply explaining her racism and then hit delete. The next day I wore the brightest shade I could find.

We All Are Different

Danny's Story

by

DENNIS GILL

We often take for granted the things we do each day,
Like walkin' and talkin' or the many games we play,
To us they are so natural that we may not realize
How fortunate we really are to be free and fit and wise.

Let's stop and look around us from a different point of view,
At all those with "differing needs" who find some things hard to do;
The diverse problems that they have may not be plain to see,
But remember they're a part of this great big family.

Chorus
We all are different, some more, some less,
One person's strength is another's weakness;
We're all a part of God's master plan,
At times we all need a helpin' hand.

So next time you see someone little bit different from you,
Please won't you try and understand what they might be going through;
Their challenges may not be yours, but yours may not be theirs,
Practise the Golden Rule, it will help lessen their fears.

—Lyrics of the song "We All Are Different" by Dennis Gill

Of the approximately 7.5 billion people who presently live on Planet Earth, basically all are different, even identical twins! Setting us apart are facial features, skill sets, heights, weights, temperaments, cognitive abilities, musical tastes, food preferences, and "a hundred things you have not dreamed of," to borrow a phrase from John Gillespie Magee's "High Flight" and use it in an entirely different context.

At times we all need a helping hand. How very true is that statement? During "Snowmageddon 2020" in the St. John's Metro Area, and the COVID-19 pandemic across Canada, it was certainly revealed and exemplified in the highest order. As the English poet John Donne wrote in 1624, "no man is an island": everyone must rely on the company and comfort of others in order to thrive.

Every person on each of the seven continents has differing needs, diverse problems, and challenges. One may need help with physical mobility, another may have a problem focusing on a given task, and another may find maintaining good mental health a challenge—the list is infinite.

Our son Danny was born "perfectly healthy and normal" on June 9, 1980, but developed frequent epileptic seizures, petit mal and grand mal, after his initial immunization at three months, which led to subsequent profound developmental delays both intellectually and physically. His grand mal seizures still persist, way too often, to this day and are often prolonged, painful, and distressing. He received no further immunizations except annual flu shots. It should be noted that we fully realize the value and importance of vaccines and that negative consequences from them are very rare; however, they are not 100 per cent trouble-free. Since Danny's seizures started immediately after his first immunization, and worsened after his second, we curtailed others.

Though Danny cannot walk or talk, and is totally dependent on us and others for his many needs, he has truly blessed our nuclear and extended family. For four decades he has taught us to be better human beings by way of caring, sharing, loving, and compassion, to cite just four traits. What is so heart-wrenching about Danny's story is how different his life could have been had he not been so negatively affected when he was so very young. But, as a verse in the Bible indicates, "we have toiled on and in our toil rejoiced." We have been down the disAbility road in the real world. Through it all, we have kept a positive attitude and dealt head-on with the various challenges which have beset us. Our lives have been abundantly enlightened and enriched.

In our home on Pilley's Island off the northeast coast of Newfoundland, my wife Roxann and I lovingly and meticulously care for Danny 365 days a year, twelve hours a day—down from twenty-four hours a day in the years prior to 2002. Though there is the rare exception, we all live by a regimen that consistently features an 8:30 p.m. "be home curfew"! Since 2002, by choice and by necessity, we have hired three part-time respite attendant care workers for 168 hours biweekly, courtesy of the Newfoundland and Labrador government's Department of Health and Community Services, to whom we are most grateful. They attend to Danny's personal and hygiene needs, dressing him, preparing his meals, feeding him, and responding to his limited communications. Danny lives in his own apartment in our home and looks forward to daily walks in his wheelchair, rides in his wheelchair-friendly van around three times a week, and going for a meal or snack at an area restaurant at least once every ten days.

During the score of years of this arrangement, we have only had nine different workers, and they have been excellent, a big plus for outport Newfoundland and Labrador. Two have since retired from the workforce, two relocated because of their spouses' employment and health, respectively, and two moved on to other fields of work. Each of Danny's caregivers has had friends and relatives in our historic and picturesque community of two hundred and fifty. We conservatively estimate that Danny has connected directly with around twenty families who have all come to embrace him—indirectly, of course, we know every single family in town!

Pilley's Island is a picturesque community with a colourful history. It was settled in 1870, and a pyrite mine operated here from 1887 to 1908, during which time the population grew to around eight hundred. Huge ore carriers, mainly from the US, would enter the harbour through The Narrows en route to the mine site to be loaded via rail cars on a tramway. This mine was the first in Newfoundland to be equipped with electric lights throughout the surface and underground workings; remnants of the old mine are readily viewable to this very day. In 1904, Sydney Herbert, who grew up in proximity to the mine, went to St. John's, wrote the exam, and became the very first Rhodes Scholar in the Dominion of Newfoundland. The Grenfell Mission started a hospital here in 1911 that had excellent operating and sterilizing rooms, running water, sewage disposal, and a nurse's residence upstairs; surgeons and physicians came from the United States. The Pilley's Island Hospital served residents in much of Green Bay during that era when the only other hospitals were in St. Anthony and St. John's.

Pilley's Islanders have valiantly served in the Boer War, World Wars I and II, the Korean Conflict, the Gulf War, Afghanistan, and as Peacekeepers in many of the world's troubled areas. Some have paid the supreme sacrifice. Fishing and logging were predominant occupations for decades but have diminished substantially. Today, there are teachers, accountants, mechanics, administrative assistants, business owners, construction employees, carpenters, nurses, rotational workers, home care personnel, other walks of life, and a fair number of retirees. The earliest settlers were diligent and resilient, and their descendants are some of the friendliest and most down-to-earth people in all of Canada.

Today's visitors can hike to the Lookout; take in the Pilley's Island Heritage Centre Complex, which is outstanding; walk Newfoundland's Shortest Trail; stay at Colleen's B&B, which has very modern accommodations with a superb view; visit the Bumblebee Bight Inn and Brewery, the newest brewery in our province, strategically located between the one in Twillingate and the one in Deer Lake; have a meal of "Bragg's Famous Chicken & Chips" at Spencer's Diner, Causeway Express; "swarve" over The Dock, up The Route, Across The Bar, around Turkey Neck Shore, through The Outside, up Lover's Lane, down The Bight; and chat with the locals known as "Square Buckets"! For those with children, the Pilley's Island

Playground is beautiful. In addition to the regular equipment, it has a wheelchair swing which Danny really enjoys.

Beginning in 1985, Danny attended three schools in Green Bay South: Crescent Elementary, Blackmore Elementary, and Green Bay South Academy, graduating with his cap and gown and certificate of completion from the latter in 2001. Inclusive education (IE) was not advanced, but there was some support in music, at assemblies, and at recess and lunch times for Danny. The IE model has improved substantially in Newfoundland and Labrador during the last score of years; students of varying abilities receive instruction in the same subjects and same classrooms as their peers. In the Challenging Needs class, Danny was taught and cared for by dedicated teachers and student assistants. He really enjoyed his morning and afternoon rides to and from school, erratically waving his arms, smiling, saying, "Dad! Dad! Dad!" and observing the sights and sounds along the way. The overall experience broadened his horizons by being around, and interacting with, other children and adults. Danny derived pleasure from the music and singing sessions, the eating times, moving independently in his walker in the gym, and being wheeled in his chair by other students. He did not particularly relish doing his exercises or just sitting around inactive. During his sixteen years in the education system, he learned some disciplinary measures and social skills. Both he and we connected marvellously with parents of his classmates and many others in the school community.

We have been camping enthusiasts since the mid-1970s. From the summer of Danny's birth to the summer of 1990, we spent six weeks annually in Terra Nova National Park. We went for drives to Salvage, Happy Adventure, Sandringham, Eastport, and several other Bonavista Bay communities; sun-bathed and "swam" in the waters of Sandy Pond; had sing-alongs; went for walks in the clean, fresh air; and made numerous acquaintances and some lifelong friends from all over the Island of Newfoundland.

Then, in 1990, we acquired a permanent site in Birchy Narrows Travel Trailer Park in Western Newfoundland. It was an association that had a volunteer board of directors and an executive that ran the park, organized social events, and kept an eye on things. There were forty-three blocks approximately forty feet by one hundred feet that could be tailored to each family's desires, within the bylaws. The entire park area was level, which facilitated movement for Danny in his chair, and a ramp made the park's central chalet accessible. Our activities were almost identical to those in Terra Nova, but, given that the occupants were predominantly non-transient, there was ample opportunity to mix, mingle, and get to know each other much, much better. Everybody knew Danny and treated him exceedingly well.

Even though we had a thirty-eight-foot trailer with two bedrooms and a nice bathroom, the accessibility features gradually became inadequate for Danny's multiple needs and increasing age. Two of the greatest challenges were getting Danny in and out of the bathtub and his bed without a lift and mobility within the trailer because his wheelchair would not fit through doors. So, in 2015, after twenty-five enjoyable May-to-October camping seasons, we sold out. We still have close friends in Birchy Narrows and drop by occasionally on a day outing from Pilley's Island to Corner Brook. We will forever treasure the fantastic memories we made there as a family.

Danny has been wearing caps since he was a small boy and likes to do so, forward or in reverse. We started hanging his caps in his apartment during recent years. His collection has grown slowly and steadily. The headwear came from families, friends, acquaintances, companies, and organizations. Danny has caps from the Bahamas, the RCMP, Canadian Idol, Houston Astros, NAV Canada, Nalcor-Churchill Falls, NTV, and Pepsi. His one-hundredth cap is from London, England—a memento from sister Jenna's visit there in 2013.

Danny's caps are "triple-C": connectors, a conversation piece, and a collection in which others can participate and become engaged. Oftentimes, when Danny is out and about, someone we may not know will remark about the design or colour of the headpiece, others will query, "Where did you get that one?" Every hat has a story. Take Danny's *Canadian Idol* cap. During the years while that show was popular, I worked with a company that helped some of the contestants, and the *Canadian Idol* organizers sent me the cap as a thank you for the assistance I gave. Another cap features Burj Khalifa, the tallest building on Earth, located in Dubai, United Arab Emirates. That one is a souvenir from the time Jenna and a young woman from China were selected by a major international oil company to go to

Dubai to do an important audit. A South Korean cap is very prominent, given by a veteran of the Korean War who was born in Pilley's Island and lives here to this day. Then there is "Always In Our Hearts ~ Cougar Flight 491," commemorating the helicopter that went down off Cape Spear on March 12, 2009. The pilot, Captain Matthew William Davis, was our nephew; may he rest in peace. Each and every cap Danny has fits the triple-C—they increase his attachments to his community, lead to meaningful social interactions, and are a hobby he and the whole family can enjoy!

Avid amateur photographers since 1977, Roxann and I have clicked the old Pentax Spotmatic F and newer Canon Digital thousands upon thousands of times. Photos are a tremendous tool for engaging and connecting families. For the past fifteen years we have been designing and printing our own Christmas cards, which feature family activities from the previous twelve months side by side with our own verses. Each December we enter the homes of a hundred families in Newfoundland and Labrador, across Canada, and in the US. Then, there is Facebook: check out Roxann Dennis Gill. We regularly post selected photos of Gill family pursuits and inclusive events like birthdays, boating, cod fishing, Canada Day celebrations, Pilley's Island Day, and trips to Grand Falls–Windsor, St. John's, and elsewhere. All enhance personal linkages.

Last, but by no means least, is music. That is by far Danny's greatest enjoyment in life. He absolutely adores music videos of such artists as Raffi, John Fogerty, Neil Diamond, Lorrie Morgan, Great Big Sea, Olivia Newton-John, Queen, John Prine, Jenna, and the list goes on and on. I am a self-taught guitarist and songwriter; since 1970 I have written well over one hundred and fifty originals. Several I sing for Danny, especially "We All Are Different," which I wrote for him when he was only six years old. Whether listening to his MP3s, watching artists via computer on one of his two flat screen TVs, or listening live to Dad, Danny is joyous: he smiles, sometimes claps, relaxes, and takes it all in. On the wall in Danny's bedroom is a framed poster, "Music Is My Life." Case closed!

Danny's sister and only other sibling, Jenna, was born on May 6, 1986, and convocated from Memorial University of Newfoundland and Labrador in 2009 with a Bachelor of Commerce (Co-op). She is employed in St. John's, is married, and has a young son and daughter of her own. Ever since she was a little girl, Jenna has loved Danny dearly, has helped us tremendously with his care, has been extremely protective of him, and has been very, very responsible. Jenna did receive all of her immunizations, except pertussis, after we had high-level discussions and consultations with the medical professionals.

I think it would be fair to say that Jenna's lifestyle did not suffer because of Danny's diverse challenges. Growing up she was always completely understanding of our nuclear family's unique situation. She learned and experienced love, care, empathy, and many more positive attributes which helped make her the wonderful young woman she became. In public speaking in elementary and high school, she would talk about her brother so eloquently and descriptively that many students would be in tears. Our avocation choice of family camping was such an inclusive venture that she often did and saw more than many of her friends. Before she started grade nine, we took her on a trek around Atlantic Canada and later, in the summer of 2003, journeyed westward to Niagara Falls. No doubt, as we grow older and are unable to, Jenna will play a more significant role in Danny's life. To minimize the financial burden as much as possible, we have a Registered Disability Savings Plan for Danny and have had wills and estate planning executed by a specialist lawyer.

In the forty years since Danny was born, we have witnessed superb improvements in the ways in which families can connect with other families, whatever the situation or geographic location. That is pivotal, as it greatly reduces the isolation and anxiety often prevalent among families of individuals with disabilities and increases their knowledge in matters like available programs, supportive living and housing, entering the world of work, tax credits, recreational endeavours, maximizing educational opportunities, and a multitude of miscellany. Enhancements in technology, communications, transportation, medical knowledge and facilities, accommodations for families while attending appointments away from home, better systems of support, and sustained advocacy, all the way up to the UN Convention on the Rights of Persons with Disabilities, have improved the quality of life of people with disabilities and their families.

In this province, the Newfoundland and Labrador Association for Community Living has been serving individuals who have intellectual disabilities for sixty-five years and has been engaging and connecting their families via meetings, forums, conferences, phone calls, face-to-face conversations, newsletters, awards of recognition, a website, and linkages with associations for community living across Canada. These associations have successfully fought for equal pay for equal work, almost eliminated institutionalization, effected numerous changes in day schools, colleges, and universities, launched poverty-reducing initiatives, helped create policy changes that resulted in the establishment of Support Trusts, monitored Canada's Medical Assistance In Dying legislation, founded a hotel respite program, advocated for individualized funding, promoted future planning, and worked tirelessly on legal reform and supported decision-making, to highlight ten milestones.

Through the years we have valiantly tried to increase the quality of Danny's lifestyle, utilizing all the methods at our disposal, and strived to make the best of a situation beyond our control. We have faithfully practised the Golden Rule [Matthew 7:1]: "Therefore all things whatsoever ye would that men should do to you, do ye even so to them." And, as in the Parable of the Talents [Matthew 25: 14-30], we have put our talents to the wisest of use for our darling Danny. We're all a part of God's master plan.

A Rainbow Revolution Is Coming

by

SUSAN ROSE

It is December 1997, and my partner and I are glued to the TV waiting for the announcement. To exist or not to exist is the question!

In 1996 the Canadian Human Rights Act was amended to include sexual orientation as one of the prohibited grounds of discrimination. One year later, Newfoundland and Labrador is finally on the verge of updating its own Human Rights Act to protect gay, lesbian, and bisexual residents of the province (trans rights are not yet on the radar), which will make it the third-last Canadian jurisdiction to do so.

Onscreen, Brian Tobin rises in the House of Assembly.

"Until yesterday there was an important area in which the Human Rights Code of Newfoundland and Labrador was lacking," he says. "Until an amendment was passed through the House of Assembly yesterday, sexual orientation was *not* identified as a prohibited ground of discrimination under the code. An entire segment of our population was without protection..."

"Why should gays and lesbians lose opportunities and be subjected to discrimination when other minority groups are not in this society? How could we...let this situation continue?... We could not leave this to the interpretation of the courts, so we took...the appropriate measures to include this important issue in legislation.

"I want to say to members of the House, and through the House to the people of Newfoundland and Labrador, that I am proud to be a member of this Legislature which has given, unanimously, its consent to this important evolution in the human rights of this province."

As he spoke, tears of joy and tears of relief flowed as a huge weight lifted. Hiding in closets has its price, but that day and in the months to follow we celebrated. That evening we called our families and cried together. Then we called some friends and cried some more.

My partner and I planned a celebration in our home: "Coming Out of The Classroom Closet." We were both teachers. Ann at the School for the Deaf, where she was out and proud. I in a denominational school system that was controlled by church doctrine, where I was way in the closet.

The hiding takes a toll on all of us. Some can cope more healthily than others by becoming overachievers, but, still, we carry the negative impacts for a lifetime. Many of us are in our twenties or thirties before we even come out. When you experience bullying and understand the paralyzing impact it can have on one's ability to function then you truly begin to see through the eyes of our 2SLGBTQ youth and educators in unsafe schools and communities.

In 1992, when I was teaching at Booth Memorial High School in St. John's, I was telling a colleague about caring for a friend dying of AIDS. It was an extremely difficult time for my community, so I guess I just wasn't thinking as the words rolled off my tongue in the staff room. Suddenly, a male colleague who was listening in jumped up from the table, shouting: "Oh, my fuck, are you queer?"

As he ran to the other side of the room, he added: "You probably have AIDS and are coming in here and infecting all of us!"

To this day, I can still recall the daunting feeling as my heart stopped! *Did I...just out myself?* running through my mind as I sat in a daze watching this man rant. My heart was beating out of my chest, and I knew my life had changed forever.

That year was a nightmare. I was harassed, insulted, and humiliated daily. My day began when I pulled into the parking lot late and anxious. Late, because it took so much energy and willpower to get to work, and anxious because of the constant threat of bullying that became my norm. Then I had to open my car door and sneak into school without being seen by a specific male colleague who took great pride in calling me a "dyke" as I passed his room.

It wasn't the first time I had been made to suffer as a result of my sexuality.

As a child, I began to understand that God hated me. Church doctrines taught me that homosexuals were vile and despicable, that it was acceptable to treat other human beings as slaves—all because it said so in Leviticus.

At school, I felt invisible. Why? Because I knew I was different and did not feel welcomed. My hope was simply to survive, graduate, and find a safe place where I could exist and enjoy life like my heterosexual peers. Yet I knew there was nowhere on the planet safe for me.

By the time I was in grade nine, the weight was too much to bear. I got drunk and attempted suicide, which landed me in the Waterford Hospital.

In retrospect, I was so blessed that my parents loved me unconditionally and looked out for my well-being during this time, or things could have ended differently. My mother saved me over and over again.

When my doctor at the Waterford was going to give me shock treatment, my mom refused to leave me there, checking me out and bringing me home. When I was readmitted a month later to a psychiatric unit in Corner Brook and the new psychiatrist likewise insisted on shock treatment, my mother brought me home for a second time. How lucky was I?

She decided instead to consult our trusted family physician, Dr. Ian Simpson. It turned out he had a friend at the Janeway Children's Hospital, and he explained to Mom that the psychiatric unit for youth would be a much better place for me because all the patients were my age. He was right! I spent seven months there, never once speaking about my attractions but growing in many ways through daily therapy.

In the years that followed, my mother remained a source of unlimited strength and support. She raised me to understand that hatred is learned, that compassion is key. Eventually, she told me to leave the church because it was killing me. That permission and her unconditional love were her two greatest gifts to me. Both freed my soul and gave me a chance to find peace in this universe.

Having gone through all that and been part of the lobbying efforts in the '80s and '90s to secure the rights of gay, lesbian, and bisexual citizens in this country, I refused to suffer through the harassment I was enduring at Booth in the early 1990s in silence. In meeting after meeting with my administration, my union, and my school board, though, I found no support, only more homophobia. One school board employee actually took great pride in telling me: "You should be thankful you're still teaching, so shut the fuck up and stop bothering me because I have more important things to deal with than you wanting to talk sex to kids!"

My last hope was the provincial education minister himself. The memory of my meeting with then minister Chris Decker haunted me for years.

As I walked to his office in the ivory tower that was the Confederation Building, I recall thinking: *This is about respectful work environments and doing the right thing, so relax. These people are educators, and surely they judge one on character.*

His cold response changed me forever.

"I am sorry you are being harassed by your colleagues, but if you make an issue of this I will fire you."

Walking to my car from the tower seemed to take forever as thoughts of being fired blurred every step. My mother's words of wisdom kept racing through my head:

Kids are taught to hate, Susan.

Remember to always do the right thing.

It's all about treating people the way you want them to treat you.

Yet here I was at a point in my teaching career where not one person cared that I was being abused at work! It was a very sobering moment and an extremely scary time in my life. My partner and I were expendable, and human rights for my family did not exist. Human rights were for everyone else but me.

So Tobin's announcement that gays, lesbians, and bisexuals—including teachers—would be protected here in Newfoundland and Labrador was life-changing. Fear of being caught still controlled my every move at work. What exactly would it mean, going from invisibility to out? For me, now that I was finally protected under the law, I planned to change the world through inclusive education and respect.

Because I taught youth with learning disabilities and behavioural issues, I was a big part of their day. Often my students would ask personal questions like "Are you married, Miss?" or complain "You're the only teacher we don't know anything about!" and every time they did my heart would sink as I attempted to continue teaching, wondering whether they would like me if they knew or whether they would refuse to attend my class.

In the end, despite my worries, some of the youth I taught actually got into fights defending me, and many parents made a point of telling me they were supportive of me "coming out." What a difference from just a few years prior when I was persecuted every day for my sexuality.

Gradually, my focus became helping 2SLGBTQ youth and their families navigate a toxic education system, and I decided to leave teaching in 2006 to pursue that advocacy work full-time. I guess some might say I have become the Department of Education's worst nightmare.

In 2007, I joined the board of Egale Canada, a national organization whose mission is to advance the equality of 2SLGBTQ people across Canada. Five years later we secured a contract in 2012 to train *every* principal, vice-principal, and guidance counsellor in Newfoundland and Labrador on 2SLGBTQ inclusivity in schools. It was like winning the jackpot. After being one of the last Canadian jurisdictions to enact human rights protections on the basis of sexual orientation, we were now leading the way in the country in creating safe and inclusive schools for our 2SLGBTQ kids and their families.

As an Egale Canada board member, I was granted permission to travel around the province with the Egale team and department staff. This was very important to me because I could observe daily how minds and hearts can open when experts on human rights and intersectionality are facilitating conversations. This was the largest educational training project in the history of our province and the one with the highest evaluation stats, so the training had a huge impact.

Since then, approximately one hundred schools out of two hundred and fifty have started Gay-Straight Alliances, and in some schools teachers are being very inclusive and welcoming to 2SLGBTQ kids. Some are teaching our civil rights movement, our history, and the contributions my community have made to the betterment of humankind. Others are sharing stories about same-sex couples with their students, even in primary classrooms.

These compassionate educators may not be 2SLGBTQ themselves, but they care about the well-being of their 2SLGBTQ students. Take Corner Brook guidance counsellor Gerard Lowe, who introduced himself to me after I gave the keynote address at a meeting of the Violence Prevention Initiative, saying: "I'm a white man raised Catholic from the Northern Peninsula. I haven't got a clue about gay students, but I know they are in my school and I know they are struggling. I also know I want to help them."

Still, too much depends on where a student lives and the climate of their school. Despite all the legal and policy advancements we have made, many schools in Canada today are not safe or inclusive for 2SLGBTQ kids. National student surveys provide horrifying statistics. One stat in particular jumped out at me from "Every Class In Every School: The First National Climate Survey on Homophobia, Biphobia and Transphobia in Canadian Schools," which was completed in 2011: 64 per cent of straight students said their schools were not safe spaces for queer and trans youth. They also said they were tired of watching as teachers ignored violence against their 2SLGBTQ classmates. When homophobia and transphobia are ignored, the message communicated to *all* kids is that it's okay to disrespect some people.

Students also suffer when 2SLGBTQ history, art, and literature are left out of the curriculum. "Knowledge is power" said Francis Bacon, yet most schools don't teach that he was gay. Our youth who do not see themselves reflected in their curriculum are four times more likely to attempt suicide. They have higher dropout rates and are more likely to develop drug and alcohol addictions than their heterosexual peers.

Because of the hostile environment at many schools, some 2SLGBTQ youth still hide to survive, and I continue to meet with them in junior and senior high schools across our province. When I get a call, my first question is: "Are you out to your parents?" If that's a no, I ask, "Are you out to a teacher?" If I get a second no, then for me that's a red flag and a kid I cannot ignore.

As a 2SLGBTQ Human Rights Advocate, I provide information on human rights, and through this lens the youth and their family, if the family is supportive, can often find a way forward. When a youth and/or parent contact me, it is always in a crisis. I am meeting them at their worst, trying to comfort and provide supports I know they require but are not receiving. Actually, that's when my work begins. For many, after a few years we grow together, and I have made some wonderful new friends because of this volunteer work.

The youngest student I've worked with was a kid in grade four who—after watching a show, I think *Schitt's Creek*—blurted out that he was gay in school the next day. After his announcement, the teacher sent him to the office, and administrators called his parents. When his parents connected with me, they had decided to keep him home, and the family moved to St. John's that summer. When youth have to move in search of a safe and inclusive school, they are paying the price of their teachers' and community's ignorance. But knowing kids have parents who love them unconditionally is a relief for me because I know they will survive high school.

Our education system is an extremely powerful institution. It builds character, it shapes and defines our belief systems, and, ideally, it's responsible for creating a peaceful society. Constantly working toward the betterment of humankind should be the purpose of such a system.

In conclusion I will leave you with the voice of a youth from Corner Brook Regional High. I met Jessie four years ago, and they are now a grade twelve honour student and a compassionate, brilliant person. They wrote an essay discussing the impacts they have experienced being invisible in their school curriculum and sent it to the school board.

"School climate varies widely across Newfoundland and Labrador. School climates are also largely impacted by the communities and environment that surround them. Smaller communities steeped in tradition nearly always show higher rates of abuse and harassment toward students who identify as part of the 2SLGBTQ community.... After countless studies and decades of research, our schools should reflect the state of our country in regards to acceptance as well as take ownership of the preventable harm that takes place in schools."

So the door is opening, and ever so slowly we will get there. We know the impacts of unsafe environments. We also know that cultural shifts are happening around the world. Respect and equality are the driving force.

Our heroes of today—our youth—will continue to demand their human rights. I look forward to the day when I'm reading a totally different set of outcomes for 2SLGBTQ.

My Visit

by

CHRISTINE POKER

I'm going to tell you a story about my visit to the Eeyou community in Quebec called Chisasibi. It was November 2018 when I travelled there from my community of Natuashish on the north coast of Labrador. Eeyou and Innu are the same. We are the same people; only our dialects are different.

I went to Chisasibi to visit my friends Bobby Neacappo and Harry Snowboy whom I met at a suicide conference in Montreal. They are traditional healers, and I enjoyed the teachings they shared at the conference. I decided to invite them to Natuashish so that other community members could hear what they teach and learn from them, too.

Bobby and Harry showed up and taught us about spirituality, but their visit wasn't only about them teaching us. Our local Elders also taught them about our culture, which is no different than theirs. There was a lot of laughter with the two of them and the Elders as they all shared their stories.

We taught them about our sacred *Makushan* feast—the Feast of the Caribou. They learned about the different steps to get ready for *Makushan* as we prepared and celebrated the feast with them. First, people are invited to cut the meat off the caribou bones, the leg bones, and the shoulder blades. The bones are then crushed to take out the bone marrow. This marrow or *atiku-pimin* is set aside. Some of it is eaten during the preparation of *Makushan*, usually by the ones who work on the bones. The Elders are also invited to share in this marrow. The crushed bones are then boiled in water, and the fat floods to the surface of the broth. The pot is put somewhere to freeze and await the *Makushan* community feast. The bone marrow is cut into pieces and mixed with the grease from the pot.

Everything that is done and every part of the caribou is treated with respect both while it is being prepared and also eaten. During the *Makushan*, its owner who is an Elder, an *utshimau-uskan*, performs an offering. He puts a piece of the *atiku-pimin* in the fire as an offering and to give thanks to *Atikush-utshimau*, the Master of the Caribou, for providing it to us. *Atikush-utshimau* is the one to decide who will be able to kill and receive a caribou. Finally, anything that is not eaten during the *Makushan* must be burned, and the bones are placed in the river.

In the past, every time an Elder performed the *Makushan*, a drum dance would follow, also to show gratitude to *Atikush-utshimau*.

When Bobby ate the *atiku-pimin*, prepared with caribou grease and marrow at the *Makushan*, he cried. He said he had seen this ritual done by his late grandfather. When the two of them went back home to Chisasibi, Bobby shared the story about the feast with an Elder woman. She, too, cried when she heard that we still celebrate this sacred feast of the *Makushan* in Natuashish. This really touched my heart. How lonely it is to hear and see Elders cry. Harry had the idea of inviting us to go visit Chisasibi. He and Bobby wanted us to teach them how the *Makushan* feast is prepared so they could bring the practice back into their lives.

This is the reason we travelled so far to see them in their community. My husband and I, along with some friends, flew on the plane from Natuashish to Goose Bay, and from there we drove two days to get to Chisasibi to see our friends.

When we arrived in Chisasibi, I thought about Harry's words when he had invited us.

"You will love our community," he said.

"Chisasibi is beautiful," I told him, when we got there. "It takes me back to Natuashish to the time when I first saw the houses built in our new community. I feel like I've returned home."

When we got to Harry's house, he invited all twelve of us to stay with him. He fit all of us in his home while he slept on a small mattress. The next day Harry invited my husband and our friends to go hunting with the men. He said they would go not far from Chisasibi and that it was okay to hunt the caribou. This was the beginning of his learning from the Innu. When the hunters returned, my husband was having fun with Harry, at the way he was shooting during the hunt. I could tell from their laughter that they had a good day.

The Innu hunters taught Harry how we have to keep and respect every part of the caribou. We showed him what we eat of the caribou. Harry said he was surprised that there was no wastage. He tasted the food I cooked, including the caribou head. I also prepared caribou sausage using the intestine. I was so pleased to see how happy Harry was to be learning from us. I even showed him how to cut up the caribou bones to begin preparations for the feast. From our visit, our friends had their prayers answered, and from that feast came good health.

When we were ready to go back home, Harry gave us caribou meat and bones. He was the hunter who had shot the caribou, so the gift had to come from him. I cooked the *atiku-uiash*, or meat, to take with us. Harry decided to go with the Innu men to get a letter from his Chief. The letter stated that the caribou was a gift from their nation to ours. It was to make sure no one would touch this gift of caribou meat, and that we would carry it safely to Natuashish. We left to go home and drove that day with no worries. I decided to read the letter from the Chief, and his words on the page gave me chills through my whole body because the letter was written with so much respect. I could feel it. That was the gift from his community to us.

We drove to a place called Tshipekemu. I'm not sure if I am spelling it right. The following morning after breakfast, I saw a man come up to my husband Prote to talk to him. I could not hear what he said to him. At first I didn't think anything of it.

"They will take our meat," my husband said to me afterwards.

"Why?" I asked. "We have the letter. What is wrong with Chief Davey's letter?"

Prote told me the man talking to him was a wildlife officer. In perfect English the man had told Prote he would take our meat.

"Why do you want to take the meat?" I went to ask this man. "If you want meat, why don't you hunt it for yourself?" But he never said anything to me.

My son, who had accompanied us on this trip, was angry and he swore at the wildlife officer. The officer called the police who then came and fined my son $150.00 for calling the game warden an asshole.

"You charge people when they say bad words," I said to the police. "But you see that man stealing the gift that was given to us, he is the one who should be charged. What kind of place is this anyway?"

The police officer just shook his head.

I didn't know what to think anymore. I felt like I was talking to something instead of somebody. I had seen and experienced this feeling before, the time I went to join the protest at Eimish (Voisey's Bay). We were protesting because we wanted to stop the mine from being built. We didn't want any land to be destroyed. There were Innu graves on the site that we wanted to protect. This same sadness had washed over me that time, the same useless feeling as I had watched an Elder screaming.

"This is my land," our Elder Munik said. "This is my father's burial ground. My father's grave is there." She pointed to the place, where now the ground was broken. I had listened to her talking about her father with tears in her eyes.

How could I explain how much it hurt me to see this kind of thing happening again to me and my friends when our caribou was stolen from us? There had been laughter, but now there was sadness. How quickly our happiness could be taken from us.

We the Innu treat animals with respect, like we treat each other and our Elders. In our legends, the animals are referred to as humans. That is how I learned to see animals growing up. We were not allowed to talk about animals in a disrespectful way.

"The animals hear every word you say," my grandmother would tell me. "And they will always know about how you treat them."

She told me a story about Kautetihumat, the man who went to live with caribou, a story that is still told to our children today. It is the story of a young man who one morning awoke from a dream that he shared with his parents.

"I dreamed that a female caribou wanted me to live with her. She wanted me to take her for my wife," he told his parents.

"This dream must mean you will get caribou when you go hunting," the father said to his son.

The young man set out to go hunting. He walked far, and as he walked he began to recognize the land in his dream. He kept thinking about how he had dreamed about the place. He reached a lake and saw many caribou sitting around on the ice.

This is what I dreamed, he thought to himself, as he watched one of the caribou stand and start to walk toward him. *Yes, I dreamed about this*, the young man thought as he heard another caribou say to a young caribou, "Go and watch your sister. If the man says yes, run to us, zigzag your way to us so we will know he said yes."

The small caribou slowly followed his sister who was still walking toward the man. The young man reached for his bow and arrow as he waited for the female caribou to come closer. As she approached, he aimed his bow and arrow at her.

"Don't shoot," the female caribou said to him. He thought about his dream and lowered his bow and arrow.

"Will you marry me?" the caribou said to the man.

"How can I survive if I marry you?" he said to her. "I don't eat the things you eat. No, I cannot marry you."

"If you do not marry me, when you go home you will die before you get a chance to drink any water. You will die," the female caribou said.

"I will die anyway if I marry you," the young man said. "You live outside, and I will die from the cold."

"If you come with me, you will feel at home where our herd goes."

Still the man said no.

"Turn around, and don't look at me," the female caribou said, and the man did as he was told.

"Now look at me," she said, and the young man turned to see the most beautiful woman standing before him.

"This is what I will look like if you live with me," the caribou said. "Will you marry me?" she asked again, and this time the young man said, "Yes."

When the small caribou heard the young man say yes, he zigzagged his way back to the herd to give his father the news.

"Leave your arrows here," the female caribou said to the man. "Just bring your bow."

The man left his snowshoes and arrows and followed the caribou. As they reached the herd, the female caribou said to the man, "Just do as I do." He watched her open what appeared to be the flap of a tent door. The young man also opened the flap and found himself inside the home of the caribou. He saw that they all looked like Innu—Innu means "Living Being." The young man followed his wife, and the two sat down beside her father.

"Pass me the most tender meat we have," the father said to the other caribou. They gave him a piece of meat which he roasted over the fire and handed over to the young man.

"We don't want our son-in-law to go hungry," the caribou father said.

The son-in-law did not return home that night. His parents did not worry because he would often spend nights away hunting. After a few days, however, when the son had not returned, his parents began to worry, and his father sent a couple of men to search for him. The men found the son's arrows and snowshoes and saw his tracks where he had walked with the female caribou toward the herd sitting on the lake ice.

The men returned home to report to the father that they had seen his son's footsteps walking toward the herd. The father remembered his son's dream.

"We'll drive the caribou out," one of the men said to the father, "and we'll see if your son can run as fast as the caribou."

The men laughed thinking they would get the young man home to his parents. They headed out again and set up their traps for the caribou.

The herd could see what the two men were up to.

"They are here to drive us out," the female caribou's father said. "We can only give them so much. We can only allow them to kill so many caribou."

The other caribou agreed, and, as soon as the hunters had finished setting their traps, the caribou ran toward them. When the caribou had passed through, the men ran to where they expected to find the son, but he was nowhere to be found. All they could see was a sign of his bow touching the snow. This was how they knew he was with the herd, as they could not see his footprints anywhere.

The men took the caribou they had trapped home. They told the parents that they had only seen a sign of their son's bow, but the father would not give up.

"You will go again to find my son," he told the men.

That same night the caribou had sent the small caribou to see how the young man's father was doing. When the small caribou returned, he reported that the father and mother were still crying about the loss of their son.

"We will give them more food," said the lead caribou, who was the young man's father-in-law. "Let's go back to the lake." The herd returned to the lake and sat waiting for the hunters.

The hunters came the next day and again drove the caribou herd toward their traps. The hunters were happy to get caribou, but they still did not see the young man, only signs of his bow touching the snow—his mark to let them know that he had been there.

Every night the small caribou was sent to see how the parents of the man were doing, and every night he reported back that they were still crying for their son. That was until one night when he arrived to see the Innu holding a *Makushan* and a drum dance to give thanks for the caribou they had trapped. They had killed many, and they were thanking the caribou for giving themselves up. The young caribou came back to the herd and reported that the Innu were now happy and celebrating. The young man was glad to hear that his parents were laughing and dancing.

"This is good," said the lead caribou, the young man's father-in-law. "Now we can go on our journey." And they left the lake with the young man.

The young man continued to live with the caribou, but he could still do all the things he had done back home. One day he decided to make a spear.

"I wish I had something to make a spear with," he said, and his father-in-law overheard him.

"What did my son-in-law say?" he asked his daughter.

"He needs something to make a spear," she said, and her father took something from where he sat and handed it to the man. The man looked at the arrowhead and went outside in search of a stick. As he worked to attach the arrowhead to the stick, his father-in-law began to admire the young man's spear.

"I wish I had something to paint my spear with," the young man said. Again his father-in-law asked his daughter what his son-in-law was looking for.

"He wants to paint his spear," the daughter replied, and her father turned to reach for a red rock from where he sat and handed it to his daughter. She gave it to her husband, and he crushed it to use the powder to colour the handle of his spear. His father-in-law looked at the spear with great admiration.

I will be the first to taste that spear, he thought, as he turned to talk to his daughter.

"Where will you go hunting today?" he asked her.

"We will just go up the river in the canoe," she said. The two left in their canoe, and the caribou ran in their direction. As the man and his wife paddled along, the man spotted a caribou and killed it. The father-in-law had wanted to be killed by the spear, so beautifully designed. He was happy to have tasted the spear.

After the father-in-law was killed by the spear, his spirit returned. The man continued to live with the caribou. He was told by them that he would never die. He would live with the caribou forever, and, like his wife, he would never grow old.

This is the story that the Innu believe, how the hunters saw the mark of the young man's bow still visible on the snow. This is a story that shows the Innu relationship with the caribou, a story that shows how the Innu and the caribou respect each other. This is the story that shows why it is when the Innu prepares to hunt caribou, the wife will sew good moccasins and leggings—special clothing to show respect to the animal. When the caribou sees this kind of respect, the animal, in return, will give himself up to the hunter.

I thought about this story that day when the wildlife officers and the police took our caribou meat and bones. My heart really went out to my husband as I watched him trying so hard to show the wildlife officers and the police the box where he put the sacred bones, to explain this to them, but he couldn't even get close to the boxes. They stood in his way to block him. He even tried to just point at the box, but the police kept pushing his hand down. Finally he gave up. I don't know how long he tried to show them which box the bones were in. The feeling I had was like the time I dreamed about my child and in my dream I couldn't reach him. Watching the way the police and game wardens were treating my husband felt like a knife going through my heart and being twisted so hard that I couldn't breathe. It was a helpless feeling.

I felt so confused wondering why the strangers had come to disrespect us. Many bad memories that I had for so long tried hard to forget came jumping back at me. I remembered back to the day of my first confession, kneeling down beside a priest for many hours, my knees hurting on his cement floor. I was back to those days, when the priest and his people taught me while they beat me, always telling me to do what they said was right.

I cried myself to sleep the night the boxes of caribou were taken. I felt like I had been forced to walk away and abandon something or someone very precious to me. The strangers took something I honoured and respected. But the next day I awoke with a smile. I had fallen asleep and dreamed that a lot of Innu I had never seen before had come to visit us, not to the community this time, but to *nutshimit*. They had come to see us on the land. These people talked to me and told me they had come on a long trip. They set up their tents near mine, and I could hear them speak a different language. When I woke up, I was smiling. These people are the caribou, I thought.

"Don't worry," I said to Prote. "The caribou will come to us."

My mother had told me once that she had this kind of dream. She had met the people in her dream and told them that we had been waiting for them to come to our camp. She told me they would come, and that she was dreaming about the caribou.

The people who had come to talk to me in my dream, knew what had happened to us. They knew that we had treated the caribou with respect.

"Let's not be sad," I said to Prote. "The people know what happened to us, and they will come."

Christine Poker, Mushuauskueu, Natuashish

Salaam B'y
A Story of a Muslim Newfoundlander
by
AATIF BASKANDERI

Hi! I'm Aatif, and I'm a Muslim Newfoundlander. I come from a place where few people look like me or believe in the same things as me. In spite of those differences, the people in this place always accepted and encouraged me, which led me to feel an unwavering sense of belonging to Newfoundland and Labrador.

My parents had no idea what they were getting into when my dad accepted a job offer as a chemical engineer at Come by Chance oil refinery. Moving from a landlocked Ontario town of 70,000 to Clarenville, a town of 4,000 on the water, was a dramatic change. But that town of 4,000 gave my family the most fantastic community to grow up in. I joke with my wife that I lived a Disney life as a child, where my days were filled with picking blueberries, playing in the woods, ball hockey on the street, "spotlight" in the neighbourhood, having bonfires, biking to the playground and corner store, and watching *Star Trek: The Next Generation*. At the same time, we were one of the rare families of colour in the community, let alone a Muslim family.

I loved my faith growing up. My dad taught me, my older sister, and my older brother how to read Quran—the Muslim holy book—which required learning how to read Arabic. He also demonstrated how to pray. Muslims pray five times a day in a set pattern that's fairly common globally. My mom taught us other short prayers, called *dua*, that we could use throughout the day to express thanks to God or ask for help in times of need. I loved visiting St. John's whenever we had the chance, mostly for heading to Ponderosa buffet and the Avalon Mall arcade, but also to visit the St. John's Masjid, where I could see a building that manifested my love of my faith.

While I embraced Islam, I also enjoyed learning about other faiths. As children, we had to take Religious Studies in school, which essentially meant Bible study. I appreciated the class, however, because all the prophets in the Bible were also prophets in Islam. For any homework assignments, my teachers let me do research and work on Islam, rather than adhering to the Christian beliefs they were teaching. I participated in the school choir, and, when we would sing about loving Jesus (peace be upon him), I would adjust the lines referring to him as God, which Muslims don't believe.

I never really felt left out, even come Christmastime, with the exception of being super bored on December 25. My mom made a tradition of giving us modest "New Year's" gifts, just so we wouldn't feel excluded when we returned to school post-Christmas break and our classmates were chatting about what Santa had brought them. All this engagement with both Christian and Muslim faiths made me appreciate how two groups could take different approaches but share a common goal—in this case, serving God.

When I was ten, my dad was laid off from his job at Come by Chance refinery when they came under new ownership, and we found ourselves driving across the country to Vancouver in search of opportunity. When Dad was unable to find an engineering position, Mom opened a Pakistani-Punjabi clothing store on Main Street, also known as the Punjabi Market area.

Economically, this was a tough time for us, and we struggled socially, too. While there was a large Pakistani-Canadian population in Vancouver, where we started to develop a community, there were numerous times when I was ostracized for "not being Pakistani enough." Though I didn't speak Urdu or Punjabi, my father would defend my right to be whoever I wanted to be to any other parent who openly criticized me.

I only felt like I belonged at school due to my two best friends: Josh, a Christian Indian, and Tariq, a half-Vietnamese, half-Pakistani Muslim. I saw the three of us as being misfits in our own right, people who didn't really fit into any one community.

Living in Vancouver exposed me to a level of racism I had never seen before. The only instance I recall in my Clarenville primary school was a kid calling me a "n*****" in the very crude chant of "Fight! Fight! N***** and a white!" where I was fairly positive the other child had no idea what he was saying. I didn't know what the word meant either, just that it was intended for me. It goes to show, however, how racist language and narratives seep into children at an early age.

In Vancouver, which was very diverse, the racial dynamics were much more intense. Perhaps it was also my age, but I noticed high school fights being pegged as "brown versus white." Witnessing those racial tensions, though, sparked my interest in social issues, and my sister turned me on to the work of the leaders of the American civil rights movement. I borrowed her copy of *The Autobiography of Malcolm X*, which sat on her bookshelf below a Martin Luther King Jr. poster. It was here that I started to really build my appreciation for social justice and human rights.

By the time high school came around, we were back in Clarenville. The Come by Chance refinery had changed leadership again and re-hired my dad. I returned to my old friends and the same house. While Clarenville wasn't as culturally mixed as Vancouver, my school had its own diversity, and I found that I had a sincere interest in connecting with anyone, something that had built in me from both living in Vancouver with its diversity and growing up in Newfoundland with its cordiality. I had close friends who were gay and straight, religious and atheist, nerds and jocks, who were amazingly smart and who found school difficult.

I used to volunteer as a tutor at the primary school, where a kid once pitched a question to me that I thought was fantastic. A little boy in grade four asked me during our math tutoring session: "Why are you brown?" The librarian looked over in shock, shooting the student a scowl to flag this as a rude and racist question. But, for some reason, I really appreciated the sincerity of this question from a child who looked up to me as a tutor, and my response was simply to explain that in the same way people have different eye colours and different hair colours, people have different skin colours.

Of course, the reality is much more complicated. Race is politicized, and there is ignorance, fear, and hatred that leads to discrimination—but I'm not about to drop that on a nine-year-old. Still, I never felt that ignorant ambivalence of "I don't see race" in Newfoundland. People knew I was different, and they empowered it.

For instance, one part of my high school graduation ceremonies, where I was the only brown graduate out of a hundred, was a church service. The graduation organizing committee came to me a few months in advance to ask if I wanted to do something Islamic as part of the event. I was sitting next to my atheist good friend at the time, and my first reaction was to ask: "Does that mean he gets to do something, too?" They laughed and ignored the request, but that really struck a chord with me. How was it that I was getting representation at this church service while my atheist friends, who were many more than me, were not? I then immediately knew what Surah (Quranic passage) I wanted to read in both Arabic and English translation: Surah Al-Kafirun, "The Unbelievers."

بِسْمِ ٱللَّهِ ٱلرَّحْمَٰنِ ٱلرَّحِيمِ	In the name of God, the Most Gracious, the Most Merciful, Say, "O unbelievers,
قُلْ يَـٰٓأَيُّهَا ٱلْكَـٰفِرُونَ	"I do not worship what you worship,
تَعْبُدُونَ مَآ أَعْبُدُ لَا	"Nor are you worshippers of what I worship,
أَعْبُدُ مَآ عَابِدُونَ أَنتُمْ وَلَآ	"Nor will I be a worshipper of what you worship,
عَبَدتُّمْ مَّا عَابِدٌ أَنَا۠ وَلَآ	"Nor will you be worshippers of what I worship.
أَعْبُدُ مَآ عَابِدُونَ أَنتُمْ وَلَآ	"For you is your religion, and for me is my religion."

This Surah is, in my interpretation, about how differences in faith and philosophy lead to different approaches to life and about the importance of cultivating mutual respect as long as people do no harm to each other.

I read it to honour my atheist friends and, at the same time, the Christian church I was reciting it in for acknowledging the value of my difference.

After graduation, I left Clarenville for St. John's to attend Memorial University. One week into this new world of higher education, I'm walking out of my residence dorm when I pass the TV room. A crowd has gathered around the television, and I walk in to see what's going on. It's surreal. I see flames emanating from the World Trade Center, a place I remember visiting in New York years earlier on a family visit. I see a plane go into the second tower but, to be honest, don't really grasp the gravity of what has happened.

I continue on to my English class and am the first to tell people what happened that morning. The class goes on and, likewise, life went on after 9/11 for me, which seems odd when I compare my experience to the rest of the world. I never knew the extent of the connection that people would draw between Muslims and the attack. At that moment, I was mainly concerned about my mom, who was flying back from Boston to Newfoundland the next day, and whether she was going to be able to travel safely. I realized years later that I was in a privileged bubble in Newfoundland. I did not hear any semblance of a narrative within Newfoundland linking Muslims to violence or oppression. Of course in broader media I did, but not on NTV, which was the only channel I had access to with no cable—ah, student life.

Not only did other Newfoundlanders never project any of this onto me, people kept empowering me to be who I was. Anytime I was at a bar asking for a ginger ale, more often than not, another random bar-goer would end up buying it for me. In my later years of university, I would pray in public spaces, like parks or restaurants, and people always made space for me. During Ramadan, my friends would make a big deal at sunset when I could break my fast, and we would feast together. People encouraged the fact that I didn't drink or do drugs. This was a place that gave me the leeway to be myself, a misfit who didn't need to fit into any box.

I did start to see Islamophobia in the news in my last years of university. It came to a point that I used to look at the websites of racist organizations to try to understand where these people were coming from and what fuelled their hate. Of course, one of my roommates remarked that probably wasn't a sensible idea for my own mental health.

This was also at a time when I encountered one of the few instances of someone implying I didn't belong. I lived in Labrador City for four months on a work term with the Iron Ore Company of Canada. One of the employees would get a good laugh at me being "Aatif Baskanderi from Clarenville" and would get me to say it in front of others. "Tell them where you're from," he'd say. While I never remember that man's name or his face, I do remember clearly the look on my friend Brad's face, staring over with his jaw dropped and eyes wide open, astounded at how racist this was—literally saying out loud, "That's racist!"

I never really knew how to engage with that type of behaviour at the time but appreciated that Brad made a point to say "this is wrong." As usual, I would always say that if anyone said anything racist to me in Newfoundland, like while on George Street, I would have to hold back others from jumping that person. Racist incidents in Newfoundland were really an exception to the rule, and, if they did happen, I would have an army of other people coming to my support.

I was always interested in social studies in high school, and did many social sciences and religious studies electives in university, but I had never really known that all these things could be connected to my engineering career until Memorial launched a chapter of Engineers Without Borders. Newfoundland gave me the opportunity to start on the path of connecting my studies in engineering to my passion for social justice. When I finished up my Bachelor of Engineering at Memorial, I went to do a Master of Science in Social Policy and Development at the London School of Economics and Political Science (LSE) in the UK.

In London, I was a misfit again—an engineer doing a master's in social policy in a class full of people with years of experience in the United Nations or government or NGOs. But by this time I was used to owning my uniqueness and willing to put myself in spaces that no one really pegged me in.

When I graduated, I had two great degrees but a very hard time finding a market for my skill set. Luckily, through my love of connecting with people, I made a great friend named Danny Richmond, a Jewish Torontonian living in the same dorm as I in London who worked at an NGO called the Tony Blair Faith Foundation.

They had a new project in Sierra Leone on interfaith community behaviour change education for malaria prevention, and they hired me on as project manager through their Faiths Act Fellowship. The malaria project had us working with the Sierra Leone Ministry of Health and the Inter-Religious Council to train up faith leaders on the science of malaria reconciled with their faith beliefs; they would then go educate their local communities on mitigating against the disease. While it's difficult for Sierra Leoneans to depend on their government or their under-resourced health care facilities, they did depend on their faith leaders.

Sierra Leone is about 80 per cent Muslim, 20 per cent Christian, and some Indigenous faiths, and the interfaith relations there are stronger than I have seen in any of the countries where I have travelled or lived, including Canada. The amount of respect between the different faiths is outstanding. I loved the country, perhaps the main reason being I again got to be myself the whole time and was surrounded by wonderfully kind people and a beautiful landscape with an amazing history.

After Sierra Leone, I returned to Canada and eventually landed a dream job at the British Consulate-General in Calgary leading the UK Science and Innovation Network covering Alberta, Saskatchewan, and Manitoba, as well as energy innovation nationally. I went for my interview at the British High Commission on a Friday morning and received a call with a job offer two hours later, at which point I fell to my knees astounded, thanking God and feeling a mix of joy and shock.

I have now found my career in empowering innovation. This has included working in non-profits, private industry, and government with the aim of commercializing innovations to create jobs in Canada, particularly during the current difficult economic time. I continue to use my Newfoundland-bred gregarious nature to promote innovation, where my goal is to build collaboration among diverse groups through mutual understanding and embracing inclusion.

With all these initiatives, I carry a relentless optimism and a get 'er done, no-nonsense, yet respectful attitude that Newfoundland raised me to have, and that my colleagues and partners appreciate. I always feel the pain of, and an urge to stick up for, all marginalized people that are ignorantly or hatefully targeted by society. Combining innovation with social justice is not only what the world needs, it has an economic benefit—there are jobs there!

Newfoundland taught me to be proud of who I am and where I come from. Not to feel the need to assimilate to others and maintain the status quo. It also showed me that by being myself, I could create the best connections with people. Connections based on authenticity and sincerity, instead of the fear and ignorance that can prevail when people see each other as anonymous members of large groups instead of individuals.

Newfoundlanders face their own type of discrimination in Canada, when you think of it. Some people see Newfoundland and Labrador as being a "have not" province, with people who are not as educated, in many ways a caricature of who they really are. Some Newfoundlanders may feel the need to assimilate to mainland culture. I have seen some Newfoundlanders downplay the fact they are from Newfoundland around certain people. Sometimes Muslims in Canada also feel like they are pressured to assimilate to other groups, or they just stick with their Muslim peers for fear that broader society will not let them be themselves. Of course, for one of those groups, the consequences of such discrimination are much more severe and, in some cases, lethal. Newfoundland didn't treat me like I was the same as everyone else as a mechanism to engage with me. Newfoundland knew I was different and validated it.

Newfoundland also gave me an environment where I could really understand and exercise the character of Islam, primarily in the areas of sincerity and authenticity. Newfoundlanders have very little time for phoniness. This gave me the confidence to just be myself—it became normal for me in Newfoundland, lest I be called out with a "whatta ya gettin' on with?" It also allows me, to this day, to follow through on my ambitions, even if they could be considered unique or out-of-the-box. Newfoundland and Labrador showed me and others a way to build communities of kindness that can build people up in great ways.

Between the Rock and a Harder Place

by

KY PEARCE

I was born on the west coast of Newfoundland in the mid-1990s, and I lived on the island until 2016, when I moved away to pursue a master's degree (and now my doctorate) at Queen's University in Kingston, Ontario. As soon as I could, I left home for St. John's but eventually found myself in Corner Brook attending Memorial University's Grenfell Campus. While I no longer live in Newfoundland, I feel a profound connection to the place that raised me. I hear the island's history in my words, their lilt, and the way my tongue curves to caress H's, R's, and A's like the ocean upon the shore. I cannot let go of the place my settler ancestors have called home for centuries, the land my Mi'kmaq ancestors have known as part of their world for millennia.

Despite this profound connection I feel to the island, I always knew I would have to leave. This was not so much something I was inspired or necessarily wanted to do, but something I was *told* I must do: it was decided for me because I'm queer.[1]

---

1 I use the word "queer" because my gender and sexuality don't really line up...

I realized that I was queer at a young age—I think I was in elementary school, but I don't know which year. It was a strange realization. I didn't know that queerness was an option: I had no mental category for it. By the time I entered junior high, I had a concept of "gay," but that concept was decidedly negative. In my environment to be "gay," a "dyke," or a "faggot" was always negative. It was an insult uttered against myself and others who did not fit strict sexual and gendered expectations.

LGBT, queer, and Two-Spirit people struggle to exist in rural parts of the island because some people have decided that queerness does not belong in Newfoundland, and this makes it nearly impossible to imagine a future there as queer people. Beyond queerphobia, my mother, guidance counsellor, teachers, and everyone else whom I had confided in about my queerness only said that it would get better when I left. "Once you move away for university, things will be different." These lines might sound like kind reassurance, but, for me and many others, they meant only one thing: you don't belong here.

But I do. We do.

I feel the island in my bones. My body is literally *made* of the island: made of the water that runs beneath its ground, the fish that swim along its coasts, the berries that grace the land, the herbs I grew in the garden, as well as the moose, rabbits, and geese that roam its wilderness. I am literally *made of* the island. Made of its "come in for a cup of tea...don't worry about it sure, that's the least I can do" culture. Made of its keen sense of self-reliance and its history of being downtrodden and looked down upon by a world that considers it lacking and stuck in the past. My ancestors lived on this land *thousands* of years before Western civilization emerged in Mesopotamia. If I don't belong to the island, nobody does.

To be specific, I grew up in "the bay," *deep* in the bay, as far away as you can practically get from St. John's while still being in Newfoundland. My

---

...with the expectations and requirements of the "LGBT" identities, and because I'm critical of colonial cisheteropatriarchy in our society—that is, our system of sex and gender we have inherited from European colonization that demands everyone be straight and cis-gendered according to a binary sex system, and privileges men over women.

hometown has a population of around three hundred, while the next town over boasts a slightly larger population of four thousand. I've taken classes with more students than there are people living in my hometown. You don't know what it means to say "it's a small world" until you've lived in small-town Newfoundland. In a place like that, it's impossible to be unknown.

This was a big problem for me.

The problem with the way I'm known in my small community is that it is never on my own terms. When home, I'm perceived through the lens of my family or my queerness. In my hometown there's no avoiding being seen, and thus no avoiding being recognized in this way. This is even the case in the other towns near my home. When I was growing up, the controlling gaze of my community felt impossible to escape. Teachers assumed I would perform in certain ways because my cousins did. Neighbours assumed I would behave in certain ways because my parents, grandparents, or aunts and uncles did. The problem is that these assumptions were never very accurate.

Assumptions were not limited to my family connections, but also my queerness. I was being spoken for. A particular kind of queerness spoke over me, erasing my personality and desires. One of the loudest things that it said (to anyone who would listen, including myself) is that I didn't belong there. Academics call this voice the gay (or queer) imaginary. The gay imaginary is credited with sparking a mass-migration of queer-aligned people to San Francisco or other major centres—in Canada this was often Toronto, and in Newfoundland this was St. John's. The gay imaginary firmly says that queers belong in the city.

My peers have no shortage of stories they've heard about relatives who moved away to the mainland so that they could be gay. This meant that there were not enough queers around to either create some form of visibility for queer youth, or enough queers around to show what a queer community in rural Newfoundland might be like. It was a specific crisis of representation that the Internet/media couldn't fix because we suffered not only from a lack of representation, but also from misrepresentation. We not only had few to no examples of queerness in our physical lives, but those offered by television and the Internet said our queerness was impossible; it presented a kind of queerness, entrenched in cities, pride parades, and gay bars. This is not even to mention those queerphobic sentiments we all struggle with in the forms of harassment, social exclusion, and violence.

Like most queer youth in rural Newfoundland, I found in the Internet my only meaningful source of queer representation. Positive portrayals of queerness came to me through YouTube, forums, social media, educational websites, and pen pals. These images, none of which were local, coalesced to give me an understanding of queerness that was positive and livable, but foreign. Given this, it's no surprise that I understood queerness to be mutually exclusive to Newfoundland. The Internet enabled me to access an imaginary gay life elsewhere for myself—but *only* elsewhere, and in a very "standardly gay" way. Because the only examples my peers and I had for queer people were urban queers in the media, and those friends and family members who had left Newfoundland to go be queer elsewhere, we all understood that queerness could not exist in rural Newfoundland. Many potential futures were erased by this belief.

I should clarify that there were a few queer people in my area. As I got older, people in my school "came out." By the time I was in the eighth grade, I knew of two students in my school (which included grades seven through twelve) who were not straight. Not long after I met these people, I learned one of my cousins is gay. Finally, in my last years of school there came to be younger students who had a variety of non-heterosexual identities. Despite the presence of this handful of queer people, we lacked any sense of being a queer community.

While I know I was lucky to have these people in my life, it didn't help much: they were just as lost and confused as I was. None of us knew what it meant to be queer beyond the fact that some of our peers, and in some cases families, despised us. Our environment was devoid of livable queer futures, and everywhere we looked the gay imaginary and queerphobia insisted we could not, or did not, exist.

In tenth grade, some of my friends and I started a Queer-Straight Alliance (QSA). My school's guidance counsellor, a wonderful woman who always supported us unwaveringly, was the staff sponsor of the group. A newly hired teacher surprised us by coming to our inaugural meeting, and he fit many of the stereotypes of gay men. That teacher never expressed that he was queer, but his presence at our meeting said enough for us to choose to believe he was. That teacher's presence was invaluable for me. It was profound to see an adult that I believed I could one day *be*, someone who represented a future I could conceivably live.

This gay teacher left his teaching post before Christmas. I do not know if he quit, went on some form of leave, or suddenly became ill. I was not one of his students, and, to my knowledge, no students were given a reason for his absence. In any case, what actually happened is not what matters here: what matters is that we believed he quit because of queerphobic bullying from students. We lived in an environment so hostile to queerness that a teacher had to quit their job. We did not consider this shocking; I remember accepting the news with a resigned sigh.

There's no "passive tide" of queerphobia in Newfoundland, and there is no cultural "quirk" of Newfoundland that says queers cannot exist there. Newfoundland culture is a product of the decisions we make every day. To paraphrase the famous anthropologist Clifford Geertz, culture is the stories we tell ourselves about ourselves. Newfoundland culture is what we decide it is. It depends on what we believe about ourselves and our society. A queerphobic Newfoundland is *made* when children bully a queer teacher out of a job. A queerphobic Newfoundland is made when people *decide* that our lives can only get better when we leave, and we must simply endure queerphobia until we leave. Newfoundland becomes a place queer people struggle to live when we decide to accept that rural Newfoundland is a place queers don't belong. Queerphobia in Newfoundland is not some quirk or natural part of Newfoundland culture, it is made every day in the decisions Newfoundlanders make. It is time we collectively reconsider these actions.

I planned to close my chapter by talking about the way a town near my home now flies a pride flag annually and has painted two rainbow crosswalks. I had originally decided to accept this as a victory. But it is not. What the flag's presence doesn't say is that an individual working in the municipal government called a friend of mine, an ally, and asked if it would be okay to fly the flag for just one week, or better yet just one day of pride month. What the original story did not say is that the town raised the pride flag and painted the crosswalks but took no concrete steps to support local queer people. Municipal leaders concluded that a flag and some paint were sufficient solutions to help queer people in a town where homophobic students chased off a gay teacher, homophobic parishioners chased off an openly gay minister, where queer people are told they can't even exist. I don't mean to shame these people for their insufficient actions; I mean to hold us all accountable so that we might reconsider our choices. A flag or a bit of paint is not enough to overcome the overwhelming narrative that we are not allowed to exist in rural communities. Patting yourself on the back for flying a flag and spreading some paint is an insult.

My final year in high school found me completely isolated as the last of my queer friends graduated and left for greener pastures. I had a handful of friends in my graduating class, and a smattering in the classes below, but I lost anything that came even remotely close to a queer peer group. All that remained was the promise that my life would get better once I left. I believed this message wholeheartedly because it was my only option. Finally, I did leave, with such enthusiasm that I lost a great deal of who I was.

But I left with a mission. I also left in stages.

First, I made for St. John's. It was as far as I could feasibly get from home. I studied at Memorial University, but I never found a foothold there. My academic interests soon led me to Memorial's Grenfell campus for its Social/Cultural Studies program. What I discovered at Grenfell was the world I had always wanted. I was in Newfoundland, and a place where my Newfoundlandness was not only accepted but cherished, while also amongst the vibrant queer community Grenfell hosted. Grenfell also offered me access to mentors and academic inquiry that facilitated critical explorations of my identity and the often-invisible social structures, institutions, and ideologies that have a profound impact on all our lives.

I completed my first degree with a final project titled: "Queer Experience and Identity: Mediating the Sociocultural City Using the Performativity of Identity." Looking back, it is a bit of a pretentious title. What that project was really about was how young people in rural Newfoundland manage expectations surrounding their sexuality and gender. It was born purely from a desire to understand my own experience, but I never got to answer the question *why? Why is it that we manage our behaviour in front of our communities so that they'll accept us?* The obvious answers of queerphobia and sexism didn't satisfy me for long.

When I finished my first degree, I left the island to pursue graduate studies at Queen's University. I soon realized I wasn't done with my questions about Newfoundland and queerness. Now that I was away from Newfoundland, I became fascinated with what had *pushed* me away. Slowly my master's thesis—"Gay by the Bay: Feeling Queer, Feeling Newfoundland"—emerged (the text can be found online). I interviewed several young Newfoundlanders for that project, all in different stages of their relationship with rural Newfoundland. Regardless of whether we had left Newfoundland yet or not, all of us shared a profound connection to the island but knew we had to leave.

While this chapter has primarily focused on the ways that queer people are told they cannot exist in rural Newfoundland, it has simultaneously been *about queer people existing* in rural Newfoundland. We live in these places, we call them home, and we love them. Many of us wish we could stay. Some of us even return permanently. The takeaway here is that queers in rural Newfoundland exist between "The Rock" and a harder place, in the limbo of the in-between: both here and there, living in rural Newfoundland but imagined only elsewhere, forbidden from existing but existing nonetheless. We survive, squeezed between the very rock of our island home and a harder place that has been made, where people decide that queers do not belong.

Despite the forces pushing us away, I am slowly learning about the queer people that have always existed in rural Newfoundland. I remember stories about a woman who once lived in my community who temporarily hosted a kid after their parents kicked them out for being in a queer relationship. The home this woman lived in is still pejoratively called "the lezzy hotel" by some. I consider this old, abandoned, and run-down home to be a monument to the resilience of my people and the way we find a way to live, love, and take care of one another.

To close, I want to tell you a more recent story. My brother came out as gay one summer after I returned from university—or, more accurately, my mother asked him if he was gay, and my brother decided to tell her the truth. My brother was dating another boy in the next town over, and they were inseparable. As his boyfriend became embedded in the family, he met my elderly religious grandmother who, without missing a beat, accepted him as my brother's *friend*, knowing exactly how *friendly* they were. Since then, my grandmother has met, and unconditionally accepted, several of her three queer grandchildren's partners. On his most recent visit home, my grandmother met my brother's newest boyfriend and really took a shine to him, declaring he "is the prettiest boy" she "has ever seen," and she now asks about him whenever my brother or I call.

Newfoundland has a whole system of language ready to go that allows for the existence of queers within heterosexist and homophobic requirements of religious and state institutions. Since I became an adult, my elderly relatives have begun to tell me about people they once knew who were "*that way*"—not pejoratively, but just as if it was supposed to be a secret. The same way they invoke our partners as our "friends."

Queer people continue to leave rural Newfoundland, and Newfoundland in general, in droves. Newfoundland's normal out-migration problem is much more extreme when it comes to queer people. We don't face the question of whether or not to stay in our rural communities, it is normally a question of how soon we can leave. But many of us bring our cherished Newfoundland identities with us, and many of us return. Several even stay—deciding to sacrifice the supposed promise of a happy future and hope for the best. The biggest problem is that queerness is written out of possibility in rural Newfoundland. But we continue to exist, we continue to love, and we continue to support one another.

We exist between "The Rock" and a harder place. We exist between the idea of Newfoundland and its reality. We exist between stories that tell us we cannot exist and our beating hearts that insist we do. I refuse to tell a story about how rural Newfoundland is becoming a friendlier and more welcoming place for queers. I don't believe that is true, just like I don't believe some "natural" or inherent queerphobia is the real reason we struggle to exist in these places. The most important thing we can do right now is to start listening to the stories of people who have been made to go without a voice, the people who are stuck between the rock of the island and "The Rock" that is made by our stories and decisions.

Gallons of Tea and the Candy Cart

by

ANTHONY BRENTON

It started with an anonymous letter to my psychiatrist, 306 Waterford Bridge Rd., pounded out on a '70s-era Underwood typewriter. It had all the music of a grand piano thrashed at by a thin, aged Igor Fyodorovich Stravinsky, bespectacled and balding, polarizing his instrument from the heights of violence to a tender whispering. The composition was definitely an attempt at a longer self-reflection that I continuously failed to produce while in session. The demented, surrealistic note wound its way through the mechanics. The letter grappled with dementia, paranoia, depression, anxiety and an overall slipping out of reality. I didn't sign it, nor did I give a return address, but, identifying me by my transparent terrors and obviously specific symptoms, my doctor phoned me directly to set up an appointment as soon as possible. I didn't see the trap.

When I checked in the next day, with my ever-present bookbag stuffed with nonsense, poems, and discs of writings, I was directed to the small waiting room where a conspicuous nurse sat a few chairs away. Terrible music played through a small radio as I sipped on a paper cone of water. Despite the apparently urgent meeting, I sat for just under an hour before being escorted into the solemn office of the brilliant doctor.

She had scrutinized the letter, realized it was mine, and decided that it had serious enough implications that it warranted an intense assessment and acute inpatient care.

I was examined thoroughly and grilled on the screed point by point. After this I was moved into a secondary room and interviewed by a doctor I had never met. She asked me a series of questions which I now know were a checklist for one to be committed against their will.

I was given the option to walk to a secure ward with two nurses, or to have orderlies come and strong-arm me there. I smiled at the receptionist and chose the heavenly nurses. Lights behind them bent sepia halos over their braided hair. Delicate hands folded atop youthful wombs.

We passed through the various smells of the hospital. Up staircases and down back halls. Finally, we hit a door with numbers and letters painted above it. A key was produced, and we breezed in. I was, by the grace of God, brought to a private room. The bed was neatly made with pastel sheets and a thin pillow. Next to it was a small desk and a wardrobe etched with the desperate musings of former guests.

Two men immediately took my bookbag and asked if there were any sharps or drugs in it. They sorted my papers and discs upon the desk. There were also house keys, Advil, pens, a book of Bukowski's poetry, coin money, and a record of Thelonious Monk's solo piano works.

A sedate-looking doctor and young nurse came into my room with a series of questions, and I was handed a yellow medication that melted in my mouth like the body of Christ in a psychiatric Eucharist. Satisfied that I was, metaphorically, chained to the proper bed, they left me to fall static into the fast tranquilizer.

I awoke in a blackened room with a flashlight's beam in my eyes; the orderlies were doing rounds, noting each condition at every hour, short-handed into a notepad, and moving on.

I yawned with the weight of a grown man upon my chest. This hideous he-hag, a suffocating villain draped within my innards, knotting my bowels in milk sickness. His breath into my nose was the electricity of a murderous nightmare, crossed into reality. His mouth full of sour pudding that muffled the chatter of his bizzt teeth. As my eyes readjusted to the dark, the devil vanished into dust, leather wings pounding; thus I sprang up with a huge breath. But by the fishy tab of a foam medication, I flopped back lifelessly into the soft horror of my elastic hospital bed.

Those first three days I left that tiny sanctuary of a room only for meals and toilet. I was battling the blows and temptations of my saintly namesake: Anthony's torment as described by Gustave Flaubert and illustrated by many fine artists. I peeked out like a hideous ghoul from his cave's mouth, fearful of the predators that lurked about, but sick of his own mind battering itself.

The ignorant aggression of a few patients became apparent very quickly. Men and women who shuffled up in a stop-motion animation, cartoons inquiring on cigarettes and money, gripping the television's remote control, pushing to the front of the line at meals, and cursing me off the phone, which I approached with great trepidation and loathing. As I spoke, I was convinced that worms that had been crawling out of the ears of other patients were screwing their way into my ear canal to lay their rotten eggs and raise their sickly brood. So at only the most desperate or enmaddened moments did I dare approach the filthy black crustacean, and only then with the most delicate of handling.

Other people never spoke. They paced around in slippers, face to the floor, hanging on to the edges of their robes. Filthy hair in all directions. Wounded eyes recoiling against everything.

Manic patients jogged about the ward. They ceaselessly blabbered. One would accost me and ramble in a rapid, aimless stream of consciousness: a collage of introspection, listing objects around the room, lyrics to songs, distorted memories, and fast realizations in shattered logorrhea.

A dozen or so others were merely shadows.

Television shows and music videos that played in the activity room are forever burned into my brain like the specifics of an acid trip. By a dementing Rx intake these memories were formed. Like a childhood day at the amusement park warped by a softening of reality. Forever captured in an unwanted photo album, crammed with monochromatic snaps of horrible times. Vivid etchings immortalized as if Gustave Doré were crammed into my hippocampus, suited, with his block of wood and engraving tools.

Sitting in front of the wide and loud television, a medication trolley that the patients had dubbed the Candy Cart was pushed into the room, filled with drawers, cups, and a jug of ice water. Our nurse doled out various capsules and pills around the room and disappeared—we heard the wheels squeaking down the hall.

Up from the couch, having swallowed my Rx, I looked out the gridded window at the streets below. There was a park, a bus stop, and a parking lot. I watched people come and go, free as pigeons, cross-hatched by steel mesh.

After five days I was moved into a ward room with five other men. The desk and wardrobe were one piece of furniture now, and stood as a partition between roommates. I was no doubt loathed, as my friend had lugged in my typewriter for the purpose of musical writing. The nurses told me that they could hear it all the way down to their desks but thought not much of it. I worked on a series of poems and vignettes, slapped at the keys, paced around, and yanked out papers that I hid under my bed until I received a visitor who would collect them for their compilation in a banker's box.

I truly believed that I was in an inescapable purgatory and that nothing but the Lord's will could usher me out. Thus, I begged to attend church in a Holy Trinity panic. A nurse escorted me down a long, beat-up hallway and into a small chapel. To gaze upon her then was like looking directly into the sun.

The pews were scantily occupied by men drooling into their Bibles, ladies bunching up long flowery dresses, and fools hollering as the priest read psalms. The grumbling flock grunted and scratched their asses.

In the grip of a church-house funeral flashback, I shook like a bird just lit down from flight! All the dearly departed filling my belly with a delayed loss, curdling in a disgusting cheese.

I sat amongst the forlorn singing "There Is Power in the Blood." What tone-deaf and unprepared vocalists were we? A freaked-out choir in muscle spasms, clenched jaws, sweats, vertigo, and disorientation.

The priest towered before us. His was a pitying breath. Enrobed, his skull became static with rolling video-lottery technicolored wheels. The true cross glistened its sharp pulp in his dust-blown pupil. His haircut like waves of bent waters. The white of dried salt crusted in the corners of his mouth.

In my pew I wept for the dead, beside my accompanying nurse. She was the Mother of Jesus there, and Mary Magdalene, too: a virgin and a whore, a double saint. She wore an expression of total serenity upon her face and held me as I wailed, lamenting my poor soul and the mystery of the after-life. Sick by the monstrousness of unknowing!

She seemed certain in her rapt attention. I did not, however, find religion again. My apostasy remained, regardless of my blind terror of hell. The power of the blood of the lamb did not attract me. The magnetic hands of Christianity fell soft to the floor, its carpet scuffed with cigarette-butt soles.

At my word we left. Down the hall and up the stairs we returned to my ward, through the daunting steel door.

In my room, I squeezed off my shoes and sat upon the bed. I pondered God and my doctors. I scrutinized the communion and the Candy Cart. I thumbed through the Bible and the Compendium of Pharmaceuticals and Specialties. Night followed day. Weeks became a month.

And, by my doctor's flawless devotion to Hippocrates, I had plateaued. The medication eased into a tiny sacrament. The nurses turned their faces away, with the heights of empathy, for the new cases admitted. The doctors became aloof interviewers for a few moments every three or four days, none too excited, the case no longer exceptional.

How I pined for cold beer and a warm woman, a tailor-made cigarette! A private washroom. An unsupervised shower.

By a boiled kettle I fixed some tea and plotted my discharge.

Thus, I talked my way out. I explained that the therapeutic value of hospitalization had indeed run its course. That the other patients were hindering my convalescence by their erratic behaviour: their constant hustling, the unpredictable gibberish. So, the forms were filled out, the interviews concluded, my possessions collected, my prescriptions written up, and a cab called. I was out.

Never again! I thought. The locks done and undone, and, as the massive, elderly institution faded behind the knotted trees, I looked forward to clocks without schedule.

———

Several years and hospital stays later I was taken to the hospital in Grand Falls from St. John's, by ambulance. Apparently this had never been done. The driver and the doctors who received me said memory held no likeness.

On the way, the passenger-side paramedic opened my files and read them over as we sped away from the city. I saw her smile; I saw her chuckle. I lay in the bed, full of tranquilizers, and spun my way down the Trans-Canada Highway.

Upon my arrival, the psychiatric ward was filled with student nurses running therapeutic games and assisting patients. They held hands in soothing reassurance, leading the tormented up and down the halls or sitting for long minutes at the television.

A dozen or so young women wore white uniforms and sneakers, milling about the main desk with hair tied back in high ponytails. They stood in circles with wings at full display, holding books and musical instruments, faces slack in complacent medical faith. Yellow halos radiated about them, but they didn't seem to notice.

One day they were all gone, and the abundance of care was lost.

This stint held absolutely no creative insight for me. I neither wrote nor drew with any invention. I did not study the Bible—I read only popular works. I played games of bingo, watched soap operas and game shows, painted by numbers, drank decaffeinated coffee.

After I had been on the ward for two weeks, a strange decision had to be made regarding the high-dosage readjustment in my medication that targeted depression. Because of the succession of powerful antidepressants, and the minimal effect that they produced, electroconvulsive therapy was now on the table. I felt like I was, indeed, climbing the ranks of insanity.

I initially ascribed to the common misconception that the procedure did little more than literally fry the mind and leave the patient a zombified shell of a person. I envisioned a one-way street to a docile, thoughtless existence. Forever in a robe, chain-smoking out by the doors, wandering aimlessly in hospital hallways until cancer or kneejerk suicide put an end to the emptiness. But the procedure is, in reality, highly effective in turning around severe depression. Being in the state that I was in, I agreed and set in motion the ordeal.

Some days later I was awoken early, taken to the toilet, gowned, and loaded onto a bed for transport to the surgical suite. It was basically your average hospital room: bags of fluid on poles, complex machines, pastel paint job. There was a psychiatrist, an anaesthetist, an ECT nurse, and a recovery nurse. A needle was jabbed into my hand, and I was shot up with an anaesthetic and a muscle relaxant. The idea is to paralyze the body to eliminate the risk of injury. In the olden days, these convulsions could easily dislocate a bone or two. Oh! Then the cold ants ran in my veins. The abrupt sensation alarmed me, so that I turned to the nurse to stop the process. Terrified at the ice, I said "I think that...," but I was enveloped in black and sucked into a void. Passive against the electrical stimulus.

I lazily erupted on the other end, in a clean bed, mildly confused, and with tender muscles.

I recall a slight euphoric state. Or a pleasant emptiness that may have been the draining of melancholy. Or it may have been the detoxification of the now-absent Rx. But the shocks were repeated a dozen times as the inpatient calendar notched itself.

I was indeed healthy after some weeks and then released with all the blessings of my medical team.

Two of my closest friends drove from St. John's to Grand Falls to escort me home. We reflected on lunacy on the many-hour drive. And once again I was morning, noon, and night in an empty apartment.

———

In a decidedly calmer, more polite, and more mature experience, I ended up one winter on the small psychiatric unit of the Health Sciences Centre at 300 Prince Phillip Drive, down in the basement with the industrial kitchen. Still a locked ward, indeed, and still with problematic patients, though they are little more than assertive, keen to leave, loud, and strutting. It had more of a geriatric-home feel. The Olympics were playing on the television, but none of us bet on any events.

The wheels on the Candy Cart were well oiled and soundless, and I spent my days in the activity room availing of the many art supplies, drawing out the confusion, the delirium, and the damned depression in abstract self-portraiture. These artworks I gave away as highly personal gifts, no doubt to belly laughs, cringing lips, and the inevitable toss.

I was locked in pharmaceutical manacles and behind steel doors when, upstairs in the emergency department, a dearest friend was felled by misdiagnosis and malpractice, and died with her red and orange curls splayed upon her hospital bed. I decided to cut it short. Things were no longer about me. So many people I adored needed all the love they could get, and I had to be involved. Within two days I had talked myself out of the ward to join the funeral procession.

My tongue had indeed become a silver key, ready to render useless the locks of asylum doors.

———

That first stint of incarcerated time left me with something of a shell shock. Being in a situation where I had absolutely no control, against an army I had no idea how to battle. I was traumatized by lock and by drug, by following a nurse and the door clicking shut behind me. "Prison - Hell" scratched upon its paint. "My body is Santa's head chopped off" crudely pencilled onto the wall above my pillow.

Despite the trouble, however, with each subsequent revisit I knew the building as a convalescent home. A sanctuary of acute care.

So the action became clear for each new stint: detoxify from useless medication, avail of the saintly and angelic nurses, listen to the testament of the doctor, take my proper dole from the Candy Cart, let time heal all wounds. Watch TV, read Dante, look out the windows, nap during the day, slowly pace the halls, reject cigarettes, forget cold beer, wait for my woman, but holler "LOVE!" from the madhouse windows.

And when the time is correct, collect the walking papers, clear-headed, and stroll out into the vast expanse: free and balanced, another law-abiding citizen on the bus.

Who Says You Can't Go Home?

by

PAUL DAVID POWER

Home.

There's something about that word, especially for Newfoundlanders. Whether we've lived in another part of the world for a year or twenty, for most, the word "home" immediately conjures that image of "the Rock."

Maybe it's the unique landscape of rolling hills, craggy cliffs, dense forests juxtaposed against miles of barren bogs. Maybe it's the distinct salty air and rhythmic sound of the crashing, foaming waves of the cold Atlantic that surrounds our island. Or, perhaps it's the people. Whether it's family or a distant acquaintance you run into on the street, they always feel like familiar friends ready to invite you into their kitchen for a cup of tea. No need to impress here.

Whatever the reason—more often than not—when you encounter someone living away, the first thing they usually say is how much they would love to move home. There's a life-long connection. But can you really go home again?

As a Newfoundlander I appreciated my life here. After a university education at Memorial and then a short stint in Toronto to get a journalism degree I settled into a life here in Newfoundland—here at home—working in communications with the provincial government. A government job: the pot of gold at the end of a rainbow for the Newfoundlander. I was with that job for eight years. Writing speeches, news releases, advertisements, designing graphics and excelling with promotions, awards, accolades, and true security. I was set.

And then—the unthinkable—I left Newfoundland.

About a year before I had met the love of my life, Jonathan. It had started out as a pretty casual thing. But as time went by we evolved from casual dating to couplehood, to calling ourselves partners. Now you have to understand this was a pretty big deal for me. It was my very first long-term, open gay relationship. There was something about Jonathan that gave my life a piece that was missing: fulfillment in a good relationship both emotionally and physically.

I was born with a physical disability. A combination of genetic and developmental defects in the womb caused my legs not to develop as they should. My legs are shorter than the rest of my body. The bones are somewhat fused rather that easily able to bend at the joints. The muscles around those bones are weak. As I aged it became apparent that for me to walk it would require the use of full-length leg braces and crutches for support. It's a physicality I have lived with all of my life.

And with that physicality came awkward stares, inappropriate questions from strangers about my medical circumstance, and above all, in the gay world, I was viewed by most as someone who could be a "friend"—but let's not go too far. Physical intimacy with the guy on crutches was not the top fantasy for most guys you encounter down at the local gay bar.

Jonathan was different. He made me feel attractive both inside and out. And I felt lucky to be with a man who was not only physically attractive but also had a great heart. It just added to the perfectness of that time of my life here at home.

Then, Jonathan received a promotion and transfer from work all the way to Calgary, Alberta. An opportunity away. He wanted me to go with him. He wanted me to leave home. The decision was mine—and it was a difficult one. But, as the saying goes, I did it for love.

What a life change. We did well in Calgary—but I was never totally at ease. Life was different. Three-hour traffic jams, a work lifestyle that saw you leave at 6 a.m. and return at 8 p.m. And casual visits with family or friends were impossible with an astronomically expensive flight lasting eight hours each way.

Sure, I missed home. But as time went by home started becoming wherever Jonathan was. If anything, it strengthened our relationship and reliance on each other as a couple. Two Newfoundlanders making it on their own out West. We were there for five years.

Eventually another work transfer would find us in Moncton, New Brunswick, and life got even more settled and domesticated. We bought a house. We both had jobs we liked. We spent our nights like an old married couple making dinner and binge-watching sci-fi. Weekends were filled with the usual errands, taking pride in our home improvement handiwork and gardening, loving the home we were creating. Life was good. And because of the proximity more frequent visits were possible from family and friends in Newfoundland. It was the best of both worlds.

And then, on September 24, 2013, at 6:30 p.m., I walked into the bathroom of our house and found Jonathan. He had died. Suddenly. An aortic dissection. I called an ambulance. Went to the hospital. Was told they could not revive him. I was sent home. The chicken I had cooked for dinner was still sitting on the stove. It all took less than two hours.

The days and weeks following are a blur. Like living outside my body. This could not be happening. How could everything change so quickly? Jonathan, where are you? I don't remember who was around. I don't remember how I slept—or if I slept. I don't even remember who made what arrangements. When faced with such a shock the mind really does shut down.

We held Jonathan's memorial where else but home—Newfoundland. I stayed back in Newfoundland after the memorial for a few weeks. But eventually I had to return to our house in Moncton. To my job. To a life that no longer really existed. I still remember walking into our house for the first time since losing Jonathan. It was eerily quiet, still, cold, and dark. This wasn't our home anymore. And as much as I tried to pretend, it never felt like our home again.

I left the house that had transformed from a happy home to a cold mausoleum and moved into my own apartment. In fact, after Jonathan passed I tried five different apartments. But none ever felt right. No matter how many times I tried to make the space like our house, no matter how many times I set up furniture and knick-knacks the way Jonathan would like them, no matter how many of Jonathan's sweaters and shirts I kept hanging in the closet, no matter what location I decided to live, it never felt like a home.

After about a year I thought I had finally come up with a solution to this sensation of homelessness. Go back to Newfoundland. I had received a job offer to return to the provincial government. I decided I would go back to my life before Jonathan. Back to the same province, the same job, the same neighbourhood—all before I met Jonathan. I would go home. But sometimes what we plan in our heads doesn't always turn out as we expected.

I moved back and started my "new" job. It was like walking back in time when I entered the government offices where I had spent eight years working. There was the familiar marble slab floor. The elevator that always took too long. The third-floor door that jiggled on its hinges when you pulled too hard. The familiar. This was what I needed—to reclaim my previous life. To feel at home.

A lot of things were familiar, but a lot had changed, too. My first day began with a new boss who could not have been older than twenty-three telling me what a good job he and his former colleague had done in these positions. How they were an unstoppable, successful team. He explained that it's very rare to find this kind of partnership and told me not to feel pressured to live up to his legacy. He showed me to my new office—a dark, sparse, windowless room with nothing more than a desk, chair, and dated computer.

After getting settled in I started receiving my assignments. Familiar assignments resembling those I had done during my previous eight years in the position. Write a news release praising government and the minister. Go through the website and see how we can improve it. Write a briefing about how government is heading in the right direction when it comes to our economy.

I must have done this a thousand times before. But as I sat down and started to write, I couldn't do it. And, if I did do it, it wasn't done very well. It wasn't important. How well the minister was liked wasn't important to me. The latest spin on how government was going to boost our economy seemed hollow. Spending eight hours behind a screen writing bureaucratic lingo was mind-numbing.

I did a crappy job. It's no wonder that about a month in I got that dreaded meeting request from Human Resources. I don't know why, but for some reason I had no idea what it would be about. I thought perhaps it would be that I and my new Doogie Howser boss just weren't connecting. Maybe they were going to offer some support.

I remember walking into that room with the HR manager and the lady who had hired me, and there were serene looks on both their faces. Pity. This could not be good.

The HR manager began a long-winded speech about job performance and about halfway through I realized, for the first time in my life, I was being fired. I was shocked. Devastated. But, deep down, not surprised. I was asked for my ID, someone went and got my coat, and I was escorted out of the building. I went to my car. I sat. Nowhere to go.

Sometimes things happen for a reason whether we like them or not. Erasing the last nine years—escaping the pain of grief by returning to a previous life—it didn't work.

So here I was back in good ol' Newfoundland without a clue what to do with my life. This is not how "moving home" was supposed to go.

For the next little while I spent a good amount of time feeling sorry for myself. Days passed just lying in bed watching TV. And then one morning I was forced to get up. Something was beeping in one of my unpacked boxes, and it was driving me crazy. I went to the box, ripped off the packing tape, opened the flaps, and there on top was my laptop—with a red light blinking with the battery dying. I took it out and plugged it in. I stared at it for the longest time. I opened it. I called up a blank page and began to type. And I typed. I typed for three days.

It was the first time since Jonathan died where I got lost in an activity. An activity that captured and held my attention. An activity that I wanted to complete. An activity that seemed meaningful. I wrote about loss; I wrote about anger. I wrote about the whole pointlessness of life. I also wrote something I had been avoiding for a long time. Something I refused to accept. Jonathan was gone. And he was not coming back. I wept.

Despite the difficulty of this exercise, something magical happened. I made a discovery. What I was searching for all this time was not a physical location but a purpose—a passion—a reason that made me want to get up in the morning. For so long my identity had been tied with Jonathan. With what we wanted to do. Where we wanted to live. Where we wanted to be in the future. For the first time I accepted that there was only one person left to make these decisions: me.

For years I had been involved with the theatre scene, both acting and playwriting. It's a hobby I started in Newfoundland and had continued while Jonathan and I were in Calgary and Moncton. But not once did it dawn on me to take that hobby further.

Those three days began a ripple effect. What I had come up with was a play. A play about grief. A play about disability. A play about healing. I showed it to a great friend who was a playwright and who also became a close mentor. He encouraged me to work further on it and to apply for funding to actually get paid to write the piece. It was a full-time approach to a career I had never really considered. I received the funding, and it, in turn, laid the groundwork for a whole new career path.

Doors that I didn't even know existed started to open. Doors that led to becoming a professional theatre artist. Doors that led to projects I felt passionate about, including advocating and demanding diversity for persons with disabilities on our stages. Doors that led to a new life beyond Jonathan.

Today I am a proud Newfoundlander living and working as a theatre artist at "home." And it does feel like home.

I started off this piece by asking if you can really go home again. The answer is yes. But be sure it's a future you're after and not a past.

About the Authors

Aatif Baskanderi (he/him) was born in Sarnia, Ontario, and moved to Clarenville, Newfoundland and Labrador, at the age of five. He completed his Bachelor of Electrical Engineering and Master of Technology Management degrees at Memorial University and a Master of Social Policy and Development at the London School of Economics, leading to a diverse career centred on innovation for social good. As an engineer with a keen interest in social justice, he embarked on a journey to connect the two. This led him to multiple engineering roles, including building smartphones at BlackBerry, researching Fair Trade farmers in Palestine, working on malaria prevention in Sierra Leone, informing science policy in Canada, the UK, and Europe, leading Engineers Without Borders across Canada, and fostering innovation in large enterprises and new start-ups. He currently lives in Brampton, Ontario, with his wife, Dr. Nazia Sharfuddin.

Leila Beaudoin (she/her) is a Tunisian-Newfoundlander who grew up on the Northern Peninsula. An award-winning journalist, her reporting experience spans two national broadcasters, both CTV and CBC, and extends to the "other side" in Communications. She holds a B.A. in English from Memorial University and a journalism degree from the University of Regina, but she got her true start in journalism when she was working as an au pair in the South of France, learning French through toddlers and navigating a new country as a 24-year-old woman on her own. She uses her platform to create space and works to elevate BIPOC voices.

Anthony Brenton (he/him) is an author, husband, and father living in Conception Bay South, Newfoundland and Labrador. He has published various works, including short stories, articles, verse, lyrics, graphic works, and novels. His work often borders on the surrealistic, absurd, and poetic. He draws from his experiences with mental illness and the insight that comes along with it. He has two cats that take care of the vermin.

Julie Bull, PhD, (they/them) is a queer, non-binary Inuk artist from NunatuKavut, who currently lives on Epekwitk (Prince Edward Island). They are an adjunct professor at Memorial University of Newfoundland and at Cape Breton University. In March 2020, they were awarded a residency at the Banff Centre for Arts and Creativity in the *Indigenous Storytelling and Spoken-Word* program. They put those skills to work in the summer of 2020 where they were a top winner at the PEERS Alliance/PRIDE PEI OUTspoken Poetry Slam as well as a performer in the Island Fringe Festival's *Pounding the Pavement: Celebrating and amplifying artists from the fringe*. They also self-published their debut poetry collection, *(h)in(d)sight 2020*, at the end of 2020, and are the profile writer for *The Buzz: PEI's Guide to What's Going On*. Learn more: www.juliebull.net.

Michelle Butler Hallett (she/her) is a novelist, history nerd, disabled person, and an ankylosing spondylitis patient. Author of the novels *Constant Nobody, This Marlowe, deluded your sailors, Sky Waves*, and *Double-blind*, as well as the short story collection *The shadow side of grace*, she writes fiction about violence, evil, and love. Her short stories are widely anthologized in *Hard Ol' Spot, The Vagrant Revue of New Fiction, Everything Is So Political, Running the Whale's Back*, and *Best American Mystery Stories 2014*. She lives in St. John's.

Born in 1981, **Marcella Cormier**, MÉd, (she/her) is a proud Franco-Newfoundlander who grew up in DeGrau on the Port-au-Port Peninsula during the golden years of French Newfoundland and Labrador's linguistic, political, and cultural revival. For nearly twenty years, she has been a teacher and administrator with the province's only French First-Language school district. After obtaining her French First-Language High School diploma at home, her conviction that her people's language and culture could survive through education led her to leave the province to continue her post-secondary studies in her first language. She later returned to her place of origin to contribute educationally and culturally to her community's development. She credits her family with instilling the love of her language in her and with helping shape her strong sense of identity. She currently resides in Conception Bay South, Newfoundland and Labrador, and occasionally freelances in writing fiction and non-fiction, editing, and revising.

Dennis Gill (he/him) is a retired high school teacher, vice-principal, and principal of Dorset Collegiate, Pilley's Island, Newfoundland and Labrador. Since his retirement from the education profession, he has been a photojournalist and an executive assistant with a privately owned company. He and his wife, Roxann, who have made their home for the past four decades in the picturesque outport community of Pilley's Island, population two hundred and fifty, are the parents of two children: Daniel and Jenna. Danny has profound intellectual and physical disabilities and epilepsy; they have learned much from devotedly and lovingly caring for him for forty years. For half a century Dennis has volunteered extensively at the local, provincial, and national levels. A self-taught guitarist, singer, and songwriter, he has composed well over one hundred and fifty originals. On January 27, 2013, he was both humbled and honoured to be presented with the Queen Elizabeth II Diamond Jubilee Medal.

Ainsley Hawthorn, PhD, (she/her) is a cultural historian, author, and multidisciplinary artist raised in Steady Brook, Newfoundland and Labrador, and now based in St. John's. Since completing her doctorate in Near Eastern Languages and Civilizations at Yale University, she has lectured on her research at universities in Germany, Austria, Italy, Canada, and the United States and been quoted in *El Mundo* (Spain), *Apartment Therapy* (US), the *Toronto Star* (Canada), *Activa Magazine* (Portugal), and *The News Lens* (Taiwan), among others. Passionate about using her academic knowledge to bring new ideas about culture, history, and religion to general audiences, she co-hosts the radio series Apocalypse Then for CBC, blogs for *Psychology Today*, and has contributed to a variety of other publications, including the *Globe and Mail*, the *National Post*, and the *Newfoundland Quarterly*. She is currently completing her first solo-authored non-fiction book, *The Other Five Senses*.

Gemma Hickey (they/them) is a multi-award-winning international author and celebrated human rights activist from Newfoundland and Labrador who has made headlines worldwide as an advocate for the 2SLGBTQ+ community and survivors of religious institutional abuse. Their highly acclaimed memoir, *Almost Feral* (Breakwater 2019), chronicles their 908-kilometre walk across the Island of Newfoundland and the uncharted emotional terrain travelled within.

Daze Jefferies (she/her) is a sixth-generation white settler artist, writer, and researcher born and raised in the Bay of Exploits on the northeast coast of rural Ktaqamkuk (Newfoundland). Working with archives, found beach materials, queer ephemera, oral histories, sound, poetry, sculpture, theory, performance, and illustration, her research-based creative practice engages with the ocean as a body of loss to form washy, wayward, and withheld counter-narratives of trans and sex worker histories at the water's edge. Her research-creation and multidisciplinary projects have been exhibited at Eastern Edge, The Rooms, Unscripted Twillingate, Inverness County Centre for the Arts, and Cape Breton University Art Gallery. Co-author of *Autoethnography and Feminist Theory at the Water's Edge: Unsettled Islands* (2018), she has recent publications in *Riddle Fence*, *Understorey*, *HELD*, *The Dalhousie Review*, *Arc*, and *Feral Feminisms*. Her debut poetry collection, *We Hold a Body of Water Together*, is forthcoming.

Michelle Keep (she/her) is an eternal optimist and romantic. She flew halfway across the country to be with her partner at the tender age of eighteen, and they've been together ever since. They now share that romance with others, full time, having gone on to become *USA Today* and *Wall Street Journal* bestselling authors. Her past job as a stripper taught her all about the art of sensuality, and their romantic suspense novels have been read hundreds of thousands of times across the globe. When she's not writing or teaching herself new skills, she volunteers her time to make the world a better place. She's the President of the Canadian Freelance Union, Board Secretary of the St. John's Status of Women Council, and has previously volunteered with the Safe Harbour Outreach Project, an organization that supports people with lived experience in the sex industry.

Ilga Leja (she/her) was born in Germany, the daughter of Latvian parents displaced by the Second World War. She grew up in the Baltic community of Corner Brook. A former librarian, she has worked primarily in government and academic libraries in Ontario and Nova Scotia. A graduate of Dalhousie University and Memorial University of Newfoundland, she has more recently turned her attention to conducting research relating to the Newfoundland Baltic community. This has included collecting oral histories and original documents from some of the Latvians and Baltic Germans who were among the first to arrive in Newfoundland. Currently working as a textile artist and knitwear designer, she manages an online knitting design business at ilgaleja.com. She lives in Halifax, Nova Scotia.

Anne Malone (she/her) is a visually impaired Guide Dog handler who envisions and advocates freedom from disability for people who live with sight loss. In her writing and speaking, she invites the sighted world to view blindness not as a debilitating condition, but rather as simply a different interface with the environment. An ardent supporter of the arts, she worked for many years in administrative roles at Eastern Edge Gallery and St. Michael's Printshop. Currently, she serves on the Board of Directors of Power Productions, a St. John's-based theatre company with a mandate of establishing diversity and accessibility in the performing arts. She and her Guide Dog, Cheryl, live in St. John's, where they work together to hack the complex and challenging urban environment in their beloved home city.

Robin McGrath (she/her) is the sole author of thirty publications, including *Salt Fish and Shmattes: A History of the Jews in Newfoundland and Labrador from 1770*. She is the editor of four books, has contributed to forty-two others, and has published hundreds of articles, reviews, and newspaper columns. She was an Associate Professor at the University of Alberta and currently lives in Harbour Main, Newfoundland, where she continues to write.

Stephen Miller (he/him) is a writer and journalist based in Newfoundland. His experience with opiate addiction and incarceration inform much of his work, including a recent radio documentary for CBC that saw him go back inside Her Majesty's Penitentiary with musician Séan McCann to capture a performance and interview inmates. He spends most of his free time with his family and small circle of friends and resides quite happily with his partner and their adorably overweight cat, Bella. He hopes to one day publish the novel he's been working on *forever.*

Tyler Mugford (he/him) is an Inuk raised in Cartwright, on Labrador's south coast, and currently residing in Happy Valley–Goose Bay. His passion for creating and telling stories from and about Labrador led him to journalism, which he spent two years studying at CNA in St. John's. After graduation, he moved back to Labrador and started work as a reporter for CBC on the morning radio show Labrador Morning. He is now interested in working for the NunatuKavut Community Council in order to learn more about Indigenous affairs and further his interest in storytelling.

Delores V. Mullings, PhD, (she/her) is an Associate Professor and Interim Associate Dean of Undergraduate Programs at Memorial University in the School of Social Work. She is a member of a large extended family, caregiver for her mother, and the mother of two living children. She has a demonstrated history and extensive expertise in Equity Diversity Inclusion leadership in community-based organizations and academic institutions, including education and evaluation. She is a human rights and anti-racist consultant and trainer, as well as a public speaker. Her scholarly interests fall under the umbrella of anti-Black racism and critical race theory and explore decolonizing postsecondary education, mothering, parenting, mental health and wellness, 2SLGBTQ+ concerns, elders, immigrants, settlement and integration, and human rights policy. Her research informs her teaching and learning pedagogy in her partnerships with community-based organizations and interdisciplinary scholars, both nationally and internationally.

Tori Oliver (she/her) is a 23-year-old autistic woman originally from the town of Gull Island, Newfoundland, but currently residing in St. John's. She is a member of Memorial University's Class of 2020, having pursued a psychology major. Life on the spectrum in early childhood made it hard to identify her struggles and express herself. She thus became motivated to use writing as an emotional outlet and has published several compositions since 2014. In her free time, she enjoys playing video games, completing diamond paintings, and walking with her dog, Rosie. Her contribution to this anthology serves to advocate for others like herself, striving for a world where autism and its differences are further understood and accommodated.

Ky Pearce (they/them) is a queer poet, activist, and scholar of Mi'kmaw and settler ancestry. They were born on the west coast of Newfoundland in the mid-90s and now live in Katarokwi (Kingston, Ontario), where they are currently working on their PhD in Cultural Studies at Queen's University. Their primary research interests revolve around queer studies, queer theory, Indigenous literature, 2Spirit critique, queer Indigenous studies, affect theory, and political economy.

Christine Poker (she/her) is an Innu filmmaker from Natuashish, Labrador. She is also a mother, grandmother, artist, writer, and addictions counsellor. Her greatest love is filmmaking. For the last ten years, she has produced films of Innu legends. The films are made with all-Innu crews directing, filming, and creating sets and costumes. When she finishes writing a script, she takes it to a circle of Elders to provide advice. She makes these films for Innu youth to see and hear the legends and to know that the Innu language is important. The films are a gift to her community, to ensure that the stories that have been passed on from one generation to another for thousands of years are not lost as Elders pass away.

Paul David Power (he/him) has spent the past twenty years working as a writer, actor, director, and communications professional in various media and for diverse organizations—including dramatic script for the stage. His formal training includes holding a BA in English with a concentration in theatre and a BAA in Journalism. He has a long history in raising awareness and understanding about disability issues through his work as a playwright, columnist, director, and actor.

Susan Rose (she/her) worked as a Special Education teacher in St. John's from 1985 to 2006, teaching students from grades four to twelve. In 1992 she began to lobby government for 2SLGBTQI rights in the education system. Since 2006 she has been volunteering her time consulting and guiding students and their families when their school and community are not safe places for them. She has served as President, and is currently Vice President, of Egale Canada. In 2017 she received the Newfoundland and Labrador Human Rights Award for her work in education. In 2019 she received the Memorial Alumni Tribute Award for Outstanding Community Service. In January 2020, she was invested into the Order of Newfoundland and Labrador for her work in education and human rights. Most recently, in April 2021 she received the Patricia Cowan Award from her peers, the NLTA, for Support and Promotion of Education. In addition to her human rights work she owns and operates a tourism business, Coastal Cottages, where she enjoys her summers hiking, mountain biking, and birdwatching along the coast.

Alex Saunders (he/him) will soon be eighty, is a single grandparent, and is of mixed Inuit, Innu, and Irish/English ancestry. His mother survived the Spanish Influenza of 1918. An ex-Navy serviceman, he has travelled both sides of the Atlantic Ocean and continued his connection to the sea as an international fisherman, travelling the waters of Greenland, Iceland, the Faroe Islands, Scotland, and the North Sea, before going on to manage a fish company. He has won three writers' awards: the 2016 Emerging Northern Writers' and Artists' Award, the 2017 Lawrence Jackson Writers' Award, and the 2019 Percy Janes First Novel Award. He has served as guest editor for *Them Days* (Happy Valley–Goose Bay, Labrador) and has completed three novels, one of which, *Aullak: A Labrador Experience*, is used in schools from Goose Bay to Nain.

T. J. Smith (he/him) is a 34-year-old man who was born and raised in St. Anthony, Newfoundland and Labrador, at the very top of Newfoundland's Northern Peninsula. He spent thirteen years in Nova Scotia playing hockey and graduating from St. Mary's University. In 2018 he returned home to be closer to family and friends, his core support system. He still takes antidepressants each night and lives with depression and anxiety. He has accepted this is a part of him, but it will not define him. He has one son, Nash, who is eight years old and lives with his mother in Nova Scotia. They remain tight as father and son.

Hailing from the Mi'kmaq Community of Flat Bay, **Ivan J. White** (he/him) is an emissary for his culture, heritage, and people. Artistically, he has worked as writer, musician, and filmmaker in both amateur and professional capacities. Formally educated in the field of marketing and practised in the areas of media and communications, he has been exploring the intersections of business, arts, and Mi'kmaw identity since his teenage years. These themes come out of a desire to better understand his place in his community and his role as a Mi'kmaw. A storyteller at heart and advocate for his people by upbringing, he remains close to his home community of Flat Bay and is likely heard before he is seen on the issues that involve his people. He currently lives in St. George's with his wife, Crystal, and their two lovely children, Isabella and Ivan Jr.

Acknowledgements

This anthology is the product of twenty-five imaginations, twenty-five lived experiences. As these stories arrived in my inbox one by one, I was amazed over and over again by the creativity of their writing and the range of their approaches. I hope that all of the authors will be as delighted by this collection and the company they find themselves in as I am.

Generous grant funding from the Canada Council for the Arts and the City of St. John's provided a professional level of pay for all the authors. If you have paid taxes in Canada, about one-tenth of one cent of each of your tax dollars goes to the Canada Council and from there to individual artists and arts organizations across the country. Thank you for making books like this one possible.

From the moment I conceived this anthology, I knew it belonged with Breakwater, and I'm grateful to Rebecca Rose and her team for greeting this project with such boundless enthusiasm. Thanks are also due to Heather Elliott and Matthew LeDrew for writing letters in support of my grant applications, to Ray Critch for providing legal advice throughout the publishing process, and to everyone who helped me to connect with potential contributors: Hope Colbourne, Camille Fouillard, Donna Francis, John Gushue, Dale Gilbert Jarvis, Bushra Junaid, Rebecca Russell, and Jen Winsor.

Finally, I want to express my appreciation to my family and friends for supporting all of my wild endeavours, especially my mother Maureen Dunn, father Paul Dicks, step-mother Jennifer Dicks, mother-in-law Rosalind Bartlett, and siblings Christian and Erin, Aislinn and Gage, Katie, and Brett, and, most of all, to the person who is by my side through every step of every project, who celebrates with me in my successes and commiserates with me in my setbacks, my partner, my confidante, my soulmate, Andrew. I love you.

Ainsley Hawthorn, Editor